D0471604

Additional praise for *The Visual Organization: Data Visualization, Big Data, and the Quest for Better Decisions*

"In Too Big to Ignore, Phil Simon introduced us to the rapidly emerging world of Big Data. In this book, he tackles how we need to see, handle, and present this mountain of information, one unlike the old, familiar, transaction data that business people know quite well. *The Visual Organization* shines a much-needed light on how businesses are using contemporary data visualization tools."

Brian Sommer
Enterprise Software Industry Analyst; ZDNet Contributor;
CEO of TechVentive, Inc.

"The fourth wave of computing is upon us, and the visualization of information has never been more important. *The Visual Organization* arrives just in time. Simon's book helps enterprises learn from–and adapt to– this new adapt world. A must read."

Larry Weber
Chairman and CEO of Racepoint Global and best-selling author

"Once again, Phil Simon has raised the bar. Like his other books, *The Visual Organization* takes a very current topic and instructs the reader on what not only what is being done, but what can be done. Simon provides a wealth of advice and examples, demonstrating how organizations can move from data production to data consumption and, ultimately, to action."

Tony Fisher
Vice President Data Collaboration and Integration,
Progress Software; Author of *The Data Asset*

"Today data is the new oil. Organizations need ways to quickly make sense of the mountains of data they are collecting. Bottom line: today visualization is more important than ever. *The Visual Organization* is a checkpoint on current dataviz methods. Simon's book represents insightful thought leadership that is sure to help any organization compete in an era of Big Data."

William McKnight
President, McKnight Consulting Group; Author of *Information Management: Strategies for Gaining a Competitive Advantage with Data*

"Through fascinating case studies and stunning visuals, *The Visual Organization* demystifies data visualization. Simon charts the transformative effects of dataviz. Only through new tools and a new mind-set can organizations attempt to compete in a rapidly changing global environment."

Chris Chute
Global Director, IDC

"A rollicking and incisive tour of the organizations pioneering the next big thing: putting visual data at the center of the enterprise. Simon's highly readable account points the way towards incorporating visualization into your own endeavors."

Todd Silverstein
Entrepreneur and founder, Vizify

"Sure, Big Data is cool, but how can it move the needle? Today, it's essential to uncover insights far too often unseen, but how do you actually do that? *The Visual Organization* answers those questions—and more–in spades. Simon demonstrates how, when done correctly, dataviz promotes not only understanding, but action."

Bill Schmarzo
CTO, EMC Global Services; Author of *Big Data:*
Understanding How Data Powers Big Business

"Data visualization is a secret sauce for visionary executives in today's time-starved economy. Simon's book provides the Rosetta Stone on how to get there."

Adrian C. Ott
CEO, Exponential Edge, and award-winning author
of *The 24-Hour Customer*

"Phil Simon's latest book, *The Visual Organization*, superbly shows the potential of data visualization and how it can spark an organization's imagination. As Simon makes clear, visualization is how organizations can ask the right questions needed to create real value from their big data efforts; instead of fumbling about with them as too many do today."

Robert Charette
President, ITABHI Corporation

The Visual Organization

Wiley & SAS Business Series

The Wiley & SAS Business Series presents books that help senior-level managers with their critical management decisions.

Titles in the Wiley & SAS Business Series include:

Demand-Driven Inventory Optimization and Replenishment: Creating a More Efficient Supply Chain by Robert A. Davis

The Executive's Guide to Enterprise Social Media Strategy: How Social Networks Are Radically Transforming Your Business by David Thomas and Mike Barlow

Economic and Business Forecasting: Analyzing and Interpreting Econometric Results by John Silvia, Azhar Iqbal, Kaylyn Swankoski, Sarah Watt, and Sam Bullard

Executive's Guide to Solvency II by David Buckham, Jason Wahl, and Stuart Rose

Fair Lending Compliance: Intelligence and Implications for Credit Risk Management by Clark R. Abrahams and Mingyuan Zhang

Foreign Currency Financial Reporting from Euros to Yen to Yuan: A Guide to Fundamental Concepts and Practical Applications by Robert Rowan

Health Analytics: Gaining the Insights to Transform Health Care by Jason Burke

Heuristics in Analytics: A Practical Perspective of What Influences Our Analytical World by Carlos Andre Reis Pinheiro and Fiona McNeill

Human Capital Analytics: How to Harness the Potential of Your Organization's Greatest Asset by Gene Pease, Boyce Byerly, and Jac Fitz-enz

Implement, Improve, and Expand Your Statewide Longitudinal Data System: Creating a Culture of Data in Education by Jamie McQuiggan and Armistead Sapp

Information Revolution: Using the Information Evolution Model to Grow Your Business by Jim Davis, Gloria J. Miller, and Allan Russell

Killer Analytics: Top 20 Metrics Missing from Your Balance Sheet by Mark Brown

Manufacturing Best Practices: Optimizing Productivity and Product Quality by Bobby Hull

Marketing Automation: Practical Steps to More Effective Direct Marketing by Jeff LeSueur

Mastering Organizational Knowledge Flow: How to Make Knowledge Sharing Work by Frank Leistner

The New Know: Innovation Powered by Analytics by Thornton May

Performance Management: Integrating Strategy Execution, Methodologies, Risk, and Analytics by Gary Cokins

Predictive Business Analytics: Forward-Looking Capabilities to Improve Business Performance by Lawrence Maisel and Gary Cokins

Retail Analytics: The Secret Weapon by Emmett Cox

Social Network Analysis in Telecommunications by Carlos Andre Reis Pinheiro

Statistical Thinking: Improving Business Performance, Second Edition by Roger W. Hoerl and Ronald D. Snee

Taming the Big Data Tidal Wave: Finding Opportunities in Huge Data Streams with Advanced Analytics by Bill Franks

Too Big to Ignore: The Business Case for Big Data by Phil Simon

The Value of Business Analytics: Identifying the Path to Profitability by Evan Stubbs

Visual Six Sigma: Making Data Analysis Lean by Ian Cox, Marie A. Gaudard, Philip J. Ramsey, Mia L. Stephens, and Leo Wright

Win with Advanced Business Analytics: Creating Business Value from Your Data by Jean Paul Isson and Jesse Harriott

For more information on any of the above titles, please visit www.wiley.com.

The Visual Organization

Data Visualization, Big Data, and the Quest for Better Decisions

Phil Simon

Cover Design: Wiley
Cover Image: © iStockphoto/sebastian-julian

Copyright © 2014 by John Wiley & Sons, Inc. All rights reserved.

Published by John Wiley & Sons, Inc., Hoboken, New Jersey.
Published simultaneously in Canada.

No part of this publication may be reproduced, stored in a retrieval system, or transmitted in any form or by any means, electronic, mechanical, photocopying, recording, scanning, or otherwise, except as permitted under Section 107 or 108 of the 1976 United States Copyright Act, without either the prior written permission of the Publisher, or authorization through payment of the appropriate per-copy fee to the Copyright Clearance Center, Inc., 222 Rosewood Drive, Danvers, MA 01923, (978) 750-8400, fax (978) 646-8600, or on the Web at www.copyright.com. Requests to the Publisher for permission should be addressed to the Permissions Department, John Wiley & Sons, Inc., 111 River Street, Hoboken, NJ 07030, (201) 748-6011, fax (201) 748-6008, or online at http://www.wiley.com/go/permissions.

Limit of Liability/Disclaimer of Warranty: While the publisher and author have used their best efforts in preparing this book, they make no representations or warranties with respect to the accuracy or completeness of the contents of this book and specifically disclaim any implied warranties of merchantability or fitness for a particular purpose. No warranty may be created or extended by sales representatives or written sales materials. The advice and strategies contained herein may not be suitable for your situation. You should consult with a professional where appropriate. Neither the publisher nor author shall be liable for any loss of profit or any other commercial damages, including but not limited to special, incidental, consequential, or other damages.

For general information on our other products and services or for technical support, please contact our Customer Care Department within the United States at (800) 762-2974, outside the United States at (317) 572-3993 or fax (317) 572-4002.

Wiley publishes in a variety of print and electronic formats and by print-on-demand. Some material included with standard print versions of this book may not be included in e-books or in print-on-demand. If this book refers to media such as a CD or DVD that is not included in the version you purchased, you may download this material at http://booksupport.wiley.com. For more information about Wiley products, visit www.wiley.com.

Library of Congress Cataloging-in-Publication Data

Simon, Phil.
    The visual organization : data visualization, big data, and the quest for better decisions/ Phil Simon.
        pages cm. — (Wiley and SAS business series)
        Includes bibliographical references and index.
      ISBN 978-1-118-79438-8 (hardback); ISBN 978-1-118-85841-7 (ebk);
ISBN 978-1-118-85834-9 (ebk) 1. Information technology—Management.
2. Information visualization. 3. Big data. 4. Business—Data processing. I. Title.
      HD30.2.S578 2014
      658.4′038—dc23
                                                                    2013046785

Printed in the United States of America

10 9 8 7 6 5 4 3 2

Other Books by Phil Simon

Too Big to Ignore: The Business Case for Big Data

The Age of the Platform: How Amazon, Apple, Facebook, and Google Have Redefined Business

The New Small: How a New Breed of Small Businesses Is Harnessing the Power of Emerging Technologies

The Next Wave of Technologies: Opportunities in Chaos

Why New Systems Fail: An Insider's Guide to Successful IT Projects

To my <u>other</u> favorite W.W.

It's an <u>honour</u> working with you.

Fondly,

G.B.

A good sketch is better than a long speech.
Quote often attributed to Napoleon Bonaparte

Contents

List of Figures and Tables

(continued)

Preface: A Tale of Two IPOs

*Every word or concept, clear as it may seem to be,
has only a limited range of applicability.*
—Werner Heisenberg

Christian Chabot had to be at least a little nervous when he woke up in Manhattan on the morning of May 17, 2013. More than a decade's worth of work would be coming to fruition in only a few hours. In 2003, Chabot—along with Chris Stolte and Pat Hanrahan—founded a little data-visualization company by the name of Tableau Software. (Tableau had started in 1996 as a research project at Stanford University funded by the U.S. Department of Defense.) Chabot served as the company's CEO, a position that he still holds today. At 9:30 a.m. EST on that May morning, Tableau would go public on the New York Stock Exchange with the apropos stock symbol of $DATA. Adding to the day's tension, Chabot and his team would be ringing the opening bell to commence the day's trading.

Now, under any circumstances, any company founder/CEO would be anxious about such a historic occasion. Chabot, however, was probably more restless than most in his position. Tableau's public launch was taking place in an environment best described as ominous. This initial public offering (IPO) was by no means a slam-dunk. To Chabot, the halcyon days of the dot-com era must have seemed like a million years ago. And, more recently, May 17, 2013, was almost exactly a year to the day after Facebook went public in arguably the most botched IPO in U.S. history. It was a day that would live in infamy.

Facebook was originally scheduled to begin trading on Nasdaq at 11:00 a.m. EST on May 18, 2012. In short, all did not go as planned. Trading was delayed for half an hour, a veritable lifetime on Wall Street. Amazingly, some investors who thought they had bought $FB shares didn't know *for hours* whether their transactions were actually executed. Aside from investor consternation, as Samantha Murphy wrote on Mashable, "The IPO caused a series of issues for finance sites, including Nasdaq.com and etrade.com."[1]

That was a bit of an understatement.

Once trading finally began, things continued to spiral downward for Mark Zuckerberg's company. Originally priced at $42 per share, $FB quickly lost one-third of its value during that fateful day. The Securities and Exchange Commission investigated the glitches, ultimately fining Nasdaq $10 million. Lawsuits were soon filed. Many early Facebook investors like Peter Thiel sold virtually all their shares as soon as they legally could—and looked shrewd for doing so. At one point in 2012, the stock slid under $20 per share, and only in August 2013 did Facebook rise above its IPO price. As of this writing, investor sentiment finally seems to have shifted.

The Facebook IPO debacle—and resulting media frenzy—reverberated throughout the financial markets in mid-2012 and well into 2013. Its effects were felt far beyond the offices of Mark Zuckerberg, COO Sheryl Sandberg, rank-and-file employees, and investors. The Facebook IPO allegedly deterred many a company from listing on the NYSE and Nasdaq. Generally speaking, Wall Street analysts believed that the fiasco poisoned the short-term IPO well for everyone, especially technology companies. In the aftermath of the Facebook IPO, many high-profile companies, including Twitter,* reportedly adjusted their own plans for going public. Of course, there were a few exceptions. Enterprise software companies Workday and Jive Software bravely went public in October and December of 2012, respectively. Their stock prices have held up relatively well after their IPOs, as did Big Data play Splunk.

APPLES AND COCONUTS

On many levels, Tableau Software is the anti-Facebook. Yes, both companies rely upon cutting-edge technology to a large extent, but that's just about where the similarities end. In many ways, the two are apples and coconuts, and no intelligent investor would ever confuse the two.

Facebook is a consumer company based in Silicon Valley with a world-famous CEO. Tableau is an enterprise technology company based in Seattle, Washington. Compared to Zuckerberg, relatively few people would recognize Tableau's CEO on the street. Tableau doesn't sport anywhere near 1.2 billion users. Nor do its eponymous products seem terribly sexy to John Q. Public. In fact, most people would probably consider them a bit drab. At a high level, Tableau's offerings help people and organizations visualize data. This data need not be transactional, structured, and internal to an enterprise. Rather, Tableau can handle data from a

---

* On September 12, 2013, Twitter announced its plans to finally go public. On November 7, 2013, the company began trading on the NYSE.

wide range of sources, including proprietary relational databases, enterprise data warehouses and cubes, open datasets, spreadsheets, and more. Tableau's products "look" at data and allow users to easily create dashboards and highly interactive data visualizations. With a few clicks, users can publish and share them.*

DAY ONE

The dubious IPO environment did not deter Chabot, Tableau's senior team, and its investors. They decided that the company would buck the IPO trend and ignore the pall that Facebook cast over the market. Tableau would roll the dice and go public.

So, how would Tableau pan out?

That was the big question for Chabot and company on May 17, 2013. Fortunately for Tableau's top brass, its first day of trading was spectacular and even redolent of the dot-com era. The company saw its stock skyrocket an astonishing 63 percent.[2] When trading closed for the day, Tableau's market capitalization exceeded a whopping $2 billion.

Facebook notwithstanding, first-day bumps in a stock's first day of trading are relatively common, although 63 percent is a pretty big one. Company founders, early investors, and employees with equity or stock options celebrate early jumps like these—and rightfully so. At the same time, though, these gains are often fleeting, as investors are tempted to cash out and take profits. (Groupon and Zynga are but two recent examples of stocks that rose early only to quickly come crashing down to earth.) It was reasonable to ask, "Would Tableau's stock price maintain its lofty valuation?" In short, yes. After its initial jump, $DATA stabilized, largely holding on to its first-day gains.

I was watching the market the day of Tableau's successful IPO with considerable interest. Its opening and subsequent performance didn't surprise me. By way of background, I'm far from an expert on investing. I certainly don't purport to understand all the vicissitudes of the stock market, much less predict it with any accuracy. I don't read these tea leaves well, and my own investment record is borderline deplorable. (It pains me to think about how much I paid for $AAPL. Just think of me as the antithesis of Warren Buffett.) In a year, $DATA may trade at a fraction of its current price. We may be laughing at Wall Street's $2-billion-dollar valuation of a data-visualization company. After all, there's plenty of precedent here. The Street is far from perfect. Exhibit A: during the dot-com boom, Pets.com sported a market capitalization north of $300 million. Whoops.

Sometimes, however, Wall Street gets it right. While it's still early, Tableau appears to be one of those cases.

---

* For some particularly cool ones, see http://tinyurl.com/cool-tableau.

THE DAWN OF A NEW ERA?

The importance of Tableau Software's wildly successful IPO is difficult to over-state. It underscores the burgeoning importance of dataviz. Now, make no mistake. Many large, publicly traded software vendors like IBM, Oracle, SAP, and Microsoft sell applications that allow their clients to visualize data—and have for a long time. However, each of these vendors hawks a wide array of other business and technology solutions. IBM, Oracle, SAP, and Microsoft make their money by selling many different products and services. These include databases, back-office ERP and CRM applications, consulting, and cus-tom software development. To each of these corporations, sales of proper data-visualization applications represent relatively negligible lines of business.

By contrast, Tableau is a different breed of cat. As of this writing, it is *exclu-sively* a dataviz company. Its products don't generate and store data, *per se*. Rather, at a high level, Tableau's solutions help organizations and their employ-ees represent and interpret *existing* data, possibly making key discoveries in the process. Equipped with data presented in such a compelling format, employees are more likely to make better business decisions.

Whether more pure dataviz companies ultimately go public is immaterial. I for one don't expect a wave of similar IPOs in the next few years. For many reasons, many companies choose to remain private these days. (Not want-ing to deal with onerous government regulations and needling activist inves-tors are usually near the top of the list.*) Many more start-ups and private companies actively seek exit strategies, perhaps "acqui-hires" by cash-flush behemoths like Facebook, Google, Twitter, and Yahoo.

One need not be an equities expert to understand that many factors explain the rise and fall of any individual stock. (As for me, I know enough to be dangerous.) At a high level, there are two types of variables. There are macro factors like the general economy, the unemployment rate, and the GDP growth. Then there are company-specific ones, including an organization's competition, cash flow, and strength of its management team. At the risk of simplifying, though, the immediate and blistering success of the Tableau IPO manifests a much larger business trend. Thousands of companies use Tableau, with more coming on board every day.

Now, Tableau may be the *only* pure data-visualization firm to go public (again, as of this writing), but it is hardly unique in its objectives:

- To make data more understandable

- Along with other tools, to allow organizations to get their arms around increasing data streams

---

* As I write these words, Dell is trying to go *private*.

▓ To promote data discovery

▓ Ultimately, to help people make better business decisions

As we'll see in the following pages, Tableau is just one of many companies that offers new and exciting ways to represent and interpret data, especially the big kind. Increasingly, dataviz is becoming a critical and even sexy topic. Awash in a sea of data, many organizations want—nay, *need*—tools that help them make sense of it all.

Powerful tech companies like Amazon, Apple, Facebook, Google, and Twitter understand data visualization, but they are hardly alone. Powerful dataviz is *not* the sole purview of Google-sized companies. As you'll see in this book, a wide array of organizations is representing data in amazing ways, deploying powerful data-visualization tools and building new ones. For instance, progressive and tech-savvy institutions like the Massachusetts Institute of Technology and the *New York Times* are hiring proper dataviz specialists and engineers.* The *Wall Street Journal* is hiring visual journalists.[3]

And this trend shows no signs of abating. In fact, it's just getting started.

Today, data and dataviz are downright cool. In a few years, we may look back at May 17, 2013, as the dawn of a new type of company: the Visual Organization.

And that is the subject of this book.

Phil Simon
Henderson, Nevada
January 2014

NOTES

1. Murphy, Samantha "Nasdaq Delayed Facebook IPO for 30 Minutes," Mashable, May 18, 2012, http://mashable.com/2012/05/18/facebook-ipo-delay, Retrieved June 19, 2013.
2. Cook, John, "Strong Debut: Tableau Closes First Day of Trading Up 63%," GeekWire, May 17, 2013, http://www.geekwire.com/2013/strong-debut-tableau-closes-day-trading-63, Retrieved June 10, 2013.
3. http://www.philsimon.com/blog.

---

* Job listing: http://jobs.awn.com/jobseeker/job/13838346

Acknowledgments

Kudos to Tim Burgard, Sheck Cho, Stacey Rivera, Helen Cho, Evelyn Martinez, Andy Wheeler, Shelley Sessoms, Chris Gage, and the rest of Team Wiley for making this book possible. Additional kudos to Karen Gill, Johnna VanHoose Dinse, and Luke Fletcher.

Paula Bales, Stephanie Huie, Justin Matejka, Drew Skau, John T. Meyer, Jimmy Jacobson, Porter Haney, Joris Evers, Scott Kahler, Ernesto Olivares, and Scott Murray were generous with their time and expertise.

I am particularly grateful to Melinda Thielbar for helping me crystallize the Four-Level Visual Organization Framework in Chapter 6. Knowing a true data scientist has its advantages.

A tip of the hat to Adrian Ott, Terri Griffith, Bruce Webster, Scott "Caddy" Erichsen, Dalton Cervo, Jill Dyché, Todd Hamilton, Ellen French, Dick and Bonnie Denby, Kristen Eckstein, Bob Charette, Andrew Botwin, Mark Frank, Thor and Keri Sandell, Michael DeAngelo, Jennifer Zito, Chad Roberts, Mark Cenicola, Colin Hickey, Brian and Heather Morgan, Michael West, Kevin J. Anderson, John Spatola, Marc Paolella, and Angela Bowman.

Next up are the usual suspects: my longtime Carnegie Mellon friends Scott Berkun, David Sandberg, Michael Viola, Joe Mirza, and Chris McGee.

My heroes from Rush (Geddy, Alex, and Neil), Dream Theater (Jordan, John, John, Mike, and James), Marillion (h, Steve, Ian, Mark, and Pete), and Porcupine Tree (Steven, Colin, Gavin, John, and Richard) have given me many years of creative inspiration through their music. Keep on keepin' on!

A very special thank-you to Vince Gilligan, Bryan Cranston, Aaron Paul, Dean Norris, Anna Gunn, Betsy Brandt, Jonathan Banks, Giancarlo Esposito, RJ Mitte, Bob Odenkirk, and the rest of the cast and team of *Breaking Bad*. You took us on an amazing journey over the past six years. Each of you has made me want to do great work.

Finally, my parents. I wouldn't be here without you.

How to Help This Book

Thank you for buying *The Visual Organization*. I truly hope that you enjoy reading it and have learned a great deal in the process. Beyond some level of enjoyment and education (always admirable goals in reading a nonfiction book), I also hope that you can apply your newfound knowledge throughout your career.

And perhaps you are willing to help me. I am a self-employed author, writer, speaker, and consultant. I'm not independently wealthy and I don't have a large marketing machine getting my name out there. My professional livelihood depends in large part on my reputation, coupled with referrals and recommendations from people like you. Collectively, these enable me to make a living.

You can help this book by doing one or more of the following:

▪ Review the book on *amazon.com*, *bn.com*, *goodreads.com*, or other related sites. The more honest, the better.

▪ Mention the book on your blog, Facebook, Reddit, Google+, Twitter, LinkedIn, Pinterest, and other sites you frequent.

▪ Recommend the book to family members, colleagues, your boss, friends, subway riders, and people who might find it interesting.

▪ Give it as a gift.

▪ If you know people who still work in newspapers, magazines, television, or industry groups, I'd love a referral or reference. Social media hasn't entirely replaced the importance of traditional media.

▪ Visit *www.philsimon.com* and read, watch, and listen to your heart's content. I frequently blog, post videos, record podcasts, and create other interesting forms of content on a wide variety of subjects.

▪ Check out my other books: *Why New Systems Fail*, *The Next Wave of Technologies*, *The New Small*, *The Age of the Platform*, and *Too Big to Ignore*.

I don't expect to get rich by writing books. Michael Lewis, John Grisham, Stephen King, and Phil Simon. *Hmmm . . . which one doesn't belong in that group?* I write books for four reasons. First, I believe that have something meaningful to say. I like writing, editing, crafting a cover, and everything else that goes into writing books. To paraphrase the title of an album by Geddy Lee, it's my favorite headache. Second, although Kindles, Nooks, and iPads are downright cool, I really enjoy holding a physical copy of one of my books in my hands. Creating something physical from scratch just feels good to me. Next, I get a sense of satisfaction from creating a physical product. Finally, I believe that my books will make other good things happen for me.

At the same time, though, producing a quality text takes an enormous amount of time, effort, and money. Every additional copy sold helps make the next one possible.

Thanks again.

Phil

The Visual Organization

PART ONE

Book Overview and Background

Part I lays the foundation for the entire book. It covers why dataviz matters more than ever and includes the following chapters:

- Introduction
- Chapter 1: The Ascent of the Visual Organization
- Chapter 2: Transforming Data into Insights: The Tools

Introduction

It's not what you look at that matters, it's what you see.

—Henry David Thoreau

Professional writers and speakers like me live interesting lives. I'd hazard to guess that most of us work from home, although some maintain proper offices. And when you work from home, strange things can happen. For one, it can become difficult to separate work from leisure. There's no boss looking over your shoulder to see if you've completed that TPS report. *Did you get that memo?* If you want to take a nap in the early afternoon as I routinely do, no one's stopping you. In a way, people like me are always *at work*, even though we're not always working. It's fair to say that the notion of work-life balance can be challenging. Lines usually blur. Maybe they're even obliterated.

In many ways, working from home could not be more different from working for "the man." Even today, many rigid corporate environments block employees from visiting certain websites via services like Websense. And forget the obvious sites (read: porn). At many companies, there's no guarantee that employees can access websites that serve legitimate business purposes, at least without a call to the IT help desk to unblock them. Examples include Twitter, Facebook, Tumblr, and Pinterest. Of course, many employees in industrialized countries sport smartphones these days, minimizing the effectiveness of the Websenses of the world. As a result, many companies have reluctantly embraced the Bring Your Own Device movement. That genie is out of the bottle.

We home-based employees, though, don't have to worry about these types of restrictions. No one stops us from wasting as much time as we want on the Web, the golf course, or anywhere else for that matter. In an increasingly blurry world, though, what does it *really* mean to waste time? That's a bit existential. Let me rephrase: Are my tweets generally work related? Have they changed over time? If so, how?

ADVENTURES IN TWITTER DATA DISCOVERY

Twitter tells me that, since 2010, I have tweeted more than 17,000 times as of this writing, or about ten times per day. I'd wager that more than 70 percent of my tweets were work related. (Yes, I have been paid to tweet. Lamentably, I don't command Kim Kardashian-type rates for my 140 characters.* *Maybe some day*.) Twitter has let me connect with interesting people and organizations, many of whom you'll meet in this book. In the course of researching this book, I searched Twitter for a random sample of thoughts, typically with the hashtag `#dataviz`. At least to me, Twitter is an exceptionally valuable business service that I would gladly pay to use. While we're at it, let's put Twitter client Hoot-Suite in that same boat.

At the same time, though, I unabashedly use Twitter for reasons that have absolutely no connection to work. If you go to `@philsimon` and follow me (please do), there's a good chance that you'll see a few tweets with `#Rush` and `#BreakingBad`, my favorite band and TV show, respectively. What's more, I've tweeted many of these things during times and days when I probably should have been working. I could delude myself, but I won't. A few of my favorite celebrities and athletes have engaged with me on Twitter, bringing a smile to my face. I'll say it: Twitter is fun.

But let's stick with work here. Based on what I'm doing, I suspect that my tweets have evolved over time, but how? It's presumptuous to assume that the content of my tweets is static. (I like to think that I have a dynamic personality.)

To answer this question, I could have accessed my archived tweets via Twitter.com. The company made user data available for download in December 2012. I could have thrown that data into Microsoft Excel or Access and started manually looking for patterns. Knowing me, I would have created a pivot table in Excel along with a pie chart or a basic bar graph. (Yes, I am a geek and I always have been.) The entire process would have been pretty time consuming even though I've been working with these productivity staples for a long time. Let's say that Twitter existed in 1998. If I wanted to visualize and understand my tweets back then, I would have had to go the Microsoft route.

Of course, it's not 1998 anymore. Answering these simple questions now requires less thought and data analysis than you might expect. Technology today is far more powerful, open, user-friendly, ubiquitous, and inexpensive compared to the mid-1990s.

---

* Reportedly, a mind-blowing $10,000 per tweet.

Like many companies today, Twitter relies upon a *relatively* open application programming interface (API).* At a high level, APIs allow devices, apps, and Web services to easily interact with one another. They also facilitate the near-instant flow of data. Lately, APIs have become all the rage. Myriad people use them every day, whether they know it or not. Facebook, LinkedIn, FourSquare, Google, and scores of other companies effectively use APIs for all sorts of reasons. And forget massive tech companies with billion-dollar valuations. Many start-ups are based on "the Twitter fire hose," including the aforementioned HootSuite. Open APIs encourage development of third-party products and services, a topic I discussed in great detail in *The Age of the Platform*.

One such service is Vizify, a start-up founded in 2011 and based in Portland, Oregon. The company is a proud graduate of both Seattle TechStars and the Portland Seed Fund. I fittingly "met" company cofounder and CEO Todd Silverstein over Twitter in June 2013 while researching this book. Vizify quickly and easily lets users connect to different social networks like Facebook, Twitter, FourSquare, and LinkedIn.

It took about three minutes for Vizify to pull my photos, education history, current occupation, work history, home page, tweets, and other key profile data that I've chosen to make publicly available. Of course, users aren't obligated to connect to any individual network. (I passed on FourSquare.) After the initial load, users can easily remove pictures or other information they would prefer not to share. By accessing open APIs, Vizify allows users to create free and interactive visual profiles. Mine is shown in Figure I.1.

If you want to see my full multipage profile, go to https://www.vizify.com/phil-simon. In case you're wondering, users can change the colors on their profiles. I went with that particular shade of green as a homage to *Breaking Bad*.

A snazzy visual profile is all fine and dandy, but it still didn't answer my Twitter question. Fortunately, Vizify also allowed me to effortlessly see the evolution of my tweets over time. A screenshot from that part of my profile is shown in Figure I.2.

Figure I.2 proved what I had suspected. First, I use Twitter for both business and personal reasons. Second, my tweets for #BigData began to increase in October 2012. At that time, I was knee-deep into the research for my previous book, *Too Big to Ignore: The Business Case for Big Data*. Before then, I didn't tweet about #BigData very often, much less the title of the book (#TooBigToIgnore).

But not everything changes—at least with me. For instance, my tweets about #BreakingBad and #Rush have remained fairly constant over time, with a few notable exceptions. (*Did I really go a whole month in early 2013 without mentioning Canada's finest export on Twitter?*)

---

* It used to be more open and has recently earned the ire of many developers for allegedly heavy-handed tactics. For more on the Twitter API, see https://twitter.com/twitterapi.

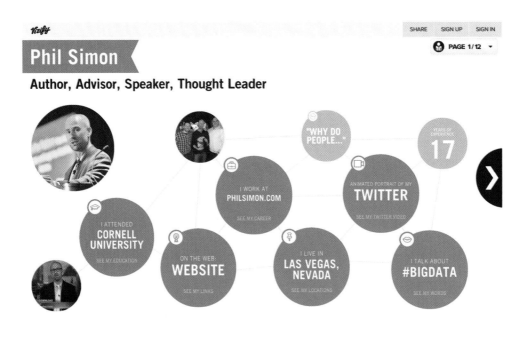

Figure I.1 Vizify Phil Simon Profile
Image courtesy of Vizify

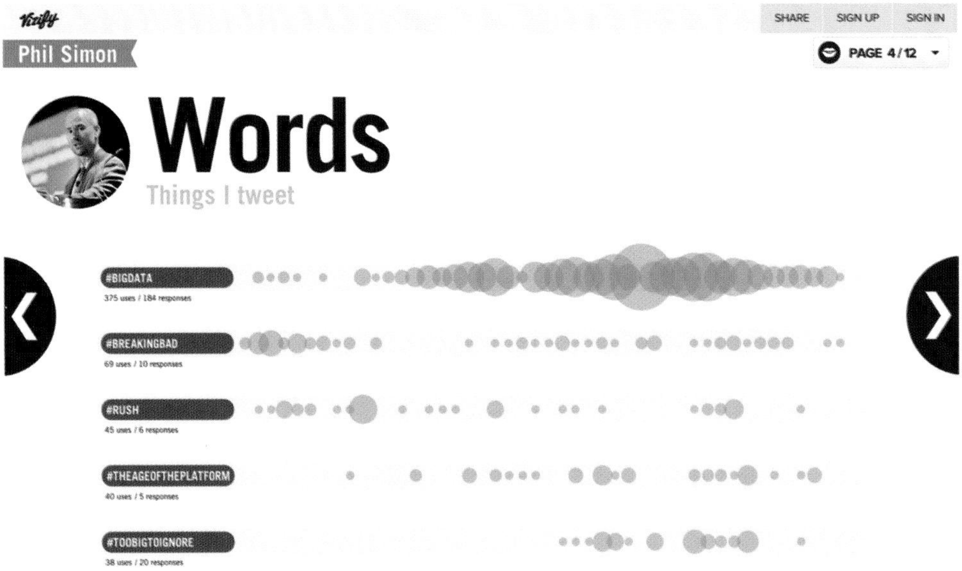

Figure I.2 Vizify Representation of @philsimon Tweets
Image courtesy of Vizify

▶ NOTE
Vizify allows users to customize their public profiles, as well as see their other frequently used Twitter hashtags. Figure I.2 shows a snapshot of my top-five hashtags as of June 2013.*

Even though this was a one-time experiment, I could see using Vizify on a regular basis. My tweets will continue to evolve, probably mirroring my professional endeavors and newfound personal interests. Case in point: my publisher has scheduled this book to be released in early 2014. If I run Vizify again around that time, I would assume that many of my tweets will contain the hashtag #dataviz. Fortunately, that won't be difficult to discern.

So, my tweets have changed over time, but (as you can probably tell) this process just whet my appetite. I was still curious about my Twitter habits, and other questions remained, like this one: what were my peak tweeting hours? It took only a few clicks to answer that question. Vizify created a personal 30-second video analyzing my tweets.† A screenshot from that video is presented in Figure I.3.

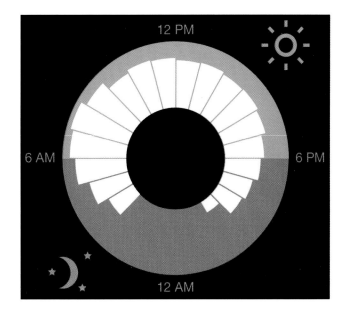

Figure I.3 @philsimon Tweets by Hour of Day
Image courtesy of Vizify

---

* Vizify even lets users create 30-second Twitter videos based on pictures tweeted. To see mine, go to https://www.vizify.com/phil-simon/twitter-video.

† To see my video, go to https://www.vizify.com/phil-simon/twitter-video.

Since I have always been a morning person, it's no shocker that my first tweets start as early as 6 a.m. On most days, I wake up by 5 a.m. and promptly make myself a cup of coffee. I check my e-mail and tweet new posts or articles I've written for my clients or my own sites. I intentionally break up my normal day to give my weary eyes a rest by hitting the gym around 10 a.m. By 6 p.m., I've already put in more than a full day. I'm rarely in front of my computer after that time, although, like many people, I have recently embraced the two-screen experience of tweeting when I watch television. (It's a sign of the times. For many TV viewers today, "It is a common practice to tweet while watching. Nielsen has new research that confirms for the first time that tweets can increase a TV program's ratings."[1])

Vizify confirmed what I expected: I am not much of a late-night tweeter, although I occasionally schedule tweets and let HootSuite auto-tweet for me. (I generally try to space out my tweets, and I don't follow anyone who tweets 34 times per hour. It's fair to say that I have developed my own Twitter philosophy. I'd even call myself a bit of a Twitter snob.)

Aside from my most frequently used hashtags, Vizify also identified my most frequent targets—that is, the people about whom I tweeted most often. I have particular affection for author and professor Terri Griffith (@terrigriffith) and blogger Jim Harris (@ocdqblog). In Jim's case, the feeling is mutual.*

Vizify let me indulge in what was mostly an intellectual exercise. (I can't say that my boss forced me to geek out.) I was curious about my tweeting history and decided to play around with a new toy, hardly an uncommon occurrence for me. And there is a slew of other toys. For instance, Ionz lets users easily "self-visualize" their Twitter data, and Visually lets users do something similar with their Facebook data. But data visualization is anything but the sole purview of geeks like me with admittedly too much time on their hands. Social networks are becoming more interactive, data driven, and visual.

Twitter senior management pays close attention to what its ecosystem and competition are doing, as it should. Not that Twitter is alone here. For instance, in June 2013, Facebook added verified accounts, support for hashtags, and Vine-like video capabilities to its Instagram app. Seem familiar? Facebook clearly "borrowed" these features from Twitter. Such is life in the Age of the Platform; frenemies and coopetition are the norm. During that same month, Twitter added enhanced native analytics of its own.† I have presented my own in Figure I.4.

I'll spare you any more analysis of my tweets. You get it. This little yarn only serves to illustrate one of the key points in this book: it's never been easier or more essential to visualize data.

---

* You can watch Jim's video here: https://www.vizify.com/jim-harris-1/twitter-video.

† To see yours, just go to http://tinyurl.com/analytics-twitter and log in.

Figure I.4 @philsimon Twitter Analytics
Source: Twitter

CONTEMPORARY DATAVIZ 101

Incessant social media, memes, and nonstop content permeate our lives. With seemingly every new hot topic or trend, there's no shortage of definitions, many of which come from people and organizations with vested interests in *their* definition winning (read: consulting firms, software vendors, and thought leaders).

In both *The Age of the Platform* and *Too Big to Ignore*, I devote a fair amount of space to defining in plain English my key terms *platforms* and *Big Data*, respectively. There's so much noise and confusion out there on each topic. I feel the need to do the same here with *data visualization*.

▶ **NOTE**

In this book, contemporary *data visualization*, or *dataviz*, signifies the practice of representing data through visual and often interactive means. An individual dataviz represents information after it been abstracted in some schematic form. Finally, contemporary data visualization technologies are capable of incorporating what we now call Big Data.

Primary Objective

There's a surfeit of data-oriented terms in the business world right now because data is just plain hot. Let me be absolutely clear here: modern-day dataviz is *not* just a synonym or a fancy term for data mining, business intelligence, the many forms of analytics,* or enterprise reporting.

Delineating among all these terms isn't terribly important here. Chapter 2 returns to this subject. For now, suffice it to say that these concepts aren't completely unrelated to one another. In fact, there's a great deal of overlap among them. The most obvious: each is predicated on data in one form or another.

Views on the "proper" goal of dataviz vary considerably. For instance, consider the words of Vitaly Friedman, the editor-in-chief of *Smashing Magazine*, an online periodical for professional Web designers and developers:

> The main goal of data visualization is its ability to visualize data, communicating information clearly and effectively. It doesn't mean that data visualization needs to look boring to be functional or extremely sophisticated to look beautiful. To convey ideas effectively, both aesthetic form and functionality need to go hand in hand, providing insights into a rather sparse and complex dataset by communicating its key aspects in a more intuitive way. Yet designers often tend to discard the balance between design and function, creating gorgeous data visualizations which fail to serve its main purpose—communicate information.[2]

Communicating information is unquestionably important, but not everyone believes in its primacy (read: that it should be *the* goal of dataviz). Dataviz pioneers Fernanda Viégas and Martin M. Wattenberg have suggested that the ideal dataviz goes beyond promoting understanding and communication. Those are short-term goals that should buttress the long-term aims of making better business decisions and even prediction. We'll see in Part II how Visual Organizations use dataviz to do much more than understand what's currently happening.

Dataviz applications are certainly important, but it's best to think of data visualization as more than the output of some software program. So argues Nathan Yau in his 2013 book *Data Points: Visualization That Means Something.* Yau stresses the importance of thinking of dataviz more as a medium than a specific tool. "Visualization is a way to represent data, an abstraction of the real world, in the same way that the written word can be used to tell different kinds of stories," he writes. "Newspaper articles aren't judged on the same criteria as novels, and data art should be critiqued differently than a business dashboard."[3]

I could quote other dataviz experts *ad infinitum,* but I won't belabor the point: opinions on the topic are far from unanimous. For the purposes of this book, dataviz shares the same *ultimate* goal with data mining, business intelligence (BI), analytics, and enterprise reporting: to make more informed

---

* These include standard analytics, Big Data analytics, visual analytics, not to mention industry-specific analytics like retail, health care, and manufacturing.

business decisions. Contemporary dataviz is primarily a means of exploring data and discovering valuable insights. It is not about reporting *per se* nor is it about creating pretty graphs or charts for the sake of doing so. In other words, the most valuable data visualizations today are often based on the premise that employees don't knowing exactly what they're looking for, much less what they'll find. By exploring the data, employees are *more likely* to discover interesting tidbits or revelations that should drive better decision-making and outcomes. (You won't find too many absolutes and guarantees in this book. I'm a big fan of probabilistic thinking.)

Benefits

To be sure, data doesn't always need to be visualized, and many data visualizations just plain suck. Look around you. It's not hard to find truly awful representations of information. Some work in concept but fail because they are too busy; they confuse people more than they convey information, to paraphrase the late George Carlin.* Visualization for the sake of visualization is unlikely to produce desired results—and this goes double in an era of Big Data. Bad is still bad, even and especially at a larger scale.

John Sviokla serves as the vice chairman of Diamond Management & Technology Consultants. As he writes on the *Harvard Business Review* blog,[4] dataviz confers three general benefits:

1. Great visualizations are efficient. They let people look at vast quantities of data quickly.
2. Visualizations can help analysts or groups achieve more insight into the nature of a problem and discover new understanding.
3. A great visualization can help create a shared view of a situation and align folks on needed actions.

At a high level, Sviokla is spot-on. Consider the following example, as it demonstrates how quickly even a simple dataviz can communicate information. Figure I.5 shows a comical visual of six prominent companies' 2011 org charts.

Would it be hard to write a few sentences on each organization's structure? Of course not. In early 2011, Apple revolved around one iconic man. Even after Steve Jobs's death, his presence is deeply felt throughout the company. For its part, Oracle is still a litigious company. Microsoft is composed of warring factions. Looking at the six images in Figure I.5 represents a quicker and certainly more humorous way of summarizing each company than even my witty text probably could.

---

* You can watch his rant on language here: http://tinyurl.com/carlin-language.

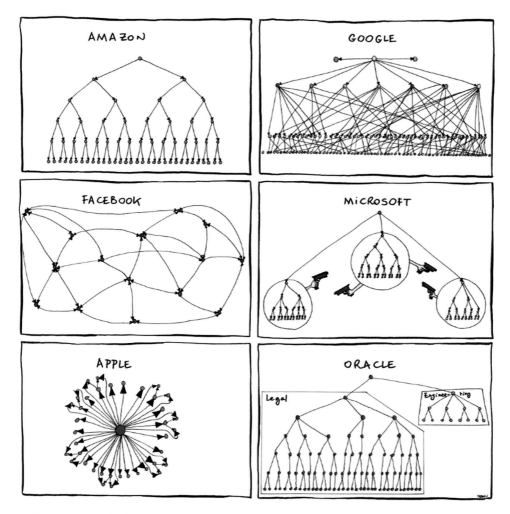

Figure I.5 Organizational Charts (2011)
Source: Manu Cornet

I would add that, for the purposes of understanding large, unpredictable datasets, *interactive* data visualizations are generally superior to static infographics, dashboards, and standard reports. (I should know. I've designed thousands of the latter in my consulting career for my clients.) By definition, presenting even Small Data in predetermined, static, noninteractive formats limits what users can do with—and ultimately get from—data. This has always been the case. In other words, these types of formats generally preclude people from interacting with the data.* They can't drill down and around. They can't explore, nor can they ask iterative and better questions, and ultimately find answers.

---

* Good report writers know that it's not terribly difficult to add some level of interactivity to static reports. For one example of how to do this, see http://tinyurl.com/phil-crystal.

More Important Than Ever

Like all sentient beings, we humans have *always* processed information in different ways, or at least attempted to do so. Many researchers have proven that there is something unique about how we *see* information, as opposed to how we hear it. Many excellent studies and books have informed our current understanding of the workings of the human brain, and I certainly won't attempt to summarize them all here. *The Visual Organization* is in no way a book about the behavioral sciences, neurology, or cognitive psychology. I will, however, concisely mention a few of the more important works in those fields.

> There are myriad questions that we can ask from data today. As such, it's impossible to write enough reports or design a functioning dashboard that takes into account every conceivable contingency and answers every possible question.

"The human visual system is a pattern seeker of enormous power and subtlety," writes Colin Ware in his classic text *Information Visualization: Perception for Design*. "The eye and the visual cortex of the brain form a massive parallel processor that provides the highest bandwidth channel into human cognitive centers. At higher levels of processing, perception and cognition are closely interrelated, which is why the words *understanding* and *seeing* are synonymous."[5] Our brains are wired to process information better in a visual manner.

That humans tend to comprehend visual information quicker than raw data doesn't mean that all visualizations are created equal. On the contrary, we understand certain types of graphical representations better than others. Researchers William S. Cleveland and Robert McGill proved as much in September 1984. Cleveland and McGill published a paper in the *Journal of the American Statistical Association* titled "Graphical Perception: Theory, Experimentation, and Application to the Development of Graphical Methods." Cleveland and McGill studied the visual clues that people are able to decode most accurately. The two ranked these clues in the following list:

1. Position along a common scale, e.g., scatter plot
2. Position on identical but nonaligned scales, e.g., multiple scatter plots
3. Length, e.g., bar chart
4. Angle and slope (tie), e.g., pie chart
5. Area, e.g., bubbles
6. Volume, density, and color saturation (tie), e.g., heat map
7. Color hue, e.g., news map

A slightly modified visual of this list is presented in Figure I.6. In English, it means that not all people comprehend and decode all visual cues equally. For instance, we tend to understand data positioned along a

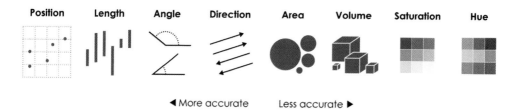

Figure I.6 Visual Cues Ranking
Source: Reprinted with permission from *The Journal of the American Statistical Association.* Copyright 1984 by the American Statistical Association. All rights reserved.

common scale better than data shown on heat maps. Note, however, that the findings of Cleveland and McGill should not be seen in absolute terms. The study suggests that absolutes are a myth and that the ability to understand visual clues is situational. For example, some people will understand a bar chart better than a bubble chart. The Cleveland and McGill recommendations are just general guidelines.

In their 2012 book *Infographics: The Power of Visual Storytelling,* Jason Lankow, Josh Ritchie, and Ross Crooks demonstrate how even very simple formatting can make certain data stand out at the expense of other data. Consider Figure I.7, a series of random numbers. Go ahead and find each instance of the number 7.

Now, with simple formatting, repeat the same exercise with Figure I.8.

In professional settings, data has always mattered, although some departments and industries have been more likely to embrace it than others. In this

```
2 1 4 3 9 5 6 7 8 2 3 6 5 9 4 0 1
6 7 9 3 4 9 0 5 6 2 5 8 4 0 5 2 6
9 8 2 6 3 5 9 3 2 9 3 7 2 6 3 4 8
8 1 6 2 3 8 7 9 5 0 2 3 9 2 8 4 3
0 9 1 8 5 4 2 9 4 7 4 6 8 4 0 2 9
3 9 2 7 3 6 6 5 2 9 4 0 4 9 4 8 6
5 2 4 3 6 4 8 1 0 3 9 4 8 4 7 3 2
8 6 2 3 0 8 7 3 6 2 5 4 4 8 3 5 0
```

Figure I.7 Preattentive Processing Test 1
Source: Lankow, Ritchie, and Crooksa

2	1	4	3	9	5	6	7	8	2	3	6	5	9	4	0	1
6	7	9	3	4	9	0	5	6	2	5	8	4	0	5	2	6
9	8	2	6	3	5	9	3	2	9	3	7	2	6	3	4	8
8	1	6	2	3	8	7	9	5	0	2	3	9	2	8	4	3
0	9	1	8	5	4	2	9	4	7	4	6	8	4	0	2	9
3	9	2	7	3	6	6	5	2	9	4	0	4	9	4	8	6
5	2	4	3	6	4	8	1	0	3	9	4	8	4	7	3	2
8	6	2	3	0	8	7	3	6	2	5	4	4	8	3	5	0

Figure I.8 Preattentive Processing Test 2
Source: Lankow, Ritchie, and Crooks

book, I contend that data visualization has never been more important. Chapter 1 will have a great deal more to say about the rise of the Visual Organization. For now, suffice it to say that representing information in schematic forms has always been essential to human understanding.

> We acquire more information through our visual system than we do through all our other senses *combined*. We understand things better and quicker when we see them.

Revenge of the Laggards: The Current State of Dataviz

Fifteen years ago, the presentation of data wasn't terribly democratic, sophisticated, and interactive, especially compared to today. Tech-savvy analysts and IT professionals generated static diagrams, graphs, and charts for quarterly or annual meetings or "special events." Back then, cutting-edge dataviz wasn't part and parcel to many jobs. There just wasn't that much data, especially compared to today.

In a way, this was entirely understandable. Yes, the late-1990s saw the advent of modern enterprise reporting and BI applications adroit at representing mostly structured data. In most organizations, however, relatively few people regularly visualized data, at least not *on a regular basis*.

My, how times have changed. Now data is everywhere. As I wrote in *Too Big to Ignore*, we are living in the era of Big Data, and many things are changing. In the workplace, let's focus on two major shifts. First, today it is becoming incumbent upon just about *every* member of a team, group, department, and organization to be, at a minimum, comfortable with data. Fewer and fewer knowledge workers can hide from quantitative analysis. Second, pie charts, bar charts, and other simple data visualizations of 15 years ago now seem quaint. They don't remotely resemble anything that qualifies as contemporary dataviz. More important, today they often fail to tell the stories that need to be told.

Next, data no longer needs be presented on an occasional or periodic basis. We are *constantly* looking at data of all types—a trend that will only intensify in the coming years. Before our eyes, we are seeing the ability to effectively present quantitative information in a compelling manner become a professional *sine qua non*. Hidden in the petabytes of structured and unstructured data are key consumer, employee, and organizational insight. *If found and unleashed*, those insights would invariably move the needle.

The PwC survey confirmed what I have long assumed. Although notable exceptions exist, only a minority of organizations and professionals currently do very much with dataviz. Most enterprises fail to present data in visually compelling ways. Far too many rely upon old standbys: bar charts, simple graphs, and the ubiquitous Excel spreadsheet. And their business decisions suffer as a result.

Why the widespread lack of adoption? I'd posit that several factors are at play here. First, while dataviz is hardly new, the landscape is. Many of the applications and services detailed in Chapter 2 are recent advents. Second, I have little doubt that the explosions of dataviz and Big Data left many CXOs overwhelmed. In this way, dataviz is much like cloud computing. With myriad options, it's natural for those in control of the purse strings to ask, "Where do we even start?"

Next, many organizations suffer from downright ignorance. Many lack the knowledge that better tools exist, not to mention that enterprises are successfully using them. (Hopefully, this book will change that, at least to some extent.) Then there are organizations whose cultures systematically ignore data and analysis. I have seen my share of those As such, their employees generally lack the willingness to try, buy, deploy, and use contemporary dataviz tools. When corporate fiat, culture, and politics dominate decision-making, what's the point of even looking at data?

For these reasons, it should be no surprise that Big Data is still in its infancy. Brian McKenna tackles this subject in an April 2013 ComputerWeekly article. About the state of Big Data, he writes that "Analytics firm SAS and SourceMedia surveyed 339 data-management professionals about their organizations' use of

▶ **NOTE**

The hype around Big Data and, to a lesser extent, dataviz still far exceeds their business realities. To quote former Notre Dame coach Lou Holtz, "When all is said and done, more is said than done." Rather than hem and haw, organizations should recognize the vast opportunity that the status quo represents. Those that act now can realize significant benefits that won't be available to them once their competition wakes up.

THE CURRENT DATA ON DATAVIZ

Sadly, most employees—and, by extension, departments and organizations—don't capitalize on the massive opportunities presented by Big Data and data visualization. So says consulting firm PricewaterhouseCoopers (PwC) in its fifth annual Digital IQ Survey (titled "Digital Conversations and the C-suite").

In 2013, PwC surveyed 1,108 respondents from 12 countries across a variety of industries. Respondents were equally split between IT and business leaders. More than 75 percent worked in organizations with revenues of more than $1 billion.*

FINDINGS

A majority of respondents (62 percent) think that Big Data can provide a competitive advantage. That's not exactly surprising, but believing in the power of Big Data is hardly the same as turning it into actual business insights—and then acting upon them. Nearly the same number of respondents (58 percent) agreed that moving from data to insight is much easier said than done.

Only 26 percent of global survey respondents are currently using dataviz. (I suspect that many of these "forward-thinking" organizations aren't exactly Google-like in their execution.) Interestingly, though, adoption—or lack thereof—is not evenly distributed among all respondents. Specifically, those that reported revenue growth in excess of 5 percent led the pack—and weren't letting up. They planned to invest more in data visualization in 2013. The same can be said of organizations in the top quartile for revenue, profitability, and innovation. The gap between the dataviz haves and have-nots seems to be growing.

OBSTACLES

Organizations face four major obstacles with respect to Big Data:

1. They are blind to the importance of visualization.
2. They are investing more in gathering data than analyzing it.
3. They are facing a talent gap.
4. They are struggling with insufficient systems to rapidly process information.

"The amount of information and data that we're collecting now is truly enormous, [especially] the volume that is outside the four walls of the organization," says Anand Rao, principal at PwC. "Organizations don't have the right people, they don't have the right structure in place, and they're still struggling with some of the tools and techniques."[6]

Rao points out that many organizations do a passable job at looking backward—that is, "hindsight analysis." Far fewer, though, predict very well. As we'll see throughout this book, dataviz can be useful in this regard.

---

* Access the entire report at http://tinyurl.com/pwc-dv-2.

data-management technology in December 2012, discovering reality still lags behind its hype. Only 12 percent of information management professionals are doing Big Data, according to a recent survey."[7] Remarkably, only 14 percent of respondents categorized their organizations as "very likely" to begin working with Big Data in 2014. Nearly one in five responded "not likely at all."

BOOK OVERVIEW

Big Data is here, leaving many organizations and their employees overwhelmed. Fortunately, new data-visualization applications are helping enterprises isolate the signal in the noise.

For instance, through interactive dataviz tools, Netflix discovers trends, diagnoses technical issues, and unearths obscure yet extraordinarily valuable customer insights. Employees at Autodesk use a remarkable and interactive tool that visualizes current and historical employee movement. From this, they identify potential management issues and see what a corporate reorg *really* looks like. Through cutting-edge dataviz, start-up Wedgies instantly serves up real-time poll results while monitoring poll traction and site issues. The University of Texas is bringing a visual type of transparency to academia. It makes unprecedented amounts and sources of institutional data available on its website. Anyone with the desire and an Internet connection can slice and dice a mountain of its data in myriad ways. And then there's eBay. Powerful data-discovery tools allow its employees to effectively "see" what ebay.com would look like as a brick-and-mortar store.

These progressive organizations are the exceptions that prove the rule. Most enterprises are woefully unprepared for Big Data. Far too many erroneously believe and act like nothing has really changed. As such, they continue to depend exclusively on reporting stalwarts like Microsoft Excel, static dash-boards, basic query applications, and even traditional business intelligence tools. In so doing, they are missing out on the tremendous opportunities that new data sources and dataviz tools can provide.

Amidst all the hype and confusion surrounding Big Data, though, a new type of enterprise is emerging: the Visual Organization. An increasing number of organizations have realized that today's ever-increasing data streams, vol-umes, and velocity require new applications. In turn, these new tools promote a different mind-set—one based upon data discovery and exploration, not on conventional enterprise reporting. Interactive heat maps, tree maps, and cho-ropleths promote true data discovery more than static graphs and pie charts.

Today, a growing number of enterprises have turned traditional dataviz on its head. In their stead, they are embracing new, interactive, and more robust tools that locate the signals in the noise that is Big Data. As a result, these enterprises are asking better questions of their data—and making better business decisions.

The Visual Organization is a largely positive and forward-thinking book. I focus more on profiling the organizations and employees who get it, not excoriating the ones that don't. (Trust me. There is no shortage of the latter.) Where warranted, I do attempt to explain the reasons behind certain types of stasis, dysfunction, and failure. These observations are based upon both my research for this book and the decade I spent as an enterprise IT consultant. Let me be clear: my goal here is *not* to harp on the negative. Rather, I merely want readers to understand the ways in which Visual Organizations differ from less progressive enterprises. As Bill Gates once said, "It's fine to celebrate success, but it is more important to heed the lessons of failure."

In the following pages, you'll meet some amazing companies and people who recognize the power of Big Data and dataviz. They are pushing the envelope and looking at problems very differently than their data-challenged counterparts. And they are seeing their efforts bear fruit.

Defining the Visual Organization

While useful and informative, many of the texts on data visualization emphasize theory more than practice. *The Visual Organization* does not. The forthcoming chapters introduce some fascinating practitioners who regularly visualize data to understand it, interpret it, and ultimately take action on it. You'll discover, as I did in researching this book, that Visual Organizations have moved well beyond simple charts, graphs, and dashboards that play nice with structured, transactional data—aka, *Small Data*.* They are using new tools to make sense of unstructured data, metadata (data about data), and other emerging data types and sources. And, as you'll see, the results are impressive.

▶ **NOTE**

Since this is a book about Visual Organizations, a short, formal definition is in order:

A Visual Organization is composed of intelligent people who recognize the power of data. As such, it routinely uses contemporary, powerful, and interactive dataviz tools to ask better questions and ultimately make better business decisions. As we'll see in Chapter 6, the notion of a Visual Organization is not binary; there are four levels. More advanced enterprises use interactive data-visualization applications to analyze Big Data. They recognize the inherent limitations of Small Data and static dataviz.

Central Thesis of This Book

The Visual Organization is based on a simple premise. The Data Deluge has arrived, and it isn't going anywhere. More than ever, employees and organizations

---

*Examples include a list of sales or employees. Think orderly and Excel-friendly data.

have to process and understand unprecedented amounts of information—*or at least try*. Complicating matters, new types and sources of data are flying at us faster than ever. Consider this amazing fact from *The Human Face of Big Data*, a fascinating book by Rick Smolan and Jennifer Erwitt. Today the average man is exposed to more data in a single day than his fifteenth-century counterpart was in his entire lifetime! According to an oft-cited March 2013 U.N. study, today more people can access cell phones than toilets.* Out of an estimated 7 billion people on the planet, roughly 6 billion can use mobile phones. Only 4.5 billion can say the same about working commodes.

Alternatively stated, data is streaming at us with increasing variety, velocity, and volume, with no discernible end in sight. These are the well-documented three *v's* of Big Data. Against this backdrop, intelligent organizations have realized several things. First, data visualization is becoming essential, and not just to manage discrete events. Visual Organizations benefit from *routinely* visualizing many different types and sources of data. Doing so allows them to garner a better understanding of what's happening and why. Equipped with this knowledge, employees are able to ask better questions and make better business decisions. As companies like Amazon, Apple, Facebook, Google, Twitter, Netflix, and others have shown, discoveries from Big Data can represent a huge competitive advantage. To do this, they have had to buy and build new tools. Yes, old standbys like Microsoft Excel spreadsheets, charts, dashboards, key performance indicators, and even mature business intelligence tools still matter. *By themselves, however, they are no longer sufficient to cope with the Data Deluge†.*

This is not a book about how to visualize data *per se*. Rather, it is a book about Visual Organizations.

Bottom line: we live in a world rife with Big Data. Organizations and their employees need different applications to find the needles buried in the haystacks, comprehend immense and dynamic datasets, and ultimately make better business decisions.

Cui Bono?

In any given month, I typically talk to a wide variety of people: CXOs, consultants, freelancers, mid-level managers, entry-level employees, unemployed professionals, journalists, fellow authors and speakers, professors, and college and graduate students. Some live in the United States, others abroad. They work at organizations that run the gamut: tiny start-ups, small businesses, and large corporations. And they work for nonprofits, government agencies, and the private sector. Although the conversations vary, I have noticed a recurring

---

* To read more, go to http://tinyurl.com/un-toilets.

†Doug Laney of Gartner coined the three v's in February of 2001. For more on this, see http://tinyurl.com/gartnervs.

theme over the past few years: most people are simply overwhelmed by data. They are struggling to cope with this deluge.

I wrote *The Visual Organization* for all of these people.

At its core, this book demonstrates how intelligent people and organizations are making better business decisions via contemporary dataviz new data visualization applications. Contemporary dataviz is no longer just nice to have or fodder for quarterly presentations. Organizations are increasingly embracing new dataviz tools, Big Data, and, most important, a new, data-driven mind-set. Visual Organizations and their employees are handling the Data Deluge better than their "visually challenged" counterparts. Finally, they distinguish between traditional reporting and data discovery.

In the forthcoming chapters, I'll demonstrate that dataviz is becoming indispensable, but make no mistake: it is no elixir. It does not solve every conceivable business problem. No matter how insightful, no matter how much data they present, data visualizations do not always provide the right answer, much less guarantee flawless execution. Often a dataviz only serves to clarify an existing issue, and there's no guarantee that it will shed light on every possible problem.

Limitations aside, the need for—and power of—dataviz has never been more pronounced, a fact that the Visual Organizations profiled in this book and their employees completely understand.

Methodology: Story Matters Here

Of all the companies started around the time of the dot-com boom, Amazon remains one of its few survivors. Calling it a *survivor*, however, is the acme of understatement. The company is nothing short of a titan—the Walmart of the Internet. And Amazon is causing unexpected ripple effects for a slew of companies and industries.

As I write these words, Oracle and its CEO Larry Ellison are forging partnerships with longtime rivals Microsoft and Salesforce.com.* The companies are putting aside their acrimonious histories with one other. They have struck an important alliance that attempts to preserve their footholds in the enterprise. At the core of their newfound and unexpected cooperation: a common fear of Jeff Bezos's firm. Amazon is a threat to them all. Ellison, Salesforce.com head Eric Benioff, and Microsoft big kahuna (at least, as of this writing) Steve Ballmer clearly understand the old Arabic proverb, "The enemy of my enemy is my friend."

Despite Amazon's longstanding prominence, the purportedly definitive text on was only recently written. Magazines like *Wired* have covered different

---

* The Oracle alliance put Salesforce.com's cloud-based CRM software atop Oracle apps and infrastructure. Cats and dogs living together...

aspects of the company very well and in some depth. Nearly 20 years after its founding, Amazon lacks the equivalent of an authorized tell-all, a comprehensive window into its vast business. Up until recently, the books written about the company have been at best incomplete and at worst disappointing. That finally changed in October 2013. *Bloomberg Businessweek* reporter Brad Stone published his much-anticipated book *The Everything Store: Jeff Bezos and the Age of Amazon*. The book is the closest thing available to a comprehensive company biography. Stone interviewed hundreds of former executives and operations, and I have eagerly followed the status of his book since it was announced.

As an author and occasional journalist, I am familiar with these types of press-related obstacles. (Maybe privacy isn't *completely* dead after all.) In researching previous books, I have contacted folks at high-profile companies, some of whom I would even call *friends*. My requests to speak on the record to employees in the know were politely denied, whether it was about privacy at Google or about Big Data at Facebook. In each case, these folks kindly told me that, as much as they may want to help me, their employers took controlling the message very seriously. I was disappointed but not offended. I understood. Access to senior management about proprietary or sensitive subjects isn't easy to come by, especially if the result is a book or an article.

None of this should be surprising. Steve Jobs only agreed to an authorized biography with Walter Isaacson when the former faced his imminent mortality. For years Jobs denied requests by authors and publishers to do the same thing. Like Jobs, Bezos is by all accounts a very private person, and Amazon follows the lead of its iconic CEO. Letting journalists and authors into their walled gardens ultimately serves no real business purpose. The risks far outweigh the rewards. Companies on that level aren't exactly hurting for PR, and flying under the radar suits them just fine. Sanctioned books like *In the Plex: How Google Thinks, Works, and Shapes Our Lives* by Steven Levy are the exceptions that prove the rule. (Levy's access to Google was unprecedented.)

In 2009, the AMC Network launched a new slogan: Story Matters Here. I couldn't agree more. For a book like *The Visual Organization* to work, I would have to do a good bit of research. That meant identifying organizations visualizing their data in interesting ways, making better business decisions as a result. In the Internet age, I knew that that wouldn't be terribly hard to do. Aside from my personal connections, I could use Google, Facebook, Twitter, LinkedIn, and other indispensable sites for research purposes.

But that wasn't all. To do this book right, I needed to do two other things. First, I would have to find dataviz practitioners doing cutting-edge things—and then talk to them. The dozens of conversations I had with dataviz professionals inform the pages that follow, whether or not I ultimately profiled their companies and clients. I learned a great deal, as I hope you will.

I have always aspired to write more books that are more "show me don't tell me." To that end, I knew that the book's case studies would be key—and I set that bar relatively high. I was clear with interviewees from the get-go. For their organizations to be featured in the text, they would have to get specific. I would need them to provide actual examples of the dataviz tools they used to do their jobs. Platitudes just wouldn't cut it.

Now, this wasn't my first rodeo. I knew that my self-imposed second requirement would pose more challenges than my first. For instance, United Parcel Service uses technology and data in truly amazing ways. UPS routes its trucks to millions of homes and businesses each day in an efficient manner. This process requires incredibly sophisticated algorithms. I am quite certain that the company's use of data visualization is book-worthy. In June of 2013, I reached out to a friend of mine, a UPS employee for more than two decades. My friend told me exactly what I expected: UPS keeps a low profile and does not like to be featured in magazine articles and books. Including fresh UPS material and examples of its proprietary tools in this book would require approval at the highest level of the company. (Can someone say *lawyers*?) Unfortunately, my efforts to include UPS went nowhere, as did similar attempts to pioneer new dataviz research on universally recognizable organizations like the National Basketball Association, Facebook, Twitter, ESPN, Pandora, and a few others. Just because these companies are not profiled in *The Visual Organization* doesn't mean that they're not doing fascinating things with data and dataviz.

With the exception of Netflix, the case studies in Part II meet *both* of my two criteria. (I'll explain the reasons for the slightly different methodology for Netflix in Chapter 3.) Profiling only relatively forthcoming organizations with remarkable dataviz stories has resulted in a better book. Such examples will, I hope, teach the reader important lessons about the subject, including what to do, what not to do, how to do it, and more. To me, a "story-centric" approach just made sense. It is superior to one that emphasized company notoriety at the expense of specifics and transparency. In the end, I believe that how, why, and what are more important than who. *The Visual Organization* benefits from profiling organizations with compelling and specific examples of contemporary data visualization, even if a few of those organizations aren't necessarily household names. And, as I'll argue in the following pages, these lesser-known enterprises may well become more recognized and successful precisely because they understand the tremendous value that data and dataviz offer.

The Quest for Knowledge and Case Studies

One day in August 2013, a graduate student by the name of James Eichinger tweeted at me. @Ikejames101 is studying predictive analytics at Northwestern University. In a subsequent e-mail, Eichinger informed me that wanted to do his final project on data visualization, but he was encountering a major problem. In his words, "Most of the case studies [he] found are either weak or tangential to the subject."[8] As for the blog posts on sites like *Harvard Business Review*, "Not a single one [shows] impacts on business decisions, management culture, or information efficiency." I didn't entirely concur with Eichinger's assessment, but our exchange piqued my curiosity about the prevalence of proper data-visualization case studies on the Web. I slept on it.

The next morning, I performed three specific Google searches. I queried existing case studies related to three different types of major enterprise technologies. The results are presented in Table I.1, and is displayed graphically in Figure I.9.

Even though Table I.1 and Figure I.9 confirmed my suspicions, it should *not* be taken as gospel or proof that the dataviz case study landscape is entirely barren. For three reasons, I wouldn't go that far.

First, think of Google's search data here as a proxy of sorts.* Without carping over the proper definition of the term *case study*, I have no doubt that there are more than 23 dataviz stories on the Web. (How many of them are actually good, useful, and vendor neutral is another matter altogether.)

Second, quantity should never be mistaken for quality. Many of the ERP and CRM case studies on the Web aren't terribly instructive. Third, by default, Google provides increasingly personalized results based upon factors like user geography, known demographic information, individual browsing history, and others.† Sometimes identical Google searches from ostensibly similar users yield wildly different results.

Table I.1 Google Search Results on Three Different Types of Case Studies

Google Search Term (with Quotes)	Approximate Results	Notes
"Data Visualization case studies"	23	Interestingly, two of the 23 results came from www.philsimon.com
"ERP case studies"	6,670	Enterprise resource planning
"CRM case studies"	16,500	Customer relationship management

Source: Google, as of August 31, 2013

---

* As any experienced Googler knows, small changes in search terms can yield vastly different results.

† Users can easily turn this "feature" off if they like.

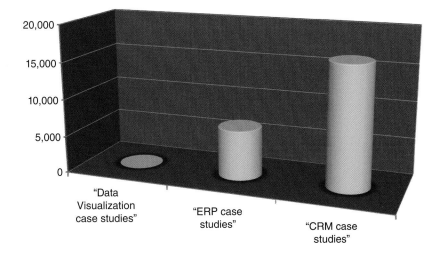

Figure I.9 Graph of Google Search Results on Three Different Types of Case Studies
Data Source: Google, as of August 31, 2013

Despite these qualifications, the differences in my little case study experiment are irrefutable. The number of CRM and ERP profiles are larger than their dataviz counterparts by orders of magnitude (717 and 290 times, respectively). Put differently, Table I.1. and Figure I.9 only illustrate what I, Eichinger, and countless others have found: profiles of organizations using contemporary dataviz and new forms of data not written by marketing departments are lacking. Data visualization is becoming critical, but how have organizations are *really* doing it? And what are the lessons? What are the pitfalls?

And that's where *The Visual Organization* steps in. It is my sincere hope that the observations, framework, case studies, interpretation, and original research in this book will help organizations use dataviz to move their needles. Academic studies and journal articles are certainly beneficial, but as of this writing there is a paucity of vendor-neutral case studies on the subject. Along these lines, perhaps this book will also make a meaningful contribution to the field of data visualization.

Differentiation: A Note on Other Dataviz Texts

The Visual Organization is hardly the first book about dataviz. On the contrary, many other researchers, authors, and practitioners have contributed a great deal to the field. It's no understatement to say that a vast body of work has been done on the topic.

In their books, Stephen Few, Edward Tufte, Alberto Cairo, Colin Ware, and Nathan Yau explain how to effectively visualize data very well. They cover the mechanics of creating graphs, charts, and, more recently, infographics, heat maps, tree maps, and choropleths. Many of these authors' books illustrate best design practices and serve as how-to guides, and I recommend checking them out. For their parts, dataviz researchers like Marek Walczak, Martin M. Wattenberg, and Fernanda Viégas have gone way beyond extending our current understanding of dataviz. They have created exciting new ways to visualize data. *The Visual Organization* does not attempt to replicate their work here.

Nor is this a text primarily about how the human brain processes data. I don't cover the science behind the mind's ability to understand information represented in a visual form. I'm the furthest thing from a neurologist. Again, a panoply of excellent books has already been written on the subject. The bottom line, as data journalist John Burn-Murdoch writes in *The Guardian*, is that "Humans are visual creatures. Peer-reviewed studies have shown that we can consume information more quickly when it is expressed in diagrams than when it is presented as text."[9]

The Visual Organization demonstrates how and why a growing number of organizations are visualizing their data to diagnose issues, discover new customer insights, and make better decisions.

Plan of Attack

The Visual Organization consists of four parts. Part I, "Book Overview and Background," examines the reasons behind the ascent of the Visual Organization. It also covers the five general categories of contemporary dataviz applications and services.

Part II, "Introducing the Visual Organization," introduces a number of diverse Visual Organizations. You'll discover how Netflix, Wedgies, Autodesk, and other enterprises have embraced Big Data and dataviz, and not just as discrete one-time "projects." We'll see how Visual Organizations have garnered profound customer insights and solved thorny business problems through new dataviz techniques and applications.

Part III, "Getting Started: Becoming a Visual Organization," takes a step back. It begins by providing a framework for readers to understand the four different levels of Visual Organizations. It then asks a key question before extrapolating a series of lessons, best practices, myths, and mistakes from the case studies in Part II. No, it's not a checklist to follow for becoming a Visual Organization, but it does present sage advice for readers interested in both reaping the benefits of dataviz and avoiding their common pitfalls.

Part IV, "Conclusion and the Future of Dataviz," concludes the book. It offers a number of careful predictions about current trends, Visual Organizations, Big Data, and the future of data visualization.

NEXT

Chapter 1 examines the ascent of the Visual Organization. It explains what's happening and why. We'll soon see that important business, cultural, technological, and human shifts are collectively causing enterprises of all kinds to change the way they think about data and traditional reporting.

NOTES

1. Snider, Mike, "Twitter Can Boost TV Ratings," *USA Today*, August 6, 2013, http://www.usatoday.com/story/tech/personal/2013/08/06/nielsen-twitter-affects-tv-ratings/2613267, Retrieved August 27, 2013.
2. Friedman, Vitaly, "Data Visualization and Infographics," *Smashing Magazine*, January 14, 2008, http://www.smashingmagazine.com/2008/01/14/monday-inspiration-data-visualization-and-infographics, Retrieved June 12, 2013.
3. Yau, Nathan, *Data Points: Visualization That Means Something*, Hoboken, NJ: Wiley, 2013.
4. Sviokla, John, "Swimming in Data? Three Benefits of Visualization," *Harvard Business Review* Blog Network, December 4, 2009. http://blogs.hbr.org/sviokla/2009/12/swimming_in_data_three_benefit.html, June 11, 2013.
5. Ware, Colin, *Information Visualization: Perception for Design*, Morgan Kaufmann, 2000.
6. Olavsrud, Thor, "4 Barriers Stand Between You and Big Data Insight," CIO.com, April 9, 2013, http://www.cio.com/article/731503/4_Barriers_Stand_Between_You_and_Big_Data_Insight, Retrieved August 27, 2013.
7. McKenna, Brian, "SAS: Data Quality, Data Governance Concerns Impede Big Data Programmes," ComputerWeekly.com April 3, 2013, http://www.computerweekly.com/news/2240180600/SAS-data-quality-data-governance-concerns-impede-big-data-programmes, Retrieved August 30, 2013.
8. E-mail from Eichinger, August 31, 2013.
9. Burn-Murdoch, John, "Why You Should Never Trust a Data Visualisation," theguardian.com, July 24, 2013, http://www.guardian.co.uk/news/datablog/2013/jul/24/why-you-should-never-trust-a-data-visualisation, Retrieved July 24, 2013.

The Ascent of the Visual Organization

Where is the knowledge we have lost in information?
—T. S. Eliot

Why are so many organizations starting to embrace data visualization? What are the trends driving this movement? In other words, why are organizations becoming more *visual*?

Let me be crystal clear: data visualization is by no means a recent advent. Cavemen drew primitive paintings as a means of communication. "We have been arranging data into tables (columns and rows) at least since the second century C.E. However, the idea of representing quantitative information graphically didn't arise until the seventeenth century."* So writes Stephen Few in his paper "Data Visualization for Human Perception."

In 1644, Dutch astronomer and cartographer Michael Florent van Langren created the first known graph of statistical data. Van Langren displayed a wide range of estimates of the distance in longitude between Toledo, Spain, and Rome, Italy. A century and a half later, Scottish engineer and political economist William Playfair invented staples like the line graph, bar chart, pie chart, and circle graph.†

Van Langren, Playfair, and others discovered what we now take for granted: compared to looking at individual records in a spreadsheet or database table, it's easier to understand data and observe trends with simple graphs and charts.

---

*To read the entire paper, go to http://tinyurl.com/few-perception.
† For more on the history of dataviz, see http://tinyurl.com/dv-hist.

(The neurological reasons behind this are beyond the scope of this book. Suffice it to say here that the human brain can more quickly and easily make sense of certain types of information when they are represented in a visual format.)

This chapter explores some of the social, technological, data, and business trends driving the visual organization. We will see that employees and organizations are willingly representing—or, in some cases, being forced to represent—their data in more visual ways.

Let's start with the elephant in the room.

THE RISE OF BIG DATA

We are without question living in an era of Big Data, and whether most people or organizations realize this is immaterial. As such, compared to even five years ago, today there is a greater need to visualize data. The reason is simple: there's just so much more of it. The infographic in Figure 1.1 represents some of the many statistics cited about the enormity of Big Data. And the amount of available data keeps exploding. Just look at how much content people generate in one minute on the Internet, as shown in Figure 1.2.

Figures 1.1 and 1.2 manifest that Big Data is, well, big—and this means many things. For one, new tools are needed to help people and organizations make sense of this. In *Too Big to Ignore*, I discussed at length how relational databases could not begin to store—much less analyze—petabytes of unstructured data. Yes, data storage and retrieval are important, but organizations ultimately should seek to use this information to make better business decisions.

OPEN DATA

Over the past few years, we've begun to hear more about another game-changing movement: open data. (Perhaps the seminal moment occurred when Sir Tim Berners-Lee gave a 2010 TED talk on the subject.*) Put simply, open data represents "the idea that certain data should be freely available to everyone to use and republish as they wish, without restrictions from copyright, patents, or other mechanisms of control."[1]

> While critical, the arrival of Big Data is far from the only data-related trend to take root over the past decade. The arrival of Big Data is one of the key factors explaining the rise of the Visual Organization.

Think of open data as the liberation of valuable information that fosters innovation, transparency, citizen participation, policy measurement, and better, more efficient government. Examples of open or public datasets include music metadata site MusicBrainz and geolocation site OpenStreetMap. But it

---

* To watch the talk, go to http://tinyurl.com/tim-open-data.

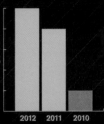

Figure 1.1 What Is Big Data?
Source: Asigra

doesn't stop there. Anyone today can access a wide trove of scientific, economic, health, census, and government data. Data sources and types are being released every day.* And, as Chapter 2 will show, there's no dearth of powerful and user-friendly tools designed specifically to visualize all this data.†

---

*To access some very large public datasets, see http://aws.amazon.com/publicdatasets.
† For some of them, see http://opendata-tools.org/en/visualization.

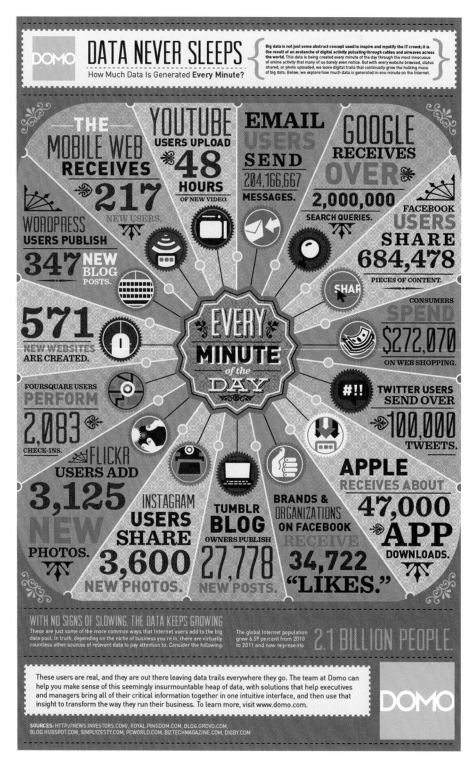

Figure 1.2 The Internet in One Minute
Source: Image courtesy of Domo; www.domo.com

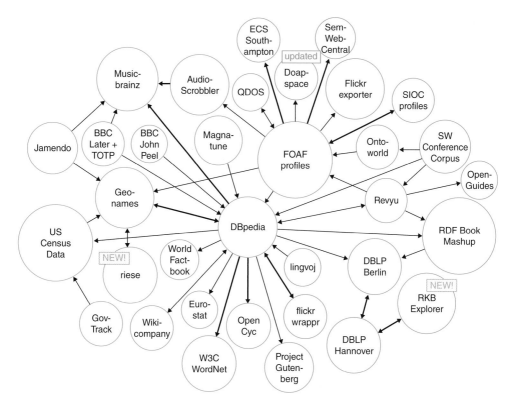

Figure 1.3 Examples of Mainstream Open Datasets as of 2008
Source: Richard Cyganiak, licensed under Creative Commons

Figure 1.3 represents a mere fraction of the open datasets currently available to anyone with an Internet connection and a desire to explore.*

Of course, the benefits of open data are not absolute. Unfortunately, and not surprisingly, many people use open data for malevolent purposes. For instance, consider Jigsaw, a marketplace that pays people to hand over other people's contact information. (I won't dignify Jigsaw with a link here.) As of this writing, anyone can download this type of data on more than 7 million professionals. Beyond annoying phone calls from marketers and incessant spam, it's not hard to imagine terrorist organizations accessing open data for nefarious purposes. Still, the pros of open data far exceed their cons.

THE BURGEONING DATA ECOSYSTEM

In the Introduction, I discussed how anyone could easily visualize their Facebook, Twitter, and LinkedIn data. I used Vizify to create an interesting visual profile of my professional life, but Vizify and its ilk are really just the tip of the

---

* For a larger visual of what's out there, see http://tinyurl.com/open-data-book.

iceberg. Through open APIs, scores of third parties can currently access that data and do some simply amazing things. For instance, MIT's Immersion Project lets Gmail users instantly visualize their e-mail connections.*

As far as I know, Google has no legal obligation to keep any of its APIs open. Nor is it compelled to regularly lease or license its user data or metadata to an entity. (Government edicts to turn over user data like the 2013 PRISM affair are, of course, another matter.) The company chooses to make this information available. If you're curious about what Google permits itself to do, check out its end-user license agreement (EULA).†

Perhaps Google will incorporate some of the Immersion Project's features or technology into Gmail or a new product or service. And maybe Google will do the same with other third-party efforts. Progressive companies are keeping tabs on how developers, partners, projects, and start-ups are using their products and services—*and the data behind them*. This is increasingly becoming the norm. As I wrote in *The Age of the Platform*, Amazon, Apple, Facebook, Google, Salesforce.com, Twitter, and other prominent tech companies recognize the significance of ecosystems and platforms, especially with respect to user data.

THE NEW WEB: VISUAL, SEMANTIC, AND API-DRIVEN

Since its inception, and particularly over the past eight years, the Web has changed in many ways. Perhaps most significantly to laypeople, it has become much more visual. Behind the scenes, techies like me know that major front-end changes cannot take place sans fundamental technological, architectural, and structural shifts, many of which are data driven.

The Arrival of the Visual Web

Uploading photos to the Web today is nearly seamless and instant. Most of you remember, though, that it used to be anything but. I'm old enough to remember the days of text-heavy websites and dial-up Internet service providers (ISPs) like Prodigy and AOL. Back in the late 1990s, most people connected to the Internet via glacially slow dial-up modems, present company included. Back then I could hardly contain my excitement when I connected at 56 kilobits per second. Of course, those days are long gone, although evidently AOL still counts nearly three million dial-up customers to this day.[2] (No, I couldn't believe it either.)

Think about Pinterest for a moment. As of this writing, the company sports a staggering valuation of $3.5 billion without a discernible business model—or

---

* Check out https://immersion.media.mit.edu/viz#.

† A EULA establishes the user's or the purchaser's right to use the software. For more on Google's EULA, see http://tinyurl.com/google-eula.

at least a publicly disclosed one beyond promoted pins. As J.J. Colao writes on Forbes.com, "So how does one earn such a rich valuation without the operating history to back it up? According to Jeremy Levine, a partner at Bessemer Venture Partners who sits on Pinterest's board, the answer is simple: 'People love it.'"[3] (In case you're wondering, I'll come clean about Pinterest. It's not a daily habit, but I occasionally play around with it.*)

It's no understatement to say that we are infatuated with photos, and plenty of tech bellwethers have been paying attention to this burgeoning trend. On April 9, 2012, Facebook purchased Instagram, the hugely popular photo-sharing app. The price? A staggering $1 billion in cash and stock. At the time, Instagram sported more than 30 million users, but no proper *revenue*, let alone profits. Think Zuckerberg lost his mind? It's doubtful, as other titans like Google were reportedly in the mix for the app.

Thirteen months later, Yahoo CEO Marissa Mayer announced the much-needed overhaul of her company's Flickr app. Mayer wrote on the company's Tumblr blog, "We hope you'll agree that we have made huge strides to make Flickr awesome again, and we want to know what you think and how to further improve!"[4] And hip news-oriented apps like Zite and Flipboard are heavy on the visuals.

Facts like these underscore how much we love looking at photos, taking our own, and tagging our friends. Teenagers and *People* aficionados are hardly alone here. Forget dancing cats, college kids partaking in, er, "extracurricular" activities, and the curious case of Anthony Weiner. For a long time now, many popular business sites have included and even featured visuals to accompany their articles. It's fair to say that those without photos look a bit dated. Many *Wall Street Journal* articles include infographics. Many blog posts these days begin with featured images. Pure text stories seem so 1996, and these sites are responding to user demand. Readers today *expect* articles and blog posts to include graphics. Ones that do often benefit from increased page views and, at a bare minimum, allow readers to quickly scan an article and take something away from it.

Linked Data and a More Semantic Web

It's not just that data has become bigger and more open. As the Web matures and data silos continue to break down, data becomes increasingly interconnected. As recently as 2006, only a tiny percentage of data on the Web was linked to other data.† Yes, there were oodles of information online, but tying one dataset to another was often entirely manual, not to mention extremely challenging.

---

* See my pins and boards at http://pinterest.com/philsimon2.

† For more on this, see http://www.w3.org/DesignIssues/LinkedData.html.

▶ **NOTE**

Some degree of overlap exists among the terms *linked data* and *open data* (discussed earlier in this chapter). That is, some open data is linked and arguably most linked data is open, depending on your definition of the term. Despite their increasing intersection, the two terms should *not* be considered synonyms. As Richard MacManus writes on ReadWriteWeb, open data "commonly describes data that has been uploaded to the Web and is accessible to all, but isn't necessarily 'linked' to other data sets. [It] is available to the public, but it doesn't link to other data sources on the Web."[5]

Today we are nowhere near connecting all data. Many datasets cannot be easily and immediately linked to each other, and that day may never come. Still, major strides have been made to this end over the past eight years. The Web is becoming more semantic (read: more meaningful) in front of our very eyes. (David Siegel's book *Pull: The Power of the Semantic Web to Transform Your Business* covers this subject in more detail.)

The term *linked data* describes the practice of exposing, sharing, and connecting pieces of data, information, and knowledge on the semantic Web. Both humans and machines benefit when previously unconnected data is connected. This is typically done via Web technologies such as uniform resource identifiers* and the Resource Description Framework.†

A bevy of organizations—both large and small—is making the Web smarter and more semantic by the day. For instance, consider import.io, a U.K.-based start-up that seeks to turn webpages into tables of structured data. As Derrick Harris of GigaOM writes, the "service lets users train what [CEO Andrew] Fogg calls a 'data browser' to learn what they're looking for and create tables and even an application programming interface out of that data. The user dictates what attributes will comprise the rows and columns on the table, highlights them, and import.io's technology fills in the rest."[6]

The Relative Ease of Accessing Data

Yes, there is more data than ever, and many organizations struggle trying to make heads or tails out of it. Fortunately, however, all hope is not lost. The data-management tools available to organizations of all sizes have never been more powerful.

Prior to the Internet, most large organizations moved their data among their different systems, databases, and data warehouses through a process

---

* In computing, a uniform resource identifier is a string of characters used to identify a name or a Web resource. It should not to be confused with its two subclasses: uniform resource locator and uniform resource name.

† The Resource Description Framework is a family of World Wide Web Consortium specifications originally designed as a metadata data model.

known as *extract, transform, and load*, or *ETL*. Database administrators and other techies would write scripts or stored procedures to automate this process as much as possible. Batch processes would often run in the wee hours of the morning. At its core, ETL extracts data from System A, transforms or converts that data into a format friendly to System B, and then loads the data into System B. Countless companies to this day rely upon ETL to power all sorts of different applications. ETL will continue to exist in a decade, and probably much longer than that.

Now, ETL has had remarkable staying power in the corporate IT landscape. Today it is far from dead, but the game has changed. ETL is certainly not the only way to access data or to move data from Point A to Point B. And ETL is often not even the best method for doing so. These days, many mature organizations are gradually supplanting ETL with APIs. And most start-ups attempt to use APIs from the get-go for a number of reasons. Data accessed via APIs is optimized for consumption and access as opposed to storage.

In many instances, compared to ETL, APIs are just better suited for handling large amounts of data. In the words of Anant Jhingran, VP of products at enterprise software vendor Apigee:

> The mobile and apps economy means that the interaction with customers happens in a broader context than ever before. Customers and partners interact with enterprises via a myriad of apps and services. Unlike traditional systems, these new apps, their interaction patterns, and the data that they generate all change very rapidly. In many cases, the enterprise does not "control" the data. As such, traditional ETL does not and will not cut it.[7]

Jhingran is absolutely right about the power of—and need for—APIs. No, they are not elixirs, but they allow organizations to improve a number of core business functions these days. First, they provide access to data in faster and more contemporary ways than ETL usually does. Second, they allow organizations to (more) quickly identify data quality issues. Third, open APIs tend to promote a generally more open mind-set, one based upon innovation, problem solving, and collaboration. APIs benefit not only companies but their *ecosystems*—that is, their customers, users, and developers.

In the Twitter and Vizify examples in the Introduction, I showed how real-time data and open APIs let me visualize data without manual effort. In the process, I discovered a few things about my tweeting habits. Part III will provide additional examples of API-enabled data visualizations.

Greater Efficiency via Clouds and Data Centers

I don't want to spend too much time on it here, but it would be remiss not to mention a key driver of this new, more efficient Web: cloud computing. It is no understatement to say that it is causing a tectonic shift in many organizations and industries.

By way of background, the history of IT can be broken down into three eras:

1. The Mainframe Era
2. The Client-Server Era
3. The Mobile-Cloud Era

Moving from one era to another doesn't happen overnight. While the trend is irrefutable, the mainframe is still essential for many mature organizations and their operations. They're called *laggards* for a reason. Over the foreseeable future, however, more organizations will get out of the IT business. Case in point: the propulsive success of Amazon Web Services, by some estimates a nearly $4 billion business *by itself*.[8] (Amazon frustrates many analysts by refusing to break out its numbers.) Put simply, more and more organizations are realizing that they can't "do" IT as reliably and inexpensively as Amazon, Rackspace, VMware, Microsoft Azure, and others. This is why clunky terms like *infrastructure as a service* and *platform as a service* have entered the business vernacular.

Students of business history will realize that we've seen this movie before. Remarkably, a century ago, many enterprises generated their own electricity. One by one, each eventually realized the silliness of its own efforts and turned to the utility companies for power. Nicholas Carr makes this point in his 2009 book *The Big Switch: Rewiring the World, from Edison to Google*. Cloud computing is here to stay, although there's anything but consensus after that.* For instance, VMware CEO Pat Gelsinger believes that it will be "decades" before the public cloud is ready to support all enterprise IT needs.[9]

Brass tacks: the Web has become much more visual, efficient, and data-friendly.

BETTER DATA TOOLS

The explosion of Big Data and Open Data did not take place overnight. Scores of companies and people saw this coming. Chief among them are some established software vendors and relatively new players like Tableau, Cloudera, and HortonWorks. These vendors have known for a while that organizations will soon need new tools to handle the Data Deluge. And that's exactly what they provide.

Over the past 15 years, we have seen marked improvement in existing business intelligence solutions and statistical packages. Enterprise-grade applications from MicroStrategy, Microsoft, SAS, SPSS, Cognos, and others have upped their games considerably.† Let me be clear: these products can without question do

---

* Even the definition of *cloud computing* is far from unanimous. Throw in the different types of clouds (read: public, semi-public, and private), and brouhahas in tech circles can result.

† IBM acquired both SPSS and Cognos, although each brand remains.

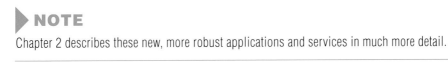

NOTE

Chapter 2 describes these new, more robust applications and services in much more detail.

more than they could in 1998. However, focusing exclusively on the evolution of mature products does not tell the full story. To completely understand the massive wave of innovation we've seen, we have to look beyond traditional BI tools. The aforementioned rise of cloud computing, SaaS, open data, APIs, SDKs, and mobility have collectively ushered in an era of rapid deployment and minimal or even zero hardware requirements. New, powerful, and user-friendly data-visualization tools have arrived. Collectively, they allow Visual Organizations to present information in innovative and exciting ways. Tableau is probably the most visible, but it is just one of the solutions introduced over the past decade.

Today, organizations of all sizes have at their disposal a wider variety of powerful, flexible, and affordable dataviz tools than ever. They include free Web services for start-ups to established enterprise solutions.

Equipped with these tools, services, and marketplaces, employees are telling fascinating stories via their data, compelling people to act, and making better business decisions. And, thanks to these tools, employees need not be proper techies or programmers to instantly visualize different types and sources of data. As you'll see in this book, equipped with the right tools, laypersons are easily interacting with and sharing data. Visual Organizations are discovering hidden and emerging trends. They are identifying opportunities and risks buried in large swaths of data. And they are doing this often without a great deal of involvement from their IT departments.

VISUALIZING BIG DATA: THE PRACTITIONER'S PERSPECTIVE

IT operations folks have visualized data for decades. For instance, employees in network ops centers normally use multiple screens to monitor what's taking place. Typically of great concern are the statuses of different systems, networks, and pieces of hardware. Record-level data was rolled into summaries, and a simple red or green status would present data in an easily digestible format.

This has changed dramatically over the past few years. We have seen a transformation of sorts. Tools like Hadoop allow for the easy and inexpensive collection of vastly more data than even a decade ago. Organizations can now maintain, access, and analyze petabytes of raw data. Next-generation dataviz tools can interpret this raw data on the fly for *ad hoc* analyses. It's now easy to call forth thousands of data points on demand for any given area into a simple webpage, spot anomalies, and diagnose operational issues *before* they turn red.[10]

Scott Kahler works as a senior field engineer at Pivotal, a company that enables the creation of Big Data software applications.

▶ **NOTE**

Visual Organizations deploy and use superior dataviz tools and, as we'll see later in this book, create new ones as necessary.

GREATER ORGANIZATIONAL TRANSPARENCY

At the first Hackers' Conference in 1984, American writer Stewart Brand famously said, "Information wants to be free." That may have been true two or three decades ago, but few companies were particularly keen about transparency and sharing information. Even today in arguably most workplaces, visibility into the enterprise is exclusively confined to top-level executives via private meetings, e-mails, standard reports, financial statements, dashboards, and key performance indicators (KPIs). By and large, the default has been sharing only on a need-to-know basis.

To be sure, information hoarding is alive and well in Corporate America. There's no paucity of hierarchical, conservative, and top-down organizations without a desire to open up their kimonos to the rank and file. However, long gone are the days in which the idea of sharing data with employees, partners, shareholders, customers, governments, users, and citizens is, well, weird. These days it's much more common to find senior executives and company founders who believe that transparency confers significant benefits. Oscar Berg, a digital strategist and consultant for the Avega Group, lists three advantages of greater transparency:

1. Improve the quality of enterprise data
2. Avoid unnecessary risk taking
3. Enable organizational sharing and collaboration[11]

An increasing number of progressive organizations recognize that the benefits of transparency far outweigh their costs. They embrace a new default modus operandi of sharing information, not hoarding it. It's not hard to envision in the near future collaborative and completely transparent enterprises that give their employees—and maybe even their partners and customers—360-degree views of what's going on.

Even for organizations that resist a more open workplace, better tools and access to information are collectively having disruptive and democratizing effects, regardless of executive imprimatur. Now, I am not advocating the actions of PRISM leaker Edward Snowden. The former technical contractor-turned-whistleblower at Booz Allen Hamilton provided *The Guardian* with highly classified NSA documents. This, in turn, led to revelations about U.S. surveillance on cell phone and Internet communications. My only point is that today the forces advancing freedom of information are stronger than ever. Generally speaking, keeping data private today is easier said than done.

THE COPYCAT ECONOMY: MONKEY SEE, MONKEY DO

When a successful public company launches a new product, service, or feature, its competition typically notices. This has always been the case. For instance, Pepsi launched Patio Diet Cola in 1963, later renaming it Diet Pepsi. Coca-Cola countered by releasing Diet Coke in 1982. Pharmaceutical companies pay attention to one another as well. Merck launched the anti-cholesterol drug Zocor in January 1992. Four years later, the FDA approved Pfizer's Lipitor, a drug that ultimately became the most successful in U.S. history.

Depending on things like patents, intellectual property, and government regulations, launching a physical me-too product could take years. Mimicking a *digital* product or feature can often be done in days or weeks, especially if a company isn't too concerned with patent trolls.

In *The Age of the Platform*, I examined Amazon, Apple, Facebook, and Google—aka *the Gang of Four*. These companies' products and services have become ubiquitous. Each pays close attention to what the others are doing, and they are not exactly shy about "borrowing" features from one another. This copycat mentality goes way beyond the Gang of Four. It extends to Twitter, Yahoo, Microsoft, and other tech behemoths. For instance, look at what happened after the initial, largely fleeting success of Groupon. Soon after its enormous success, Amazon, Facebook, and Google quickly added their own daily deal equivalents. Also, as mentioned in the Introduction, Facebook introduced Twitter-like features in June 2013, like video sharing on Instagram, verified accounts, and hashtags.* Facebook's 1.2 billion users didn't have to do a thing to access these new features; they just automatically appeared.

Social networks aren't the only ones capable of rapidly rolling out new product features and updates. These days, software vendors are increasingly using the Web to immediately deliver new functionality to their customers. Companies like Salesforce.com are worth billions in large part due to the popularity of SaaS. As a result, it's never been easier for vendors to quickly deploy new tools and features. If Tableau's latest release or product contains a popular new feature, other vendors are often able to swiftly ape it—and get it out to their user bases. Unlike the 1990s, many software vendors today no longer have to wait for the next major release of the product, hoping that their clients upgrade to that version and use the new feature(s). The result: the bar is raised for everyone. Chapter 2 will cover data-visualization tools in much more depth.

DATA JOURNALISM AND THE NATE SILVER EFFECT

Elon Musk is many things: a billionaire, a brilliant and bold entrepreneur, the inspiration for the *Iron Man* movies, and a reported egomaniac. Among the companies (yes, plural) he has founded and currently runs is Tesla Motors.

---

* Facebook also borrowed trending topics in January of 2014.

Tesla is an electric-car outfit that aims to revolutionize the auto industry. Its Model S sedan is inarguably stunning but, at its current price, well beyond the reach of Joe Sixpack. Less certain, though, are Musk's grandiose performance claims about his company's chic electric vehicle.

New York Times journalist John Broder decided to find out for himself. In early 2013, he took an overnight test-drive up Interstate 95 along the U.S. eastern seaboard, precisely tracking his driving data in the process.*

On February 8, 2013, the *Times* published Broder's largely unflattering review of the Model S. In short, the reporter was not impressed. Chief among Broder's qualms was the "range anxiety" he experienced while driving. Broder claimed that the fully charged Model S doesn't go nearly as far as Musk and Tesla claim it does. The reporter worried that he would run out of juice before he made it to the nearest charging station. In Broder's words, "If this is Tesla's vision of long-distance travel in America's future . . . and the solution to what the company calls the 'road trip problem,' it needs some work."

A negative review published in the *New York Times* has legs; this wasn't a teenager's Tumblr account. Musk quickly went on the offensive, attempting to prove that Broder got it wrong. Musk's smoking gun: the data—sort of. In a piece for the Tow Center for Digital Journalism (an institute within Columbia University's Graduate School of Journalism), Taylor Owen wrote that, "Tesla didn't release the data from the review. Tesla released [its] *interpretation* of the data from the review."[12] [Emphasis mine.]

Musk appeared on a number of television shows to plead his case and to question Broder's ability to follow simple instructions. Broder retaliated in a separate *Times* piece. The story blew over after a few days, but its impact has been anything but ephemeral. If this was hardly the first kerfuffle between a journalist and a public figure, then what was special about this one? In short, it was the cardinal role that data played in the dispute. Both Musk and Broder tried to *prove* their positions by using data.

Broder is one of an increasing cadre of high-profile reporters taking a more data-oriented approach to journalism these days. *Bloomberg Businessweek* formally refers to some of its staff as *data journalists*. *New York Times* Op-Ed columnist David Brooks has written extensively about the impact, benefits, and limitations of Big Data. But if there's a poster boy for contemporary data journalism, he goes by the name of Nate Silver.

In 2009, *Time* named the thirty-something statistician, pundit, and blogger as one of the most influential people on the planet. A picture of the wunderkind is presented in Figure 1.4.

From 2010 to July 2013, the *New York Times* licensed and hosted his blog FiveThirtyEight, and the results were nothing short of staggering. For instance,

---

* Read the entire review here: http://tinyurl.com/broder-tesla.

Figure 1.4 Nate Silver Speaking at SXSWi in 2009
Source: Randy Stewart, Seattle, WA, USA[13]

on the Monday before the 2012 U.S. presidential election, more than 20 percent of all visitors to the *Times* website read some of Silver's musings. Predictably (pun intended), his 2012 book *The Signal and the Noise: Why So Many Predictions Fail— But Some Don't* quickly became a bestseller.

In his writing, Silver frequently uses data, statistical models, charts, and graphs on a veritable bouillabaisse of topics. Beyond politics, Silver opines about subjects like these:

- Blogging: "The Economics of Blogging and *The Huffington Post*"

- Hockey: "Why Can't Canada Win the Stanley Cup?"

- Baseball: "Money on the Bench"

- Basketball: "Heat's Clutch Stats Meet Match in Spurs' Strategy"

Although the subjects change, the general methodology does not. Silver's readers observe firsthand how he uses data to support his hypotheses so convincingly, although he has his detractors. Many FiveThirtyEight fans read Silver's data-driven articles while commuting or at work. When making arguments to their own bosses and colleagues, it's likely that Silver's thought process and articles persuade them to use data and dataviz as well.

In early 2013, Silver spoke to an audience at Washington University about what Max Rivlin-Nadler of *Gawker* described as the "statistical pitfalls of accruing such a large following." After the presidential election, Silver had become so popular that he was starting to exert considerable influence over the democratic process. For some time, Silver wondered if he should do the unthinkable: cease blogging, at least about politics and elections. "I hope people don't take the forecasts too seriously," Silver said in February 2013. "You'd rather have an experiment where you record it off from the actual voters, in a sense, but we'll see. If it gets really weird in 2014, in 2016, then maybe I'll stop doing it. I don't want to influence the democratic process in a negative way."[14]

The possibility of Silver leaving the *Times* became a reality on July 19, 2013. Silver announced that he was taking a position with ESPN in August of that year. (Undue influence was unlikely the sole factor in Silver's decision; he probably attracted a colossal contract, and his love of sports is well documented.) In a statement released by ESPN, Silver said, "This is a dream job for me. I'm excited to expand FiveThirtyEight's data-driven approach into new areas, while also reuniting with my love of sports. I'm thrilled that we're going to be able to create jobs for a great team of journalists, writers, and analysts. And I think that I've found the perfect place to do it."[15]

In a way, however, Silver's departure changes nothing. No doubt that the popularity and data-driven style of his writing will continue to influence many current and future journalists throughout the world.

DIGITAL MAN

For a bunch of reasons covered in this chapter, we have become increasingly more comfortable with—and reliant upon—data and technology in our daily lives. It seems that we are almost always tethered to devices of one kind or another. This section explains the arrival of the digital man and how it has led to the Visual Organization. To summarize, as citizens, we have become more tech savvy, and not just at home. We take this newfound knowledge into the workplace. If our current employer isn't providing us with the tools we need to do our jobs, many of us will just bring our own.

The Data Deluge is transforming many areas of our lives, including journalism. To be sure, there will still be disputed stories that ultimately hinge upon "he said, she said." More and more, however, data will be able to tell more of the story.

The Arrival of the Visual Citizen

Although precise statistics are hard to come by, social networks and blogging platforms have exploded. There's no government agency that releases official or validated government statistics. For instance, Google claims that more than 400 million people use Google Plus, but it's important to take that claim with more than a grain of salt. Numbers like these are bogus for many reasons.

First, consumer-facing companies face a strong incentive to exaggerate their reported users. Next, it's not difficult for people, groups, and enterprises to create multiple accounts on any network. For instance, I created and actively manage four separate Twitter handles, each with a different purpose:

1. @philsimon: my main handle*

2. @motionpub: the handle for my small publishing company

3. @thenewsmall: the handle for my third book

4. @newsmallapp: the handle for my app, based upon the third book

At least I'm a human being, though. Fake handles are rampant. Fortunately, services like ManageFlitter allow me to detect Twitter handles likely run by spambots. With a few clicks, I can remove them *en masse*.

Even if we ignore those considerations, we're still not out of the woods yet. The question of what represents an "active user" is open to wide interpretation. The term is fuzzy; there's no universally accepted way to define it, much less monitor it for accuracy. Are you considered active if you create an account? If you log in every week? Every month? If Google automatically creates a Plus account when users sign up for Gmail, are they active users even if they never set up circles or "+1" anything?

I don't have answers to these questions and, for our purposes, exactitude doesn't matter. Social networks are huge, and hundreds of millions of us legitimately spend a great deal of time on them. In the process, we generate and consume oodles of data. As we do this, we become more comfortable with it. Increasingly these networks are presenting their data in visual, interactive formats. Mark Zuckerberg, LinkedIn CEO Reed Hoffman, Twitter boss Dick Costolo, and others know that we don't want to stare at raw data in spreadsheets any more than we have to. We do enough of that at work. We prefer to view data in more visual ways. This is why these sites allow us to easily see the page views, impressions, or "engagement" of our status updates, posts, videos, and photos. This type of data makes many of us more likely to buy Facebook or Twitter ads, sponsor a story, and promote a tweet.

In the Introduction, I described how Twitter allows users to easily represent their tweets via interactive and visual means. On October 29, 2013, Twitter went even further. The company announced that it was making its timeline decidedly more visual via an update that "will insert previews of images and Vines directly into tweets on the web and in Twitter's iOS and Android apps. To see the entire image or Vine, just tap on it."[16]

It would be folly, however, to claim that Twitter and its ecosystem collectively hold a monopoly on data visualization for social networks. Nothing could

---

* True story: I inadvertently deleted @philsimon a few years ago and started a #savephilsimon campaign under @philsimon2. It worked. The Twitter powers that be gave me @philsimon back.

be further from the truth. Facebook's famous social graph provides a visual means for both users and the company to see who is connected to whom. Zuckerberg understands that contemporary dataviz requires the deployment of *structurally different* technologies. (Behind the scenes, the social graph utilizes a graph database, not a relational designed for processing backend operations.* This difference is anything but semantic. Graph databases assume that the relationships are as important as the records.[17])

For its part, LinkedIn launched a major redesign of its member profiles in June 2013.† The goals were twofold: to make profiles simpler and decidedly more visual. Premium members can access more advanced analytics, many of which are visualized. Rather than show my own profile again, let's look at part of the new profile of Mark Kelly, the talented keyboardist for the English progressive rock band Marillion. It is shown in Figure 1.5.

A look at Figure 1.5 reveals the obvious: Kelly is endorsed most frequently for his expertise in the music industry. Aside from his duties in Marillion, Kelly serves as head of the Featured Artists Coalition, a group that campaigns for the protection of performers' and musicians' rights. As of this writing, 18 people have endorsed Kelly for this skill, including yours truly. Clicking on any image on the right takes the user to that endorser's profile.

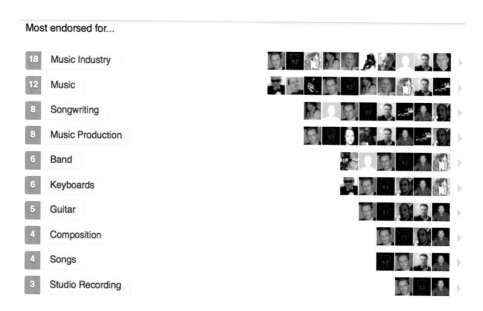

Figure 1.5 LinkedIn Endorsements of Marillion Keyboardist Mark Kelly
Source: LinkedIn

---

* For more on this, see http://tinyurl.com/fb-graph2.

† In November of 2013, Netflix relaunched its home page, making it decidedly more visual.

LinkedIn's recent redesign reflects a much larger Web trend. Today, most prominent social networks provide users with access to free, powerful, and increasingly visual analytics and data. Examples include Pinterest, Google, and Facebook.

Today, laypeople are looking at and working with data more than ever. More and more business decisions now require data. To make sense of it, data needs to become visual. Dataviz is becoming the norm. The LinkedIn redesign was a case in point. Without effective dataviz, how can we cope with the Data Deluge?

Mobility

It would be remiss here to ignore the enormous impact that mobility has had on our data-consuming and -generation habits. To be sure, the rise of smart-phones, apps, and near-constant communication has driven an increase in both the supply of—and demand for—data. Over the past five years, we have seen the explosion of tablets and other touch-based devices. While not the only show in town, the iPad reigns supreme, with more than 100 million units sold as of this writing.[18]

The full political, economic, and cultural impact of mobility is way beyond the scope of this book. For now, suffice it to say that, more than ever, mobility has made data more pervasive, visual, and even touchable.

The Visual Employee: A More Tech- and Data-Savvy Workforce

In his 2008 book *Grown Up Digital: How the Net Generation Is Changing Your World*, Don Tapscott discusses how today's young people are using technology in fascinating and unprecedented ways. Yes, there are slackers within such a large group; it's not as if they all spend their time passively watching television, texting, and eating Cheetos. Rather, "Net Geners" are constantly active. Tethered to their smartphones, they are almost always viewing, creating, and distributing data in one form or another via Twitter, Facebook, Snapchat, Vine, YouTube, Instagram, and a host of other apps and sites. They aren't just constantly consuming information; they are actively generating lots of it. As a group, Millennials are extremely proficient with gadgets.

But don't think for a minute that Millennials are the only ones interacting with data and technology on a near-constant basis. Yes, legitimate differences among generations exist. (Don't they always?) But the consumerization of IT has ushered in an entirely new and tech-centric era. We are *all* becoming more tech- and data-savvy, not to mention fidgety. According to a 2012 Pew survey of 2,254 people, 52 percent of *all* cell phone owners said they had used their mobile devices to do a variety of things while watching TV.[19]

▶ **NOTE**

As a group, consumers are becoming much more familiar with—and skilled at—using, interpreting, and representing data. Tech-savvy citizens take these skills and this data-oriented mind-set with them to work. They don't leave their brains at the door. This is causing increasing friction in organizations tied to "data-free" ways of doing things.

Navigating Our Data-Driven World

Knowing that better dataviz tools exist only gets us so far. For any organization to be as successful as possible, all of its employees need to step up. Truly understanding today's data streams requires more than just purchasing, downloading, and creating dataviz tools. Employees must actually use them.

Fortunately, there's never been greater access to user-friendly and powerful dataviz applications. The past ten years have brought about a much more democratic technology ethos into the workplace. Many employees no longer take as a given that they have to use only programs endorsed by IT. Sure, many organizations still cling to restrictive policies about the applications that employees *officially* can and can't use while on the clock. This hostility to "nonsanctioned" technologies, however, is starting to wane. Over the past decade, we've seen the rise of the Freemium model, BYOD (bring your own device), Web-based services, and open-source software. The success of workplace social networks like Yammer (acquired by Microsoft for $1.2 billion in June of 2012*) underscores a critical trend: in many organizations, the adoption of new technologies is becoming much more organic and bottom up, especially compared to the mid-1990s.

As mentioned earlier in this chapter, employees today are increasingly tech savvy. If they are dissatisfied with their employer's current applications and systems, they can and often will look elsewhere for superior alternatives. This is true with respect to many technologies, and dataviz is no exception to this rule. What's more, in most instances, there's not a great deal that IT can realistically do about employees "flying under the radar."

We are all becoming more comfortable with data. Data visualization is no longer just something we have to do at work. Increasingly, we want to do it as consumers and as citizens. Put simply, visualizing helps us understand what's going on in our lives—and how to solve problems.

A simple Google search on "best free data-visualization tools" may confirm what skeptical employees have long suspected: that their employers are a little behind the times and better options are available. This "use whatever tools are needed" mind-set is particularly pronounced at small businesses and start-ups.

* At the time, Microsoft already sold SharePoint, a workplace social network of sorts. Unlike Yammer, SharePoint needed to be deployed in a top-down manner. In this sense, it was the antithesis of Yammer.

NEXT

Chapter 2 looks at the specific dataviz applications, services, and tools that Visual Organizations are using. We'll see that the new boss isn't the same as the old boss.

NOTES

1. Auer, S. R.; Bizer, C.; Kobilarov, G.; Lehmann, J.; Cyganiak, R.; Ives, Z. (2007). "DBpedia: A Nucleus for a Web of Open Data." *The Semantic Web*. Lecture Notes in Computer Science 4825. p. 722.
2. Aguilar, Mario, "3 Million Suckers Still Pay for AOL Dial-Up," Gizmodo, July 27, 2012, http://gizmodo.com/5929710/3-million-suckers-still-pay-for-aol-dial+up, Retrieved August 27, 2013.
3. Colao, J.J., "Why Is Pinterest a $2.5 Billion Company? An Early Investor Explains," *Forbes*, May 8, 2013, http://www.forbes.com/sites/jjcolao/2013/05/08/why-is-pinterest-a-2-5-billion-company-an-early-investor-explains, Retrieved August 27, 2013.
4. Mayer, Marissa, "Your World, in Full Resolution," Yahoo's Tumblr, May 20, 2013, http://yahoo.tumblr.com/post/50934634700/your-world-in-full-resolution, Retrieved August 27, 2013.
5. MacManus, Richard, "It's All Semantics: Open Data, Linked Data & The Semantic Web," readwrite.com, March 31, 2010, http://readwrite.com/2010/03/31/open_data_linked_data_semantic_web, Retrieved August 26, 2013.
6. Harris, Derrick, "Import.io Wants to Help Turn Web Pages into Data—Fast," Gigaom, August 29, 2013, http://gigaom.com/2013/08/29/import-io-wants-to-help-turn-web-pages-into-data-fast, Retrieved August 29, 2013.
7. Jhingran, Anant, "From ETL to API—A Changed Landscape for Enterprise Data Integration," Apigee blog, October 10, 2012, https://blog.apigee.com/detail/from_etl_to_api_a_changed_landscape_for_enterprise_data_integration, Retrieved, June 27, 2013.
8. Dignan, Larry, "Amazon's AWS: $3.8 Billion Revenue in 2013, Says Analyst," ZDNet, January 7, 2013, http://www.zdnet.com/amazons-aws-3-8-billion-revenue-in-2013-says-analyst-7000009461, Retrieved August 28, 2013.
9. Hiner, Jason, "We've Entered the Third Generation of IT, Says Vmware," TechRepublic, August 27, 2013, http://www.techrepublic.com/blog/tech-sanity-check/weve-entered-the-third-generation-of-it-says-vmware, Retrieved August 28, 2013.
10. Personal conversation with Kahler, September 25, 2013.
11. Berg, Oscar, "3 Reasons Why Organizations Need to Increase Transparency," CMS Wire, July 5, 2011, http://www.cmswire.com/cms/

enterprise-collaboration/3-reasons-why-organizations-need-to-increase-transparency-011886.php, Retrieved July 20, 2013.

12. Owen, Taylor, "What the Tesla Affair Tells Us About Data Journalism," Tow Center blog, February 21, 2013, http://www.towcenter.org/blog/what-the-tesla-affair-tells-us-about-data-journalism, Retrieved September 15, 2013.

13. Nate Silver—SXSWi 2009. [CC-BY-SA-2.0 (http://creativecommons.org/licenses/by-sa/2.0)], via Wikimedia Commons http://commons.wikimedia.org/wiki/File:Nate_Silver_2009.png.

14. Rivlin-Nadler, Max, "Nate Silver Might Stop Blogging if He Starts to 'Influence the Democratic Process,'" Gawker, February 16, 2013, http://www.gawker.com/477097844, Retrieved June 21, 2013.

15. "Nate Silver Makes Move to ESPN," July 22, 2013. http://espn.go.com/espn/story/_/id/9499752/nate-silver-joins-espn-multi-faceted-role, Retrieved July 22, 2013.

16. Newton, Casey, "Twitter Timeline Becomes More Visual with Previews of Images and Vines," The Verge, October 29, 2013, http://www.theverge.com/2013/10/29/4848184/twitter-timeline-becomes-more-visual-with-previews-of-images-and-vines, Retrieved October 29, 2013.

17. Neo4j, "Social Networks in the Database: Using a Graph Database," Neo4j blog, September 15, 2009, blog.neo4j.org/2009_09_01_archive.html, Retrieved September 6, 2013.

18. Statistic Brain, "Apple Computer Company Statistics," September 22, 2012, http://www.statisticbrain.com/apple-computer-company-statistics, Retrieved June 12, 2013.

19. Reardon, Marguerite, "Trend watch: We're using our cell phones while watching TV," CNET, July 17, 2012, http://news.cnet.com/8301-1035_3-57473899-94/trend-watch-were-using-our-cell-phones-while-watching-tv/.

2

Transforming Data into Insights: The Tools

Man is a tool-using animal. Without tools he is
nothing, with tools he is all.

—Thomas Carlyle

I bet that you've heard of eBay. I'd also wager that you have probably used it at some point in your life.

Founded in 1995 by Pierre Omidyar, eBay connects individual buyers, sellers, and many small businesses. As of this writing, the 17,000-employee-company sports nearly 100 million active users around the globe. It has become the world's largest online marketplace. Anyone can buy and sell practically anything on eBay, and some attempted auctions are downright hysterical. Yes, you can buy Twitter followers to make yourself or your organization seem more popular than it is. (For under $20, you can add 12,500 followers right now.) Adam Cohen's excellent 2003 book *The Perfect Store* provides some particularly colorful items that people have tried to sell on the site over the years. My favorite: an F/A-18 Hornet fighter jet. No, not the model. *Imagine the shipping on that one*.

As of this writing, more than a staggering $62 billion worth of goods has been sold on eBay. This translates to more than $2,000 *every second*. And all of that commerce generates a staggering amount of data, in excess of 150 billion records generated each day. Certain log tables contain *trillions* of rows of data.

In an attempt to make sense of this much data, eBay has embraced Big Data and dataviz. In the process, as Gary Dougan explains, it has become a Visual Organization.*

Dougan, as of this writing, serves as the eBay's senior manager of business intelligence (BI) platform and architecture. As Dougan told Andrew Lampitt of *InfoWorld,* "Tableau brings value of data to nearly everyone internally. We've seen phenomenal growth; its usage doubles every six months. It lets users explore data across [a] variety of platforms. [It] is used more and more to support strategy."[1]

Dataviz in general—and Tableau in particular—help make data at eBay democratic and open. At eBay, data exploration, data visualization, and analytics aren't optional or nice to have. They're essential.† eBay employees use a bevy of dataviz tools to support, understand, and improve the business—and it's not hard to understand why. Think for a minute about eBay's business model. In the words of David Stone, the company's former senior manager of analytics platform, "It's not like you can stand in an eBay store and watch customers walk around. The visibility and insights into the business stem from Web logs coming off of ebay.com. By looking at those, we not only see what customers are doing; we see more than a regular retailer would see."[2]

Visual Organizations like eBay don't just buy a single application and mechanically deploy it. Rather, they first ask how they can make datasets more accessible and then see which tools achieve that goal. For instance, eBay extended Tableau's core functionality by creating Data Hub, its own Joomla-based Web portal.§ Data Hub is a secure and centralized resource that lets eBay's employees view existing datasets and request virtual datamarts. Increased accessibility to data has helped eBay optimize a broad range of its operations and garner invaluable insights into customer behavior. Thomas Carlyle's quote at the beginning of this chapter speaks volumes.

DATAVIZ: PART OF AN INTELLIGENT AND HOLISTIC STRATEGY

Depending on your current position, maybe you're skeptical about advocating or authorizing even more expensive technology purchases for your employer. Perhaps you have heard about some of the dataviz options out there and, quite frankly, your head is spinning. You might be thinking about the previously unsuccessful IT projects you've seen throughout your career. (I feel your pain.

---

* My attempts to do a more complete and original exposé of eBay for this book were politely rebuffed. The company's senior management understandably keeps this type of information close to its vest.

† Teradata, SAS, and Hadoop are just a few of the software providers eBay relies on.

§ Like Drupal and WordPress, Joomla is an open-source content management system.

I wrote a book about this subject.) Like many people, maybe you're frustrated that your company spent a fortune on a shiny new reporting tool only to find that no one bothered to learn it, much less use it. Opportunities were squandered, and Excel remained the default tool for analysis. Your wound is still sore, and you're asking yourself questions like these:

- Does my organization really need to spend a boatload of cash on new dataviz applications and specialists?

- Aren't many of these "new" dataviz applications just reporting tools reincarnated?

- Don't all these tools essentially do the same thing?

The short answers: No, no, and no. Although these are fair questions to ask, they are rooted in misconceptions and a traditional—and, I would argue, *outdated*—IT mind-set. As we'll see in Part II, Visual Organizations don't make the mistake of viewing dataviz as just another set of reporting applications. Put differently, data visualization represents just one club in the bag, but it's an incredibly important one. Think of it as a putter. Trying playing 18 holes of golf without one.

Today, organizations can do only so much with Small Data and traditional reporting tools. (Chapter 6 will have a great deal more to say about this.) Visual Organizations realize that the Data Deluge and Big Data are causing tectonic business shifts. For every action, though, there is an equal and opposite reaction. Specifically, we are seeing the emergence of a new wave of dataviz tools that help organizations and employees cope.

By itself, knowing that new and powerful dataviz applications exist only gets an enterprise so far. Visual Organizations actually use them to ask better questions and make better business decisions. Unleashing the power of dataviz and Big Data requires organizations to do much more than pay lip service to these topics.

THE TYRANNY OF TERMINOLOGY: DATAVIZ, BI, REPORTING, ANALYTICS, AND KPIS

As mentioned in the Introduction, dataviz has become topical as of late. Case in point: Gartner, "the leading information technology research and advisory company" in the world, recently added a new (if clunky) entry to its IT glossary: *Search-Based Data Discovery Tools*. The applications under this umbrella "enable users to develop and refine views and analyses of structured and unstructured data using search terms."*

---

* See http://www.gartner.com/it-glossary/search-based-data-discovery-tools.

Now, Search-Based Data Discovery Tools doesn't exactly roll off the tongue, but the announcement made headlines in business and tech circles. Big Data requires new data discovery tools, many of which are visual in nature.

While we're on the subject of terms, let's take a step back for a moment. There's a great deal of overlap among labels like dataviz, data mining, data discovery, business intelligence, analytics, and enterprise reporting. Understanding where one begins and the other ends is not obvious, and the landscape becomes nearly inscrutable when hype-heavy terms like *2.0* are thrown into the mix—for example, "data visualization 2.0."

And make no mistake: the intersection of these business expressions isn't just conceptual. It extends to many of the mature reporting and data-management applications that organizations currently use. Netflix—discussed in much more detail in Chapter 3—is light years ahead of most companies on a number of levels. However, it is fairly typical in at least one regard. Netflix employees don't rely on a single application to manage and interpret data. Rather, Netflix personnel use a multitude of tools to make sense of internal and external data. As we saw earlier in this chapter, eBay uses Teradata, Hadoop, SAS, Tableau, and Microsoft Excel, among others.

The point here is that in all likelihood your organization *already* licenses at least one reporting application that allows for a fair amount of data visualization, at least on Small Data. (Whether that application can effectively handle Big Data, though, is much less certain.)

MY DATAVIZ AND REPORTING BONA FIDES

These days, I don't create too many proper reports for my corporate clients. My consulting practice is more strategic than tactical, and I can't say that Simon, Inc. generates massive volumes of data. Up until four years ago, though, reporting of one sort or another represented a considerable part of my professional life and income.

On the client side for a few years and then as a systems consultant for more than a decade, I worked with a panoply of reporting applications and database query tools. Early in my career, I noodled with widely used commercial-off-the shelf (COTS) applications like ReportSmith, Business Objects, Crystal Reports, BrioQuery, and, of course, the ubiquitous Microsoft Excel and Access. I also used my fair share of clunky homegrown query tools, usually in mild protest and with the knowledge that far superior alternatives existed.

I then moved on to some more powerful BI applications like Cognos* PowerPlay and Impromptu, Lawson Business Intelligence, Microsoft SQL Server Reporting Services, and others. Equipped with these tools (and real-time access to enterprise data), I created more standard reports for my clients than I could count, as well as dashboards with alerts, analytics, and key performance indicators (KPIs).

---

* IBM acquired Cognos in January 2008.

Generally speaking, COTS reporting applications provided back then the ability to perform at least basic dataviz, view high-level trends, and sometimes "drill down" into the details. Indeed, this is still true today. (Of course, some were better than others, and that, also, is still true today.) And, in many cases, these same reporting and BI applications—or at least their ancestors—are still relevant. As such, it's possible and even likely that employees at your organization can already visualize certain types of data with their existing tools. They may not be able to do the same things that employees at Visual Organizations can, but you can decide that for yourself as you read Part II.

Do Visual Organizations Eschew All Tried-and-True Reporting Tools?

It's not as if Visual Organizations prohibit the use of Microsoft Excel, KPIs, standard reports, traditional dashboards, and BI tools.* (Someone at Netflix or Google is probably working on a spreadsheet as you read these very words.) The larger point is that Big Data has not rendered moot all aspects of traditional reporting. Let me be clear: used properly, those items remain useful, even valuable, at Visual Organizations.

Visual Organizations get that *useful* and *ideal*, however, are often two different things. The old boss is not the same as the new boss. The era of Big Data means that employees will need to learn new applications, terms, and skills. They will have to routinely represent much larger amounts of data from different sources. And they will have to do so in compelling, interactive, and visual formats. Most traditional reporting and BI tools cannot effectively handle Big Data yet—and they may never be able to do so. Put simply, they just weren't built to handle petabytes of unstructured data streaming at them at Godspeed.

Now, don't fret. There's every reason to believe that large software vendors will continue to improve traditional reporting and dataviz tools—and launch new ones. Fresh versions regularly ship with enhanced features and even some completely new ones. (Whether these newfangled versions and features ultimately represent improvements over prior iterations is another matter altogether. Opinions usually vary.) Management at software vendors usually isn't complacent. They realize that they must do two things to remain relevant. First, their current offerings must continue to evolve. Second, where necessary, they must develop new applications. Competition raises the bar for everyone.

However, Visual Organizations realize that, in order to make better business decisions these days, their employees need much more than a set of standard reports, *ad hoc* query capability, dashboards, analytics, and KPIs. Yes,

---

* PowerPoint, though, is sometimes a different story.

legacy reporting tools are often helpful, but *by themselves* they cannot handle the Data Deluge in any meaningful way. The widespread lack of contemporary data-discovery applications is prohibiting many organizations and their employees from finding new, hidden, and data-driven insights about their workforces, customers, supply chains, and businesses. (Of course, the absence of these tools is hardly the only inhibitor. Chapter 9 will return to this subject.) Visual Organizations appreciate this. As such, they are embracing new and contemporary dataviz tools.

Drawing Some Distinctions

There are fundamental differences among tools geared toward reporting, analysis, and data visualization. In *Taming the Big Data Tidal Wave*, Bill Franks differentiates between reporting and analytics. So, where does dataviz stack up? I have presented Franks's original comparison in Table 2.1 and have added a third column for dataviz.

Table 2.1 shows that traditional reporting and analysis tools still matter and fulfill a number of essential business functions. As such, they will remain widely used throughout the enterprise. To effectively handle—and make sense of—Big Data, however, Visual Organizations realize that they need contemporary and interactive dataviz applications. The old tools just don't cut it.

Table 2.1 Reporting vs. Analysis vs. Dataviz

Traditional Reporting Tools	Analysis	Contemporary Dataviz Tools
Provides data	Provides answers	*May* provide answers. Just as important, though, it allows users to ask deeper and arguably better questions of the data.
Provides what is asked for	Provides what is needed	*May* provide what is needed.
Is typically standardized	Is typically customized	Is extremely customizable; with an interactive dataviz, each user can discover vastly different things.
Does not involve a person	Involves a person	Involves a person; data visualizations are still subject to interpretation.
Is fairly inflexible	Is extremely flexible	Depending on the dataviz, it *may* be extremely flexible. Static infographics, however, are not.
Traditionally handles Small Data	Traditionally handles Small Data	Can handle both Small and Big Data.

Source: Modified from Bill Franks's book *Taming the Big Data Tidal Wave*, John Wiley & Sons, 2012.

THE DATAVIZ FAB FIVE

Chapter 1 discussed, among other things, the arrival of Big Data and why data visualization has grown in importance. I briefly touched upon the recent proliferation of powerful dataviz applications. (See "Better Data Tools.") To truly understand how Visual Organizations operate, a much longer discussion is required.

This chapter answers the simple question, "What types of dataviz applications and services are available today?" The short answer is that contemporary data-visualization applications fall into five buckets:

1. Applications from large enterprise software vendors, or LESVs*
2. Proprietary best-of-breed applications
3. Popular open-source tools
4. Design firms
5. Start-ups, Web services, and additional resources

Applications from Large Enterprise Software Vendors

As discussed earlier, dataviz is a *not* a recent phenomenon. For a long time, LESVs like IBM, Oracle, SAP, Microsoft, SAS, and others have developed products designed to help their clients manage and interpret enterprise information. Aside from building their own offerings, LESVs have, to varying extents, acquired competing or complementary data management, reporting, and dataviz products. Although IBM, Oracle, and others may not have branded their new releases as dataviz products *per se*, make no mistake: for a long time, just about every organization has been able to graphically represent its raw data, irrespective of a product's moniker. Table 2.2 reflects some of the more powerful and mature applications from established software vendors.

▶ **NOTE**

These five categories aren't entirely distinct. There's a fair degree of overlap among many of them. Design firms use open-source tools like D3.js to create interactive visualizations for their clients. Statisticians crunch data in R and then use Tableau to pretty it up. Best-of-breed dataviz applications work in conjunction with tools and frequently pull data from traditional databases, data warehouses, and APIs.

My main objective in this chapter is to educate readers on the five general categories of dataviz tools. That is, this chapter does *not* serve as a comprehensive list of all services, marketplaces, applications, software vendors, technologies, and open-source projects. Dataviz is a dynamic area and will remain one for quite some time.

---

* Yes, I am aware that this is pretty clunky acronym.

Table 2.2 Dataviz and BI Offerings of Established Enterprise Software Vendors

Vendor	Selected DataViz Offerings
Actuate	Makes interactive, Web-based, BI reporting tools. Actuate is also the founder and coleader of the Eclipse Business Intelligence and Reporting Tools open-source project, a development environment for presenting compelling data visualizations.
IBM	Cognos PowerPlay and Impromptu, SPSS Modeler, ManyEyes.
Microsoft	Major tools include SQL Server Reporting Services, Excel, and Access.
MicroStrategy	Visual Insight and its eponymous BI platform.
SAP	BusinessObjects BI OnDemand, SAP Lumira Cloud.
SAS	SAS Visual Analytics and a variety of traditional BI tools. JMP (pronounced "jump") combines dynamic dataviz with powerful statistics.
Teradata	Aster Visualization Module.

Based upon factors like the rise of Big Data discussed in Chapter 1, dataviz has become particularly topical. Exhibit A: the success of the Tableau Software IPO. Don't think that the soon-to-retire Steve Ballmer, Virginia Rometty, and Larry Ellison haven't noticed. LESVs are being forced to respond to Big Data and dataviz.

LESVs: The Case For

Melvin Kranzberg once famously said, "Technology is neither good nor bad; nor is it neutral." He was talking specifically about data visualization, but it's spot on here. First, the good side.

To be sure, we have seen a decent amount of innovation from LESVs in their dataviz and related offerings over the past ten years. (Of course, that innovation hasn't been evenly distributed among all the players in Table 2.2. Some vendors have done more than others, but let's keep it relatively simple here.) What's more, this trend will only accelerate as dataviz becomes more important and data streams increase.

Consider Microsoft Excel, for instance, a staple found on seemingly every computer in Corporate America. As an Excel user for the past twenty-something years, I have seen it evolve quite a bit from its early days. Remember that, up until its 2003 version, a single Excel spreadsheet could hold a maximum of 65,536 rows.* That number is now more than one million, and a few companies are working on ways to increase that number to one billion and even one *trillion*.

Beyond increasing row limits, over the years Microsoft has released many add-ins and enhancements to Excel. Generally speaking, these have brought

---

* Why? Because 65,536 equals 2 to the 16th power. Row limits are always a function of 2 to some power.

new functionality and support for new data sources. Let's consider two recent Excel dataviz enhancements. PowerPivotPro dramatically extends the power of Pivot Tables in native Excel. Think Pivot Tables on steroids. PowerMap (formerly called *GeoFlow*) allows users to create three-dimensional maps with Bing integration. (Data must be associated with a latitude and longitude or street address.) Users can then represent the data in different ways, compare it to standard charts and graphs, and build animated tours. From the Microsoft Office blog:

> Preview for Excel 2013 allows you to plot geographic and temporal data visually, analyze that data in 3D, and create interactive tours to share with others. This preview gives you an early look into the new features that provide 3D data visualization for Excel and a powerful method for people to look at information in new ways, enabling discoveries in data that might never be seen in traditional 2D tables and charts.[3]

Again, Excel still can't do everything data related, and it never will; no application can. The point here is twofold. First, Excel can do more than it could ten years ago, although it's nowhere near as powerful as Hadoop, MapReduce, and other legitimate, contemporary Big Data tools. Second, like all major software vendors, Microsoft recognizes that its tools must continue to evolve, add functionality, and continue to support new data sources. Don't expect the innovation train to stop anytime soon. These companies can throw abundant financial and human resources at any problem, and dataviz is certainly on their individual radars.

As a general rule, the dataviz applications from LESVs listed in Table 2.2 seamlessly integrate with that vendor's existing enterprise databases and data warehouses out-of-the-box—or at least with a bit of configuring. It's usually not terribly difficult to get one IBM product to "talk to" another IBM product. And mixing and matching isn't problematic if you know what you're doing. With a few clicks and the consent of the IT department, it's fairly simple to build a report in Vendor A's application that pulls data stored in Vendor B's database.* (In fact, that same report could grab records from tables in databases from Vendors C and D.) In exceptional circumstances, developers and IT professionals build bridges through unconventional means.

LESVs: The Case Against

Remember Kranzberg's earlier quote about technology and innovation. There's *always* a downside. Not every LESV will *truly* improve its dataviz products—or the related functionality within its current offerings. In the next few years we

---

* In my prior consulting days, I would frequently use different ODBC (Open Database Connectivity) drivers to link to tables in Oracle, SQL Server, and DB2 databases.

will no doubt see some smoke and mirrors, hyperbole, and maybe even a little outright deceit. Certain software vendors will simply rebrand their current offerings to play up the increasingly important dataviz angle of their products. In other words, they won't truly innovate.

Although unfortunate, this is par for the course. Historically, the sales forces and marketing folks at LESVs have felt considerable pressure to stay current with cutting-edge terminology and business trends. (The *Glengarry Glen Ross* mantra "Always be closing" is gospel in many publicly traded tech companies.) To some extent, this is understandable. Compared to truly innovating, it's always been easier—and certainly tempting—for companies to just change the names of existing products. A related stratagem is to launch "new" versions with sexier monikers but little or no new functionality. When peddling products with dated titles, sales and marketing folks aren't exactly silent. They complain that they are losing deals to competitors whose names have more sizzle.

> If it looks like a duck, walks like a duck, and quacks like a duck, it's probably a duck. Calling it a dog doesn't change that. All else being equal, best-of-breed software vendors innovate faster than large software vendors.

Make no mistake: these types of name changes are merely cosmetic. In the code and on the back end, old terminology is much stickier. Most users care much more about what an application can do and how well it does it, not what it's called.

This begs the question, why? Think about it. LESVs like IBM support many different products. They enable one-stop shopping (or at least a facsimile thereof), a strong selling point during the sales cycle. Consider Microsoft. Office, Windows, Surface, Windows, Azure, and Xbox are much higher corporate priorities than any dataviz release—*and they should be*. As a result, a very small percentage of employees at any LESV focuses on niche products—and dataviz certainly qualifies. (Note, however, that *niche* here is a relative term. For a company as large as Microsoft, even a small number is usually pretty big. If Microsoft assigns one percent of its U.S. workforce to a product or project, nearly 600 people will be working on it.*) Nevertheless, it's hard to credibly argue such a project is anywhere near top corporate priority.

Microsoft has many fish to fry. And don't forget that its enterprise clients submit myriad enhancement requests. Finally, Microsoft is also going after consumers, a market that has traditionally eluded it. (Xbox is the exception that proves the rule.) CEO Steve Ballmer must devote resources to an astonishing array of products. Judging by his recent comments on the July 2013 reorganization, Microsoft's focus is anything but singular.

---

* According to its website as of July 17, 2013, the company employs 97,811 people worldwide, 57,572 of whom work in the United States.

I am not trying to demonize Microsoft here. I am just pointing out that for *any* company its size, juggling so many balls isn't easy. Other examples abound. Yahoo found that out in 2006 when senior vice president Brad Garlinghouse wrote the now-famous Peanut Butter Manifesto. In a nutshell, Garlinghouse claimed that his employer was spreading itself too thin by trying to do everything. For his part, Larry Page cut many popular Google projects like iGoogle, Google Health, Google Reader (a personal favorite of mine), and others after reassuming the role of CEO in April 2011.

Best-of-Breed Applications

The 1990s and 2000s saw a great deal of M&A activity in the technology world. Behemoths like IBM, Microsoft, Cisco, SAP, SAS, and Oracle collectively gobbled up hundreds of niche vendors in areas such as enterprise security, CRM, ERP, BI, and others.* The reasons for these deals varied but, generally speaking, fell into three camps. First, they often allowed large vendors to augment and complement their own offerings. Second, in many cases, these deals sought to leverage existing client-vendor relationships. Many clients like one-stop shopping and a single point of contact. (As I know from personal experience, adding more parties to the mix rarely increases accountability and performance.) Third, cash-strapped vendors often found it easier to buy competing technology—and related talent—than to build their own. If you can't beat 'em, join 'em.

Despite this flurry of M&A activity, today myriad important tech companies still specialize in one type of offering. It would be a vast overstatement to claim that every company of consequence has been acquired. Today's best-of-breed vendors tend to operate with laser-like focus. That is, they don't face the "jack of all trades, master of none" problem that can frustrate clients of LESVs.

With respect to dataviz, Tableau is the Big Kahuna today. It sports more than 10,000 clients, including Facebook, eBay, Manpower, Pandora, and other prominent companies. Unlike Microsoft, best-of-breed vendors like Tableau don't sell productivity applications, game consoles, and relational databases. As "Dirty" Harry Callahan said in *Magnum Force*, "A man's gotta know his limitations." Put differently, Tableau's offerings might not be very wide, but they are quite deep. Tableau *only* sells data-visualization applications, at least for the time being.

Tableau may be the most popular best-of-breed dataviz tool on the market, but it faces plenty of competition. For instance, QlikTech delivers product self-service BI through its flagship QlikView. TIBCO Spotfire designs, develops, and distributes in-memory analytics software for next-generation business intelligence. Other emerging players include Birst, ChartBeat, Panopticon,

---

* For instance, under the watch of CEO John Chambers, Cisco has been an acquisitions machine. See http://tinyurl.com/cisco-acq.

GoodData, Indicee, PivotLink, and Visually. These companies focus on one thing—dataviz—although they go about it in different ways. That's it.

Let's look at three considerations for evaluating best-of-breed tools: cost, ease of use and employee training, and integration into the Big Data world.

Cost

There's another major difference between dataviz tools sold by LESVs and "specialty" firms like Tableau. By and large, the former have been—and remain—relatively expensive. They are often out of the reach of most small businesses and start-ups. (Of course, cost was a bigger problem a decade ago. Today, open-source software, SaaS, and cloud-based offerings have leveled the playing field to a great degree.) Compared to the aforementioned stalwarts, newer, best-of-breed dataviz tools often cost less and offer enhanced functionality.

Ease of Use and Employee Training

Any new program requires some level of employee training. I played around with some interesting dataviz tools in researching this book. One of my favorites is Visually, a one-stop shop for creating powerful data visualizations and infographics. (We'll return to Visually later in this chapter, because it also serves as a marketplace of sorts.)

As a tool, I found Visually to be powerful, intuitive, and diverse in its uses—and scads of others agree. As I researched this book, I came to know Drew Skau, the company's Visualization Architect. Over the course of a number of discussions, he described to me the wide range of customers and their needs it serves:

> Visually customers look for a full range of visualization types. The majority are looking for infographics that tell a story using charts to display data and illustrations or diagrams to convey processes and concepts. Some want interactive visualizations that range from maps or timelines to custom visualizations like in the Startup Universe (see Figures 2.3, 2.4, and 2.5). Motion graphics have been gaining a lot of popularity recently, because they engage a viewer extremely well, and do a great job of telling a story. Finally, others need help with presentations, quarterly reports, or other internal documents that need to effectively communicate data.[4]

However, with any new application, there's always a learning curve, and Visually is no exception. As someone who's taught hundreds of people how to use a spate of software applications, I know that people are often apprehensive. Some learn faster than others, but most users know that they'll have to take at least a small step or two back before maybe taking a giant leap forward. Lamentably, that fact can deter the adoption of new technologies. Many people continue to use "good enough" staples like Excel because they know how, even though superior tools exist for visualizing different types of data. Many people just don't have the time or desire to learn a new application, and they feel like they can get by with an old standby in their jobs. As I saw during my consulting career, even employees who spend a week in training learning a new reporting or BI application often revert to Excel. Changing default behaviors is never easy, and the devil you know is better than the devil you don't.

Integration and the Big Data World

Compared to the offerings of LESVs, best-of-breed data-visualization applications may not provide the same *native*, optimized, and direct integration with third-party databases and data warehouses, at least as of this writing. And this can pose a significant problem. Suboptimal connections, early-morning ETL (extract, transform, load) jobs, and clunky workarounds require more time for users to access data, represent it in a visual form, and make business decisions. In an era of Big Data, viral videos, flash sales, and trending topics, speed kills.

Aware of this limitation, best-of-breed dataviz vendors are quickly building bridges to connect all sorts of data sources. They are also supporting an increasing number of APIs. For instance, Tableau has forged partnerships with some of the largest database companies in the world, including Teradata, a large data warehousing and BI vendor. In 2013, Tableau announced direct and seamless integration with key Teradata products.

Integration with traditional enterprise databases and data warehouses is important, but today that isn't sufficient. No longer do many of even the largest companies "store" all their data internally (read: on-premises), at least in the traditional sense. Visual Organizations increasingly need tools that move beyond relational data and tightly integrate with contemporary Big Data services, many of which are based in the cloud. To this end, in July 2013, Tableau announced the launch of Tableau Online, a Web-based service that does just that. Consider the ways in which it allows for fast and relatively easy importing of—and linking to—critical sources of Big Data:

- Data already residing in online applications like Salesforce.com can be copied directly into Tableau in-memory extracts.

- Data in Amazon Redshift* or Google Big Query† can be queried directly.

- Data in on-premise data centers can be pushed into Tableau Online using vendor-provided tools.

Ten years ago, such integration would have required highly technical employees, an expensive and long-term consulting project, and considerable

---

* Amazon Redshift is a fast and powerful, fully managed, petabyte-scale data-warehouse service in the cloud.

† The Google BigQuery Web service lets users do interactive analyses of massive datasets.

IT support. Today, however, that's simply not the case, at least according to Francois Ajenstat, Tableau's director of product management.[5]

Tableau is far from the only company to play nice with other Big Data sources and companies. Dataviz start-ups a fraction of the size of Tableau also recognize the value and importance of easy integration with both enterprise data and external data sources. (We'll come back to start-ups later in this chapter.) For example, in July 2013, start-up DataHero announced that its users could now automatically pull data from their SurveyMonkey accounts via the latter's API. (DataHero also supports application programming interface (API) from MailChimp, Dropbox, Box.Net, Stripe, and other popular services.) By easily linking to survey response data, users can instantly see dynamic visualizations of and potentially gain key, real-time insights into user behavior.

There's more choice than ever in the dataviz world. Take advantage of it. Kick the tires on a dataviz product or service before signing expensive, long-term contracts with any software vendor, big or small. If possible, take advantage of a free trial. Get a little bit pregnant. See if the tool is user-friendly and can handle large datasets quickly and with minimal tweaking. Play with different applications and Web services. Decide which trade-offs are acceptable.

Popular Open-Source Tools

Relatively expensive enterprise solutions and dedicated best-of-breed applications represent two completely viable dataviz options. There is a third group worthy of discussion. A raft of free, open-source solutions exists to enable insightful and near-instant data visualization. Like many technologies today, dataviz is democratic. Start-ups and small businesses looking to save money would do well to consider some of the solutions discussed in the forthcoming section.

One word of warning: think free speech, not free beer. Freely downloading an open-source program is not tantamount to being able to effectively use it.

D3.js

D3.js is a JavaScript library for manipulating documents based on data. D3 brings data to life using programming languages like HTML, Scalable Vector Graphics, and Cascading Style Sheets. By emphasizing Web standards, D3 gives users the full capabilities of modern browsers without tying themselves to proprietary frameworks. It fuses powerful visualization components and a data-driven approach to Document Object Model (DOM) manipulation. (For some truly spectacular data visualizations, see the GitHub D3 Gallery.*)

---

* Go to https://github.com/mbostock/d3/wiki/Gallery.

The design of the current generation of data-visualization tools is heavily influenced by the advent of REST Web APIs. Historically, creating a dataviz required following this process:

1. Aggregate all the data from multiple sources
2. Crunch the numbers
3. Create a normalized/uniform table
4. Generate the visualization from this table

REST* APIs have streamlined this process, as Jimmy Jacobson told me. (Jacobson is the cofounder of Twitter survey tool Wedgies). They have made it easy to immediately pull data from disparate sources. Current tools like D3 are specifically designed to treat data responses from JSON† APIs as inputs into the dataviz process. This allows visualizations to be created in real time and displayed on any device capable of rendering a webpage, making the most current information available to anyone. In Chapter 4, we'll see some actual examples of visuals created with D3.

R

Developed by Ross Ihaka and Robert Gentleman at the University of Auckland, New Zealand, R is more than just a very powerful and popular open-source programming language. It has become a software *environment* for statistical computing and graphics, one that continues to evolve. Today, the R Development Core Team refines the core offering and pushes its development into new and exciting directions. Countless statisticians and data miners use R to develop statistical software and to perform data analysis. Polls and surveys of data miners are showing R's popularity has increased substantially in recent years.

Nicholas Lewin-Koh, senior statistical scientist at Genentech, describes R as "rich with facilities for creating and developing interesting graphics. Base R contains functionality for many plot types including coplots, mosaic plots, biplots, and others."[6]

But don't think of R as Minitab§ reincarnate. R also allows users to create robust and *interactive* graphics and data visualizations.

---

* Representational state transfer (REST) is a style of software architecture for distributed systems such as the World Wide Web. REST has emerged as the predominant Web API design model.

† JSON stands for *JavaScript Object Notation*. It is a lightweight data-interchange format. It is both easy for humans to read and write and for machines to parse and generate. Everybody wins.

§ Minitab is the first statistics package that I ever used, and it still exists today.

Others

Gephi bills itself as "The Open Graph Viz Platform." Gephi allows users to create, explore, and understand graphs. Think Photoshop, but for graphs and data. Gephi supports a wide variety of networks and complex systems and lets users create dynamic and hierarchical graphs. It began as a university student project in 2009 and has quickly become a valuable open-source software resource for visualization and analysis, particularly of large networks. Today, Gephi enables thousands of users to easily create and test hypotheses, intuitively discover patterns, and view anomalies and outliers. Think of Gephi as a *complementary* statistical tool. (Importantly, Gephi integrates with R.)

It would be remiss to ignore two prominent open-source BI solutions: Jaspersoft and Pentaho. To be sure, these are not dataviz applications *per se*. (See "The Tyranny of Terminology: Dataviz, BI, Reporting, Analytics, and KPIs" earlier in this chapter). Still, millions of people have downloaded these tools and use them to interpret data and understand their businesses.

Organizations weary of proprietary solutions can still take advantage of powerful, open-source dataviz applications. It's not an either-or situation.

These tools represent just the tip of the data-visualization iceberg. There's a veritable trove of open-source dataviz services and software programs. (See "Start-Ups, Web Services, and Additional Resources" later in this chapter.)

Design Firms

As Big Data has exploded, we've seen a corresponding rise of infographics (especially on news sites), dataviz tools, and design firms. Two of my personal favorites are Stamen and Lemonly.* Stamen has developed a reputation for beautiful and technologically sophisticated projects in a diverse range of commercial and cultural settings. The firm has done some excellent work.

Lemonly makes exciting infographics, data visualizations, interactive graphics, and even video presentations. The company's website clearly articulates its mission: "We make data easier to understand. From infographics to videos to interactive design, we help turn lemons to lemonade." Lemonly continues to push the boundaries of design, visualizing even relatively small datasets in fascinating ways.

---

* For a Quora list of some of the more renowned dataviz firms in design, see http://tinyurl .com/dv-quora.

You can spend a great deal of time perusing Lemonly's diverse and visually engaging online portfolio. Just as interesting, though, is that Lemonly eats its own dog food. The company put its 2012 annual report, colorfully titled "One Sweet Year,"* online for anyone to see. I have never seen a more insightful look into a company's financials. This is a testament not only to Lemonly's design chops, but to its remarkable level of transparency. (Privately held companies need not make this information available.) Figures 2.1 and 2.2 show a few of the data visualizations from the company's annual report.

There are pros and cons to hiring a design firm for data-visualization purposes. Contracting a firm with dataviz expertise can quickly provide desired results. To be sure, it's more palatable for organizations struggling with dataviz to test the waters on a discrete engagement than to hire a team of expensive specialists. Professional designers often find powerful and innovative ways to represent data because, quite simply, they possess the skills, experience, tools, and perspective that an organization's current staff lacks. For instance, I know of few organizations whose employees can create something as informative, interactive, and downright cool as this (see Figure 2.3).

Figure 2.3 shows the publicly available investment history of one particularly prominent individual: Netscape founder and current VC titan Marc Andreessen.† But The Startup Universe is an exceptionally useful and interactive dataviz. It's impossible to list all of the ways that users can "cut" the data. Go ahead and look at investments by company name, industry, VC firm or angel investor, date, amount, and scads of other factors. (To view the entire interactive universe, go to http://tinyurl.com/z-vizbox. Warning: it's addictive.) Drilling down and around takes zero technical skill and, arguably more important, allows users to unearth interesting insights. Consider the following figures:

Figure 2.4 shows the investments in Tableau Software by amount, time, and investor before its IPO. One such investor is New Enterprise, a global venture capital firm that invests in technology and health care. It is based out of Menlo Park, California, home to many prominent VC outfits. If you're curious about the other public investments made by New Enterprise, just click your mouse a few times and you wind up with Figure 2.5.

Figures 2.3, 2.4, and 2.5 come from Visually, a dataviz company mentioned earlier. Visually is part Web-based application and part traditional design shop, but with a neat wrinkle. The Visually Marketplace brings together marketing gurus, geeks, and design junkies based on shared interests. In this sense, it's like eBay. Infographic and dataviz buyers and sellers easily find each other.

---

* See it at http://tinyurl.com/lemon-2012.

† Remember from Chapter 1 that not all data qualifies as *open data*. Like many investors, Andreessen may very well not choose to disclose each one. Given how closely others watch his behavior, I'd bet on it.

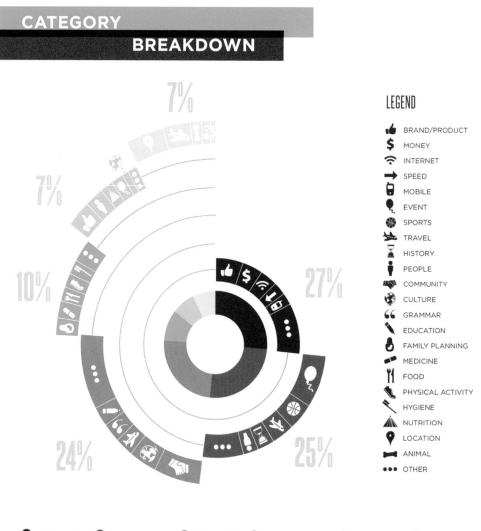

Figure 2.1 Breakdown of 2012 Lemonly Clients by Category
Source: Lemonly

CLIENT LOCATION DISTRIBUTION

& INDUSTRY TYPE

● TECHNOLOGY
● ENTERTAINMENT
● FOOD & BEVERAGE
● NON PROFIT
● HEALTH & FITNESS

GERMANY   U.K.   FRANCE

Figure 2.2 Breakdown of 2012 Lemonly Clients by Location and Category
Source: Lemonly

Figure 2.3 represents a collaboration among Visually, design firm Accurat, and graphic communication expert Ben Willers. This underscores the often participatory nature of Visual Organizations: a dataviz may not be the sole work of a mad genius. Community matters.

If you think that creating a dataviz as dynamic and interesting as the Startup Universe was simple or quick, think again. The entire process took six months from soup to nuts.* The wireframes, thought process, and trade-offs involved are nothing short of mind-blowing.

In the software world, a common bromide is "Fast, cheap, and good. Pick any two of the three." The same holds true here. If something seems too good to be true, it probably is. Depending on your budget, the cost of a leading design firm may be prohibitive. What's more, outsourcing anything minimizes knowledge transfer. When a third party does the work for you, it's unlikely

---

* To get a behind-the-scenes look of the design process, see http://tinyurl.com/startup-univ-dv.

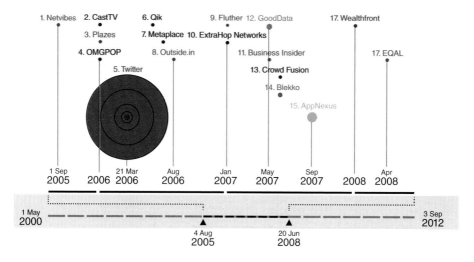

Figure 2.3 The Startup Universe: A Visual Guide to Startups, Founders & Venture Capitalists; Investment History of Marc Andreessen
Sources: Visually, Accurat, and Ben Willers

that your own employees will learn about the process and technique. Finally, when deciding upon using a design firm, ask yourself if you need to create a single, static, standalone data visualization or an interactive, dynamic tool that will frequently need to be changed. The difference is acute: a one-time cost versus recurring bills.

Organizations without the internal expertise to develop their own data-visualization tools need not go without them. Untold numbers of organizations use design firms to create powerful and customized dataviz applications.

Start-Ups, Web Services, and Additional Resources

Fifteen years today is tantamount to a technological eternity. Not that long ago, organizations would deploy enterprise applications at a snail's pace, especially compared to today. Back then, requests for information would give way to requests for proposals, final selection, and negotiations over price. Eventually, contracts were signed and consultants arrived. Up until fairly recently, most organizations would primarily deploy applications primarily from the top down using the waterfall method. It wasn't uncommon for the entire process of deploying ERP, CRM, BI, and intranet technologies to take *years*.

In my second book, *The Next Wave of Technologies*, I refer to that largely bygone era as *Enterprise 1.0.** During that time, most employees could not easily

---

* Web 1.0 still exists. Scads organizations act as if things like clouds, the Internet, and mobility don't exist.

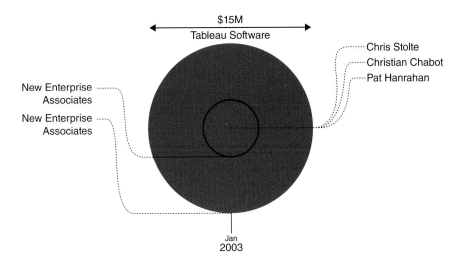

Figure 2.4 The Startup Universe: Investments in Tableau Software by Amount, Time, and Investor
Sources: Visually, Accurat, and Ben Willers

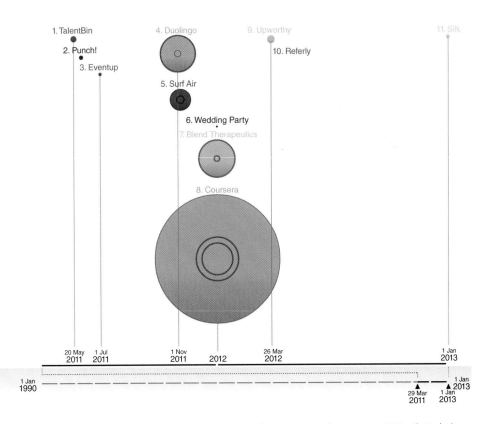

Figure 2.5 The Startup Universe: Different Investments by New Enterprise over an 18-Month Period
Sources: Visually, Accurat, and Ben Willers

play with different technologies and applications at work. With relatively few exceptions, ambitious, tech-curious employees could not easily experiment; they often had to make do with existing stalwarts. Impatient people like me had to wait for senior management to get it, often biting our tongues.

Today, Enterprise 1.0 seems quaint, like floppy disks. The early days of the Internet have long passed. Some call this more mature environment *Enterprise 2.0* or *Web 2.0*. Regardless of moniker, one thing is sure: we live in a very different technological era than we did in 1998. The seeds planted back then are flourishing. Ours is a time of constant connectivity, broadband connections, historically low start-up costs, social networks, cloud computing, SaaS, agile software development, APIs, SDKs, Big Data, open-source software, BYOD, and the Freemium model. Yes, today's seemingly endless stream of data and technology can be a bit overwhelming at times, but there is an upside. If your manager, department, organization, or CXO doesn't understand the benefit of new technologies, Web services, and applications, don't fret. People have never had access to more powerful, user-friendly, and very affordable—if not free— dataviz resources. This book's Appendix presents some of the more popular dataviz tools not covered as of yet.

I won't even attempt to evaluate the utility of the dataviz tools presented in the Appendix. By the time this book goes to print, I'm certain that some will have collapsed or ceased development and new ones will have appeared. In addition, it would be folly to claim that the Appendix presents a comprehensive list of emerging start-ups and useful dataviz tools, applications, and services. New ones are being released seemingly on a monthly basis.* As discussed earlier in this book, Big Data and dataviz are hot topics, attracting a slew of start-ups and hundreds of millions of dollars in VC funding. I am reminded of the famous quote by bank robber Willie Sutton. When a reporter asked Sutton why he robbed banks, Sutton curtly replied, "Because that's where the money is." Although he died in 1980, Sutton's words still ring true today.

> Although it's impossible to be aware of every new data-visualization release and product, Visual Organizations recognize the value of paying attention to new developments and trends.

Beyond new start-ups and open-source projects, there's no shortage of sites and blogs on dataviz best practices. Some of the more colorful names are Tableau Love and Tableau Jedi.[†]

THE FINAL WORD: ONE SIZE DOESN'T FIT ALL

This chapter has presented a fairly detailed overview of the more popular dataviz tools. While my intent here was to inform, not overwhelm, it's understandable if your head is

---

* For more, go to http://tinyurl.com/cool-dv-tools.

[†] See http://tinyurl.com/dvsites for some more good ones.

spinning at least a little bit. You may be asking yourself, "What's the *one* tool that my organization ought be using?"

Let me save you some time. There is no one such tool.

Self-described code artist Scott Murray knows a thing or two about data-visualization applications. Murray contributes to Processing, a popular open-source dataviz project. But he is no one-trick pony; Murray wears many hats. While not coding, he wrote *Interactive Data Visualization for the Web: An Introduction to Designing with D3*. He also serves as an assistant professor of design at the University of San Francisco. As Murray told Alexandra Pappas of Visualizing.org:

> It's important to pay attention to who uses certain tools, and why. For example, R is very popular in the statistics community because it evolved out of and for that community. So R makes sense to statisticians, Matlab makes sense to mathematicians, Processing makes sense to artists and designers, and Excel makes sense to people in finance and the broader public.[7]

Murray further explains that D3's rapid and diverse adoption stems in part from its flexibility. What's more, D3 is designed for a pervasive platform: the Web.

Many technologies, products, and services don't serve a particularly useful purpose or fill a critical business or consumer need. This scenario has been described as "a solution in search of a problem," one of my favorite axioms. However, to successfully navigate the era of Big Data, different audiences require different tools.

> Don't waste valuable time searching for the one dataviz tool that satisfies everyone's needs. It just doesn't exist.

NEXT

We now know why Visual Organizations have arrived and some of the tools they use. It's time to delve deeper. Part II presents detailed case studies of organizations that are solving important business problems by visualizing their data.

Part II lays the groundwork for a four-level dataviz model discussed in Chapter 6. Rather than introduce it here, I have chosen to jump right into the case studies. Should you be curious about this model, feel free to skip ahead to Part III.

NOTES

1. Lampitt, Andrew, "Big Data Visualization: A Big Deal for eBay," InfoWorld, December 6, 2012, http://www.infoworld.com/d/big-data/big-data-visualization-big-deal-ebay-208589, Retrieved August 5, 2013.
2. Tableau Software, interview with David Stone, "eBay Drives Business with Analytics," Tableau company website, http://www.tableausoftware.com/es-es/node/16230.

3. Microsoft Office Blog, http://office.microsoft.com/en-us/download-geoflow-for-excel-FX104036784.aspx, Retrieved June 17, 2013.

4. Personal conversation with Skau, September 4, 2013.

5. Henschen, Doug, "Tableau Takes Data Visualization Online," InformationWeek, July 22, 2013, http://www.informationweek.com/big-data/news/software/business-intelligence/tableau-takes-data-visualization-online/240158610, Retrieved July 22, 2013.

6. Lewin-Koh, Nicholas, "CRAN Task View: Graphic Displays & Dynamic Graphics & Graphic Devices & Visualization," January 29, 2013, http://cran.r-project.org/web/views/Graphics.html, Retrieved June 15, 2013.

7. Pappas, Alexandra, "Expert Galleries: Scott Murray," Visualizing Blog, July 23, 2013, http://www.visualizing.org/stories/expert-galleries-scott-murray, Retrieved August 17, 2013.

PART TWO

Introducing the
Visual Organization

In Part II, we'll see how Visual Organizations are embracing dataviz and a new mind-set—and seeing spectacular results. Up until now, the concept of a Visual Organization might have seemed a bit abstract. This Part concretizes the Visual Organization through three proper case studies. It includes these chapters:

- Chapter 3: The Quintessential Visual Organization

- Chapter 4: Dataviz in the DNA

- Chapter 5: Transparency in Texas

The Quintessential Visual Organization

> People are generally better persuaded by the reasons which they have themselves discovered than by those which have come in to the mind of others.
>
> —Blaise Pascal

What's the biggest Big Data company today? Is it Facebook with 1.2 billion registered users, many of whom are authentic? What about Amazon or Google? They're not exactly slouches.

It's a silly question with no correct answer. It all depends on what you're measuring. The definitive answer isn't terribly important, but one could credibly argue that the honor currently belongs to Netflix.

NETFLIX 1.0: UPSETTING THE APPLECART

Reed Hastings and Marc Randolph founded Netflix in 1997, originally as a DVD-by-mail business. At that time, the process of renting a video entailed a trip to the local Blockbuster or Hollywood Video, looking around, and hoping to find something interesting in stock. Many customers didn't find the titles they wanted. When they did, they often incurred late fees upon returning their videos. In 2000, "Blockbuster collected nearly $800 million in late fees, accounting for 16 percent of its revenue."[1]

▶ **NOTE**

In the interest of full disclosure, I treated Netflix a bit differently than the other case studies in this book. Although I asked politely, Netflix did not provide me with exclusive interviews or visuals for this book.*

The company is understandably protective about what it releases to journalists and outsiders in general. However, to their credit, the Netflix employees with whom I communicated encouraged me to use the existing public information on how the company uses Big Data and dataviz. After a bunch of sleuthing, I was able to write an interesting case study with minimal direct input from current Netflix employees.

Hastings and Randolph saw the writing on the wall. They believed— correctly, as it turned out—that the current video rental model was ripe for disruption. What's more, they had built a much better mousetrap. Netflix offered free shipping, no late fees, a massive selection of titles, and a simple interface by which customers could manage their queues—all at an affordable price. Red envelopes started appearing everywhere.

Even as Netflix started to gain traction, Hollywood Video and Blockbuster, then the powers that be, predictably pooh-poohed the very idea of DVDs by mail. It was a classic case of *The Innovator's Dilemma*. The conventional thinking was that customers would never buy into the Netflix model. They would not want to wait a few days for a video to arrive by mail; they wanted to watch videos *immediately*, or at least after a trip to the local video shop. Plus, mail gets lost. Postage costs add up. DVDs break. Customers steal. DVDs by mail would never work.

Well, we know how things played out. Hollywood Video ceased operations in May 2010. Its parent company, Movie Gallery, declared Chapter 7 bankruptcy. For its part, Blockbuster formally declared bankruptcy on September 23, 2010, although it had become essentially irrelevant long before that.

NETFLIX 2.0: SELF-CANNIBALIZATION

Even as it was cannibalizing Hollywood and Blockbuster, Netflix was laying the groundwork to cannibalize itself—specifically, its own DVD-by-mail service. To use the Silicon Valley buzzword *du jour,* the company was in the process of pivoting. Netflix began streaming video in 2007, even when most of its attention was focused on drubbing Blockbuster. (Say what you will about Netflix and Reed Hastings, you can't call either one complacent.)

---

* My contacts at the company weren't rude. They just encouraged me to take advantage of what's out there.

As it moved from physical DVD delivery to streaming, Netflix management realized that its customers were generating a mind-boggling amount of data—and not just on who was watching which shows. By all accounts, Netflix *always* has understood the importance of data. Beyond programs watched, today it collects as much subscriber data as possible, including the following:

- Where its customers watch videos through geo-location data

- The devices on which its customers are watching

- When its customers watch—that is, the time and day of week

- Within limits, what its customers are doing while they watch. (Netflix tracks every time customers rewind, fast-forward, and pause a movie or TV show.)

But Netflix doesn't stop there. It also purchases metadata from third parties such as Nielsen and collects social media data from Facebook, Twitter, and other sites. At Netflix, the default *modus operandi* is data collection. As Derrick Harris wrote in a slightly dated June 2012 piece for GigaOM,[2] here are some fascinating Netflix statistics:

- More than 25 million users (36 million as of this writing)

- About 30 million plays per day

- More than 2 billion hours of streaming video watched during the last three months of 2011 alone

- About 4 million ratings per day

- About 3 million searches per day*

Those numbers have only increased in the time since that piece was published. I don't know the precise statistics, but rest assured that Netflix does. Its infrastructure is predicated on scale, speed, Big Data, and sophisticated algorithms. As such, Netflix can compile updated stats like these very quickly, if not in real time.

The results speak for themselves. Netflix growth has been nothing short of meteoric. (Both in terms of stock price and number of subscribers, it has recovered nicely from the brief and ill-fated 2011 Qwikster debacle that effectively split its streaming and physical DVD business into two.) As Willa Paskin writes in *Wired*, "Today three times as many Americans subscribe to Netflix's streaming service as to its DVD-by-mail offering, and about 70 percent of what they watch is television. Overall, 33 million subscribers stream more than a billion hours of Netflix content every month."[3] Astonishingly, the Netflix streaming

---

* No doubt that these numbers have grown considerably in the eighteen months since the article was published.

service today accounts for roughly one-third of all nightly home Internet traffic in North America.[4]

Without a sufficiently powerful infrastructure to handle this influx of data and the tools to visualize it, Netflix would not be nearly as successful as it is today. Visual Organizations understand that adopting a new business model most likely changes the equation. Almost always, such a "pivot" requires adopting new and more robust data-management tools.

Let's discuss those tools.

DATAVIZ: PART OF A HOLISTIC BIG DATA STRATEGY

When the Netflix streaming service stopped working on December 25, 2012, many Americans took to Twitter. The microblogging service exploded with the #fail hashtag. (A common tweet that day: *Now I have to talk to my family? I wanted to watch [insert name of show]. Thanks, Netflix!*) In reality, however, the problem had nothing to do with Netflix *per se*. To make a long story short, an Amazon employee accidentally deleted key data from the Amazon Web Services, traffic apportion system. Chaos ensued.[5]

The glitch and subsequent fallout underscored the extent to which Netflix relies upon AWS. Without it, Netflix could not stream so much content to virtually any device in the world. Christmas was a case in point. In fact, Netflix has been for some time the world's largest AWS customer, reportedly using it to a greater extent than Amazon itself! As Ashlee Vance writes in *Bloomberg* Businessweek:

> Netflix is one of the world's biggest users of cloud computing,
> which means running a data center on someone else's equipment.
> The company rents server and storage systems by the hour, and
> it rents all this computing power from Amazon Web Services,
> the cloud division of Amazon.com, which runs its own video-
> streaming service that competes with Netflix.[6]

Amazon and Netflix are the epitome of frenemies. They are at once partners and competitors. But Netflix doesn't just use the data-management utilities that AWS provides. On the contrary, as Vance points out, "Netflix has built an array of sophisticated tools to make its software perform well on Amazon's cloud." To its credit, Amazon recognizes the value of these applications. It has aped many of the Netflix advances and offered them to its other business customers, most notably the 2012 Barack Obama reelection campaign.

Although much of its technology is proprietary, Netflix has customized a great deal of open-source software (OSS) to power key parts of its business. In terms of the Netflix technology infrastructure, OSS plays second fiddle only to AWS. Behind the scenes, Netflix is at the forefront of open-source Big Data tools like Hadoop, Hive, and PIG. (More on that later.)

Each new application and improvement gets Netflix closer to its ultimate goal. In other words, Reed Hastings isn't satisfied with merely determining what its customers are *currently* doing—in this case, consuming boatloads of content. Like many organizations, Netflix seeks the Holy Grail (read: the ability to make accurate predictions). Most enterprises would like to do this, but here's the difference: Netflix actually possesses the infrastructure and data to make this a reality.

A great deal of the data that Netflix captures and analyzes directly furthers its efforts to predict what its customers are likely to watch *next*. Mohammad Sabah, the company's senior data scientist, told GigaOM in June 2012 that the company "already captures JPEGs and notes the exact time that credits start rolling." What's more, Netflix is taking into account other, less obvious sources of data. In the near future, Netflix might base recommendations on elements like movie volume and even scenery. (As we'll see shortly, it already uses jacket colors.) Such movie or show metadata may well provide Netflix with even more valuable insights into what its customers will likely watch. Any of those insights inform its massive content-acquisition decisions, like its $100-million-dollar original series *House of Cards* starring Kevin Spacey and its decision to resurrect the cult TV show *Arrested Development* in 2012.*

DATAVIZ: IMBUED IN THE NETFLIX CULTURE

In a data-driven environment like Netflix, dataviz plays a key role. It must. According to its corporate blog,[7] Netflix considers data visualization to be of paramount importance. Many of Netflix's major systems contain significant dataviz components. And, like other Visual Organizations covered in this section, Netflix uses data-visualization tools on a continuous basis, not occasionally. That is, Netflix employees *routinely* look to existing dataviz tools to tweak algorithms, garner new insights, and solve pressing business issues.

Jeff Magnusson serves as the manager of data platform architecture at the company. On June 27, 2013, at the Hadoop Summit, he provided a rare window into the Netflix Big Data ethos. Magnusson presented with Charles Smith, a colleague and a software engineer. The title of the talk: "Watching Pigs Fly with the Netflix Hadoop Toolkit."† During their presentation, Magnusson and Smith laid out three key tenets of the Netflix data philosophy:

1. Data should be accessible, easy to discover, and easy to process for everyone.

2. Whether your dataset is large or small, being able to visualize it makes it easier to explain.

3. The longer you take to find the data, the less valuable it becomes.

---

* For my money, one of the smartest shows to ever grace the big screen.

† To view slides, see http://tinyurl.com/jeff-mag. Watch the video at http://tinyurl.com/jeff-charles-netflix.

These canons explain why Netflix is the quintessential Visual Organization. At the heart of its business lie some of the most sophisticated Big Data tools on the planet, including no shortage of dataviz applications. At a high level, these tools serve the interests of two critical constituencies: customers and technical professionals. It's important to note, however, that satisfying both masters ultimately benefits everyone: executives, stockholders, nontechnical employees, and others.

Customer Insights

Look at the covers of *House of Cards* and the 2010 version of *Macbeth* that ran on the PBS series *Great Performances*. At first glance, they are eerily similar. They both display older white men with blood on their hands—Kevin Spacey and Patrick Stewart, respectively—against primarily black backgrounds. Figure 3.1 illustrates the detailed color breakdown.

Figure 3.1 manifests the obvious: the covers of the two shows are much more similar than dissimilar. At the same time, though, subtle differences

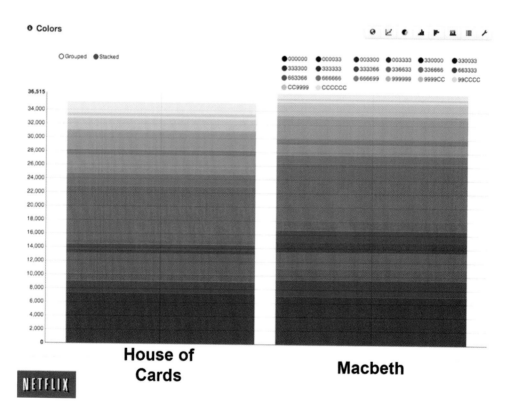

Figure 3.1 Detailed Color Comparison of *House of Cards* and *Macbeth*
Source: Netflix Technology Blog (techblog.netflix.com)

Figure 3.2 Detailed Color Comparison of *Hemlock Grove*, *House of Cards*, and *Arrested Development*
Source: Netflix Technology Blog (techblog.netflix.com)

exist—and Netflix can precisely quantify those differences. What's more, Netflix can see if they have any discernible impact on subscriber viewing habits, recommendations, ratings, and the like.

Figure 3.2 shows a similar color analysis of the *House of Cards*, *Arrested Development*, and *Hemlock Grove*, an American horror thriller and Netflix original program that premiered on April 19, 2013.

Given the cost of producing high-quality original content, why would Netflix create the cover for a new series in a vacuum? Why wouldn't decision-makers look at the company's vast trove of data? With subscribers bombarded by nearly unlimited options, why leave such a potentially critical aspect completely to chance? After all, Netflix possesses the data to make the most informed business decision possible. No, Netflix didn't invite outsiders to production meetings for *Hemlock Grove* and *House of Cards*. Still, you can bet that its head honchos carefully reviewed subscriber data when selecting the covers to these series.*

At Netflix, comparing the hues of similar pictures isn't a one-time experiment conducted by an employee with far too much time on his hands. It's a

---

* For more on this, see David Carr's excellent *New York Times'* piece at http://tinyurl.com/carr-netflix.

regular occurrence. Netflix recognizes that there is tremendous potential value in these discoveries. To that end, the company has created the tools to unlock that value. At the Hadoop Summit, Magnusson and Smith talked about how data on titles, colors, and covers helps Netflix in many ways. For one, analyzing colors allows the company to measure the distance between customers. It can also determine, in Smith's words, the "average color of titles for each customer in a 216-degree vector over the last N days."

In a word, *wow*.

How many organizations understand their customers to this extent? I would hazard to guess that few do. Most companies would love to know even half as much about their customers as Netflix does.

This begs the obvious question, how? Through Big Data and dataviz, Netflix seamlessly delivers mind-boggling personalization to each customer. At the same time, Netflix can easily aggregate data about customers, genres, viewing habits, trends, and just about anything else. Equipped with this data, Netflix can attempt to answer questions that most organizations can't or won't even ask. With respect to color and covers, these include the following:

- Are certain customers trending toward specific types of covers? If so, should personalized recommendations automatically change?

- Which title colors appeal to which customers?

- Is there an ideal cover for an original series? Or should different colors be used for different audiences?

- And plenty more.

In short, Netflix can ask better questions and make better business decisions based upon superior data, dataviz tools, and a culture that recognizes the importance of both.

Better Technical and Network Diagnostics

While it has created some of the world's mightiest Big Data tools, Netflix doesn't rest on its laurels; the company develops new ones as needed. In an interview with Maria Deutscher of *SiliconAngle*, Magnusson discussed one particularly thorny technical issue: the difficulty in understanding Apache Pig* raw code due to the complexity of certain scripts. Deutscher writes that "Netflix solved this problem with a visualization tool called Lipstick. The homegrown program transforms code into directed acyclic graphs, or DAGs, that make it easier

---

* Apache Pig is a platform for analyzing very large data sets. It consists of a high-level language for expressing data analysis programs, coupled with infrastructure for evaluating these programs. The salient property of Pig programs is that their structure lends itself to substantial parallelization. For more, see http://pig.apache.org.

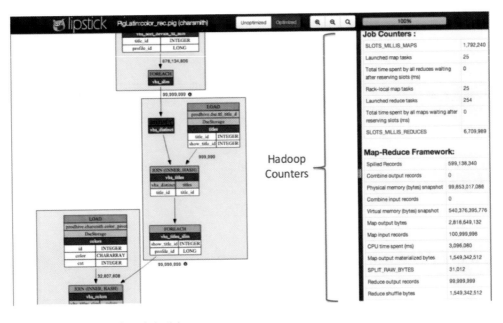

Figure 3.3 Screenshot of Lipstick
Source: Netflix Technology Blog (techblog.netflix.com)

to spot bugs in large projects.* These charts also enable developers to view MapReduce† jobs as they execute."[8] Figure 3.3 shows a screenshot of Lipstick.

Figure 3.3 illustrates an essential truth about Visual Organizations. Put simply, even techies benefit from interactive data visualizations. Via Lipstick, employees responsible for building and maintaining the company's infrastructure can better understand the following:

- Which jobs have stalled
- Whether users see the data they were expecting
- Why an individual job has failed
- Nascent trends

The ability to spot nascent trends cannot be overstated, especially for a company like Netflix with more than 30 million subscribers. As Qwikster showed, Netflix customers are not afraid to leave *en masse* if they don't like what's happening. Remember that Netflix is not AT&T or Verizon; it does not force customers to sign rigid, highly penal two-year agreements. Netflix subscribers pay by the month.

---

* At a high level, DAGs are useful for modeling different kinds of structures in mathematics and computer science.

† MapReduce is a programming model for processing large data sets with a parallel, distributed algorithm on a cluster.

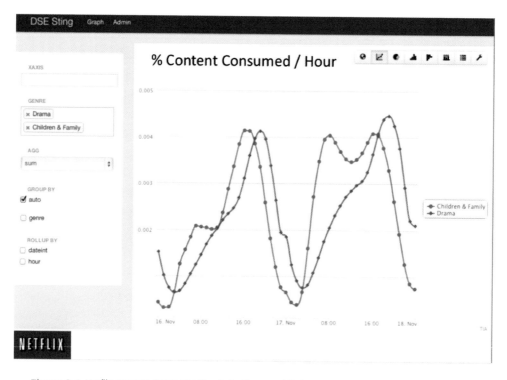

Figure 3.4 Netflix Content Consumed by Date, Hour, and Category
Source: Netflix Technology Blog (techblog.netflix.com)

As Figure 3.4 shows, Netflix can determine real-time subscriber usage patterns by any number of key factors.

Figure 3.4 illustrates that shows categorized as *children* and *drama* tend to follow roughly similar consumption patterns over time. No doubt that Netflix can add additional variables related to subscriber location, demographic, and device in *real time*. Beyond understanding customer preferences and viewing habits, Netflix employees interact with the data to investigate system issues.

Put it all together, and you begin to get a sense of just how well Netflix understands *all* facets of its subscriber base. For instance, the company can answer questions like, "Which are the most popular devices for subscribers to stream Netflix content?" The answer is shown in Figure 3.5.

Netflix knows which of its customers are watching which shows, where, on what device, and increasingly why. No, this level of knowledge is not solely due to dataviz. At the same time, though, it's hard to envision Netflix as we know it without the robust data-visualization tools it possesses—and the recognition that these tools are essential to running its business.

And Netflix just keeps going. It continues to make useful tools available to consumers. (Think of it as the antithesis of most cable companies.)

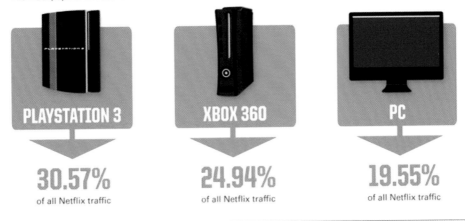

Figure 3.5 Netflix Breakdown of Streaming by Device (2011)
Sources: GigaOM and ColumnFive Media

Consider the August 2013 launch of its ISP Speed Index. The tool evaluates different aspects of ISP performance in several of the countries in which Netflix is available. Figure 3.6 shows an international ISP comparison as of July 2013.

And Figure 3.7 shows the breakdown for the United States during the same month.

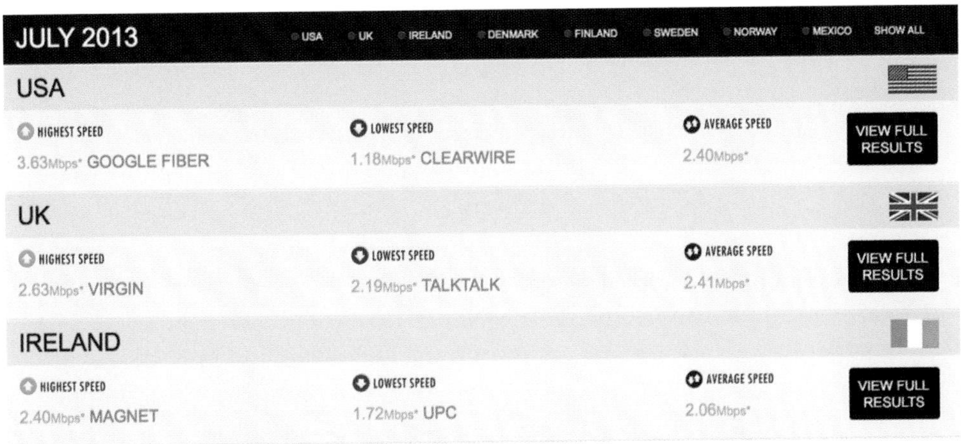

Figure 3.6 Netflix ISP Performance, Country Comparison—July, 2013
Source: Netflix Technology Blog (techblog.netflix.com)

USA ISP SPEED INDEX

JULY 2013

FIXED 🖨 📷   🗺

RANK	CHANGE	ISP NAME	AVG SPEED (Mbps*)
1	⊖	GOOGLE FIBER	3.63
2	⊖	CABLEVISION - OPTIMUM	2.53
3	⊖	COX	2.44
4	⊖	SUDDENLINK	2.40
5	⊖	CHARTER	2.20
6	⊖	VERIZON - FIOS	2.15
7	⊖	COMCAST	2.09
8	⊖	TIME WARNER CABLE	2.04
9	+2	BRIGHT HOUSE	2.01
10	-1	MEDIACOM	2.01

Figure 3.7 Netflix ISP Performance, United States—July, 2013
Source: Netflix Technology Blog (techblog.netflix.com)

The index is based on data from the more than 36 million Netflix members who collectively watch more than 1 billion streaming hours of TV shows and movies each month.* Think about it. Diehard Netflix subscribers can use the index to select their next ISP. As I write these words, perhaps an angry Cablevision customer in New Jersey is deciding to stick with his incumbent ISP because Netflix rates Comcast slower.

Embracing the Community

In keeping with Version 2.0 of the Apache License,[†] Netflix has made Lipstick and some of its open-source solutions freely downloadable to anyone with an Internet connection.[§] Although this may seem counterintuitive to many traditionalists, rereleasing improved projects back into the community is hardly uncommon in the open-source world. For instance, in *Too Big to Ignore*, I wrote about how Internet advertising company Quantcast did the same thing after forking the Hadoop Distributed File System. Quantcast created the Quantcast File System (QFS) as a cost-effective alternative to its Hadoop counterpart.

---

* For more on this, see http://tinyurl.com/netflix-isp.

[†] It is generally considered less restrictive than GPL, a free, copyleft license for software and other kinds of works. For more on the Apache License, see http://tinyurl.com/apache-z1.

[§] To download, improve, or fork your own version, see https://github.com/Netflix/Lipstick.

After spending considerable internal resources on the project, Quantcast freely made QFS available to the world at large.

Skeptics could argue that making Lipstick publicly available is just a PR move or an empty gesture. Imagine the developer reaction when a multi-billion-company keeps stealing from the cookie jar without replenishing it. (In the open-source world, this just isn't cool.) Netflix understands, however, that such a move is not just altruistic; it's concurrently selfish. External developers often take highly visible open-source projects like Lipstick in entirely new directions. In a critical way, Netflix is outsourcing potential innovation around Big Data and dataviz. To be sure, Netflix employs myriad smart cookies, but plenty of talented folks are not on its payroll. Why not take advantage of their acumen and skills?

Beyond releasing open-source projects, Netflix also uses its API to look outward. As Ben Schmaus writes on the Netflix blog:

> The Netflix API serves as an integration hub that connects our device user interfaces to a distributed network of data services. In supporting this ecosystem, the API needs to integrate an ever-evolving set of features from these services and expose them to devices. The faster these features can be delivered through the API, the faster they can get in front of customers and improve the user experience.[9]

While not *totally* open, the Netflix API is "open enough." That is, other people and companies can access it to extend Netflix core offerings. For instance, a third-party site called Instant Watcher* (IW) allows subscribers to manage their queues. Beyond simply adding movies, IW users can do things that they currently cannot do on the Netflix home page and app. For instance, they can see which Netflix movies are trending, which actors and movies other subscribers have recently searched, and which movies are expiring soon (although Netflix will no longer be providing that information in the near future). If particular third-party features like these are useful, Netflix can just ape that functionality on its home page and app.

LESSONS

This chapter represents just the tip of the Netflix data iceberg. That is, the preceding pages have covered just a few of the many ways in which Netflix embraces Big Data and dataviz, uncovering scads of valuable customer insights in the process—many of which outsiders like me are not aware of. (For obvious reasons, the company guards its data and intellectual property very closely.)

---

* See http://instantwatcher.com.

As Netflix shows, Visual Organizations understand that they can only realize the benefits of Big Data if they incur the attendant costs— new tools, new hardware, and new employee skills. Above all, a new mind-set is essential.

Even without knowing everything there is to know about Netflix, we can draw some high-level conclusions. The company clearly demonstrates critical lessons for aspiring Visual Organizations. First, harnessing the power of Big Data to the extent that Netflix has takes time. Companies like Netflix do not appear on day one, wave magic wands, instantly gain fascinating insights into consumer behavior, and mesmerize us with accurate predictions on day four. In the case of Netflix, it has taken more than 15 years for it to be able to do everything that it does today, not to mention significant investment and its fair share of bumps along the way. Yes, dataviz may result in grabbing some low-hanging fruit, but an enterprise doesn't go from "zero to Netflix" overnight.

Second, Hastings knows that dataviz is not a silver bullet. Rather, data visualization needs to be part of an integrated information-management strategy. Netflix has deployed powerful data-visualization tools to handle Big Data, but those tools are predicated on an even more powerful infrastructure (read: AWS).

Finally, realize that the path to success is not linear. A fair amount of trial and error and, dare I say, *failure* is inevitable. As the Lipstick example demonstrates, new tools need to be created because old ones no longer suffice.

NEXT

The data side alone of the Netflix story could fill a sizeable tome by itself. Maybe one day Hastings will let the world in on what goes on there. Nevertheless, it's time to move on to other Visual Organizations. Netflix is hardly alone in its appreciation for data, data exploration, and dataviz.

NOTES

1. Anderson, Mae, and Liedtke, Michael, "Hubris—and Late Fees—Doomed Blockbuster," NBC News, September 23, 2010, http://www.nbcnews .com/id/39332696/ns/business-retail/t/hubris-late-fees-doomed-block-buster/#.UgZSI1OE6AI, Retrieved August 10, 2013.

2. Harris, Derrick, "Netflix Analyzes *a Lot* of Data About Your Viewing Habits," Gigaom, June 14, 2012, http://gigaom.com/2012/06/14/netflix-analyzes-a-lot-of-data-about-your-viewing-habits, Retrieved June 25, 2013.

3. Paskin, Willa, "The New Rules of the Hyper-Social, Data-Driven, Actor-Friendly, Super-Seductive Platinum Age of Television: Rules 9 & 10,"

Wired magazine, March 19, 2013, http://www.wired.com/underwire/2013/03/netflix/, Retrieved August 10, 2013.

4. "Netflix Accounts for 1/3 of Nightly Home Internet Traffic, Apple's iTunes Takes 2%," Apple Insider, May 14, 2013, appleinsider.com/articles/13/05/14/netflix-accounts-for-13-of-nightly-home-internet-traffic-apples-itunes-takes-2, Retrieved June 25, 2013.

5. http://news.cnet.com/8301–1023_3–57561454–93/amazon-apologizes-for-netflixs-christmas-eve-streaming-outage/.

6. Vance, Ashlee, "Netflix, Reed Hastings Survive Missteps to Join Silicon Valley's Elite," *Bloomberg Businessweek*, May 09, 2013, http://www.businessweek.com/articles/2013–05–09/netflix-reed-hastings-survive-missteps-to-join-silicon-valleys-elite, Retrieved June 25, 2013.

7. Moore, Brian, "What Is Garbage Collection Visualization?," The Netflix Tech Blog, May 22, 2013, http://techblog.netflix.com/2013/05/garbage-collection-visualization.html, Retrieved June 10, 2013.

8. Deutscher, Maria. "Netflix's Jeff Magnusson on Big Data Visualization," SiliconAngle, July 13, 2013. http://siliconangle.com/blog/2013/07/12/netflixs-jeff-magnusson-on-big-data-visualization, Retrieved July 12, 2013.

9. Schmaus, Ben, "Deploying the Netflix API," The Netflix Tech Blog, August 14, 2013, http://techblog.netflix.com/2013/08/deploying-netflix-api.html, Retrieved August 20, 2013.

CHAPTER 4

Dataviz in the DNA

*Progress is impossible without change, and those who
cannot change their minds cannot change anything.*
—George Bernard Shaw

A fter reading the previous chapter, you might be feeling a little intimated. Netflix is a company worth nearly $21 billion as of this writing. As you read a few pages ago, Netflix gathers the types of insights about its subscribers about which most other organizations can only dream. It's only natural for you to be a bit apprehensive. Maybe you're even asking yourself a question like, Is *that* what it takes to be a Visual Organization? Fortunately, as you'll see in the following pages, the answer is a definitive no.

These days, stories of start-ups receiving millions of dollars in venture capital (VC) funding permeate the business headlines. Many pundits openly wonder whether we have entered another tech bubble redolent of the late 1990s. For instance, Groupon said no to Google's $6 billion offer prior to going public in November 2011. More recently, in November 2013, Snapchat reportedly rebuffed Facebook's acquisition offer. Evidently, $3 billion wasn't a sufficiently high number. Later that month, Dropbox announced that it was seeking $250 million of additional funding that would value the company at a remarkable $8 billion.[1]

The bubble question is a fair one, but it's easy to forget that popular start-ups like Snapchat, Dropbox, Instagram, Tumblr, and their ilk still represent the exceptions, not the rule. Most start-ups don't receive proper VC funding, much less to the tune of tens of millions of dollars. The vast majority of start-ups need to bootstrap—at least at first. No matter how brilliant, very rarely are untested ideas by themselves sufficient to raise substantial money.

Of course, that reality hasn't deterred millions of people from eschewing traditional corporate life in pursuit of their own dreams. Technology costs have dropped by orders of magnitude. Popular books like *The Lean Startup* and *The $100 Startup* espouse DIY virtues. Culturally speaking, the United States places far less of a stigma on failure compared to other countries. Many people have decided to just go for it.

In this chapter, we'll see that one need not be a behemoth like Netflix to embrace the notion of a Visual Organization. The focus here is on a single start-up that does start-up dataviz well, even with relatively modest revenues and a small headcount. At least to some extent, an organization's awareness and mind-set vis-à-vis data visualization can trump its paucity of financial and human resources.

THE BEGINNINGS

Founded by Jimmy Jacobson and Porter Haney in 2012 and based in Las Vegas, Nevada, Wedgies is a five-person start-up that lets users easily create simple polls via Twitter. The company is on a mission to rid the world of boring and unwieldy surveys.

As Haney describes the company's beginnings, "Jimmy and I sat down at my kitchen table and looked to build something useful to the people around us. We saw people asking a ton of questions on Twitter and Facebook and getting open-ended responses back. We decided to build Wedgies to aggregate and visualize those responses in real time."

Hardly neophytes to the world of technology, Haney and Jacobson knew what they signing up for before starting Wedgies. As mentioned earlier, tech start-up costs had decreased by orders of magnitude since 2000. Long gone are the days of paying tens or hundreds of thousands of dollars per month for infrastructure (read: servers, databases, and the software to manage each). "Most websites and mobile apps these days run off the same cloud services that power Dropbox," Jacobson says. "Once configured correctly, the difference between running 1 or 100 servers is a command and a bump in monthly billing. This lets us focus on the lifeblood of our start-up: our customers."

Like many consumer services today, Wedgies has embraced the freemium model. Anyone can create a simple Wedgie for free with just a few clicks. Premium options include:

- Brand customization: Customers can change pictures and colors to better reflect their individual brands.

- Enhanced sharing: Customers can enable voting on their own sites, not just http://www.wedgies.com.

▩ Editing: Customers create polls with more than five options, as well as multiple choices.

▩ Fraud busting: Wedgies uses algorithms to detect multiple votes. This allows customers to collect better data.

UX IS PARAMOUNT

Wedgies understands the importance of a very visual and intuitive user interface. This is becoming norm today; no one is building ugly websites like Craigslist.

By way of background, Web 2.0—aka, *the Social Web*—has exploded over the past six to eight years. One of the consequences of the maturation of the Web is that design and user experience (UX)* have become white-hot topics. UX conferences and books are popping up almost on a daily basis. The rationale isn't hard to understand. Long gone are the Web 1.0 days in which consumers visit websites because they were novelties or there were no legitimate alternatives. Over the past five years, we have seen a veritable monsoon of consumer-oriented websites, services, devices, content, and apps with no end in sight. Rare is the company that fails to recognize the importance of providing user-friendly, social, and visual user experiences—and Wedgies is no exception. In this über-crowded milieu, differentiation is essential, and a superior UX a potential means to that end.

> UX remains largely a hygiene factor.

Despite its cardinal importance, UX remains largely a hygiene factor. Let me explain. Today there are no guarantees for success, but this much is true: ignoring or dismissing UX will almost certainly result in failure. In other words, even if Haney and Jacobson build the world's greatest UX, the odds are still stacked against them. Most start-ups fail, even ones that seem to have all of the right ingredients, such as solid business models, experienced leadership, strategic partnerships, etc.

Great design doesn't change the fact that ours is a crowded world. They call it *Big Data* for a reason. Limitless content on just about any topic is available to anyone with a smartphone. No one is going to stare at boring bar charts, much less share them. For Wedgies to gain any sort of traction, it needed to be both easy to use and easy on the eyes. Wedgies are designed to be not only visually compelling, but brain-dead simple to create and share.† With a single click, users of Wedgies can create polls, download their visualizations in a high-quality PNG

---

* User experience (UX) relates to someone's emotions while using a particular product, system, or service.

† This is even more true as of November 12, 2013, as the company launched a new version of its flagship product. Users can now add any image to their online polls.

format, and easily share them with friends and on their social networks. Users can quickly leverage the results of their polls through a variety of means.

Haney and Jacobson did their research before starting the company. They know that the human mind is conditioned to identify and recognize faces. "Using faces in our visualizations helps us quickly focus on interesting trends," Jacobson says. Wedgies sorts faces in its visualizations based on two criteria. First, which option did users choose in a poll? Second, did any people vote together in blocks? Wedgies refers to this latter group of users as *frenemies* because they might not always agree, but they vote on the same groups of polls. They are obviously sharing the polls with one another, as shown in Figure 4.1.

By including faces and geography, Wedgies has discovered something interesting: its users spend more time examining the data in front of them. This

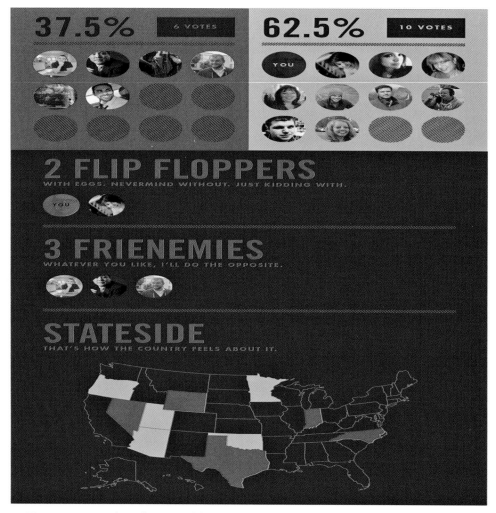

Figure 4.1 Frenemies Poll Data Breakdown
Source: Wedgies

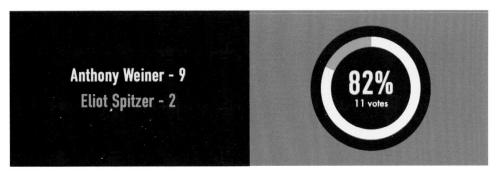

Figure 4.2 Poll: Who's the More Despicable Politician?*
Source: Wedgies

increases site stickiness and incentivizes others to continue using Wedgies— not an easy thing to do in a crowded landscape in which attention is a precious currency.

Creating a Wedgie is downright fun. For instance, in the summer of 2013, I was curious to see what the public thought of two disgraced New York politicians running for office: Eliot Spitzer and Anthony Weiner. In the public's eye, who was more disgraceful? I created a Wedgie, and the results of my highly unscientific poll are represented in Figure 4.2.

Sating my curiosity is one thing, but other people are using Wedgies to collect valuable data for more professional purposes. For instance, on July 28, 2013, *USA Today* reporter Jeff Gluck was covering a NASCAR race at the Indianapolis Motor Speedway. Unlike most events, this one took place on a dirt road. Gluck created a Wedgie asking his followers if they liked the new surface. The Wedgie is presented in Figure 4.3.

Soon after Gluck created his NASCAR Wedgie, it exploded. Within 15 minutes, he had collected more than 1,400 responses.[†] It's interesting to note that Gluck used this in the post-race press conference to determine which questions to ask the drivers. In effect, the Wedgie allowed him to collect data and to do his job better. (We'll return to this example later in the chapter.)

THE PLUMBING

While nowhere near the size of Netflix, Wedgies has more in common with the streaming video giant than one might think. Each company has built its technical infrastructure in similar conceptual manners. In the case of Wedgies,

---

* To see the Wedgie for the poll, go to http://tinyurl.com/wedgies-weiner.
† To see the Wedgie for the poll, go to http://tinyurl.com/nascar-wedgies.

JEFF GLUCK WANTS TO KNOW...

Did you enjoy tonight's NASCAR race on dirt?

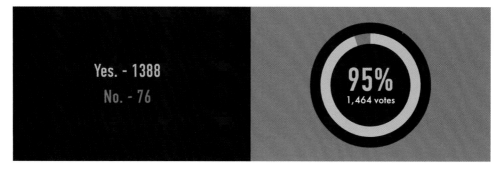

Figure 4.3 Jeff Gluck NASCAR Poll
Source: Wedgies

it doesn't matter if an individual Wedgie generates 10 responses or 10 million. Like Netflix, Wedgies is designed for the long term; it does not require regular Band-Aids or spaghetti code.

Let's cover some of the specific ways that Wedgies uses different dataviz tools to handle its operations.

Embracing Free and Open-Source Tools

Jacobson and Haney are astute users of free and open-source tools. Yes, the Wedgies' team could easily build extremely sophisticated dataviz or analytics applications from scratch. As Wedgies grows, perhaps that day will come. For now, though, the company gets by with Google Analytics and its aforementioned internal dashboard. With regard to the former, Wedgies is hardly alone. Untold millions of individuals and businesses use Google Analytics to understand their traffic sources, most popular webpages, demographic breakdowns, and the like—including yours truly. It more than suits the current business needs of Wedgies. As for the latter, Jacobson used a mix of D3 and a few of the open-source charting libraries mentioned in the Appendix.

All else being equal, web-native companies are more likely to recognize the importance of data, dataviz, open-source software, and cloud computing. A company today needs to be prepared for instantaneous and massive increases in usage and scale.

Wedgies' dataviz tools allow employees to wrap their heads around problems and trends not easily surfaced in traditional tabular data, allowing employees to respond as needed. In Jacobson's words, "Social data is a great example of this. It's very easy to see how many Twitter followers someone has, but basic data like this doesn't tell us how engaged that person's fans are. Even the number of retweets means little." In other words, there is no way to really know if the person retweeting read the content or engaged with it in any meaningful way. "It's not uncommon for us to see an expert in a field get better engagement out of a Wedgie than a brand with hundreds of thousands of followers on Twitter."

Google Analytics may not be the most powerful analytics tool ever created, but it certainly gets the job done for a wide variety of companies.

Let's return to Figure 4.3 for a moment. As Gluck's NASCAR poll was gaining traction, behind the scenes Jacobson was able to see what was happening and react accordingly. He consulted both Wedgies' internal dataviz tools and Google Analytics to gauge site performance and look at metrics. The latter is presented in Figure 4.4.

Jacobson understands that start-ups often only get one bite at the proverbial apple. Speed kills, and stories can "trend" or "go viral" in minutes. As such, keeping an eye on things is more critical. Fortunately, dataviz makes that easier than ever. Reflecting on the NASCAR poll, Jacobson says:

> We knew that Gluck was a popular NASCAR reporter with a decent number of Twitter followers. We looked at his numbers after he signed up with us, but weren't expecting that his Twitter followers would be so engaged. Gluck created his Wedgie and our dashboard showed that it quickly started getting a lot of votes. We checked Google Analytics and confirmed that we had over 500 people on site at that very moment. More than half of the clicks came from mobile devices. Thirty seconds later I had scaled up our cloud servers to handle that load and we watched the data pour in.

Does this example seem simplistic compared to Netflix does? Of course. Still, it underscores the fact that Wedgies understands the significance of dataviz, a true sign of a Visual Organization. Only when we *see* what's happening can we react in real time. If Jacobson had not monitored the status of Gluck's Wedgie and had failed to respond accordingly via Amazon Web Services (AWS). It is entirely possible that the poll would have crashed, damaging the Wedgies brand in the process.

Should Wedgies continue to grow, gain more customers, and raise more capital, Jacobson and Haney will evaluate whether purchasing—or, more likely, renting—another, more powerful analytics application makes sense.

Google Analytics

Go to this report

**http://www.wedgies.com - https://wedgies.com
www.wedgies.com**

My Dashboard

Sep 9, 2013 - Sep 9, 2013

Visits

4,540
% of Total: **63.50% (7,150)**

Visits

1 ▬▬▬▬ 6

Visits by Source

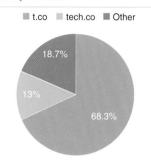

Visits by Visitor Type

Visits by Social Network

Social Network	Visits
Twitter	3,100
reddit	134
Facebook	84
Facebook Apps	7
Tumblr	4
TweetDeck	4

Visits by Device Category

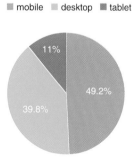

© 2013 Google

Figure 4.4 Wedgies's Google Analytics, September 9, 2013
Sources: Wedgies, Google

Extensive Use of APIs

Chapter 2 showed that today ETL is not the only way to move and access data—and it often is not the best way. Jacobson agrees with this general premise and has made APIs a key part of Wedgies' infrastructure. As he explained to me:

> Companies have recently realized the benefits of providing users with low-level access to their own data. Giving developers the tools they need to solve problems and visualize data means that company itself doesn't need to implement the same features. The transition from SOAP/XML* to REST/JSON as a standard for web APIs has made it even easier to scale this approach. Now companies like Salesforce.com are generating revenue by providing marketplaces for developers who build apps on top of their APIs and platforms. It will be really exciting in the future when governments are also providing this level of access to the data we generate as citizens. The same tools and apps developed to visualize consumer data will be valuable in visualizing civic data.[2]

Note how Jacobson talks about *external* data sources, not just the data that Wedgies "owns." (For more on the increasingly important issue of data ownership, see the Coda.) Through open APIs, perhaps future incarnations of Wedgies will draw upon even more repositories of information.

LESSONS

This chapter has demonstrated that even small companies like Wedgies are embracing dataviz. On the front end, Wedgies' very visual design lets users create compelling yet simple data visualizations of their polls. Behind the scenes, the company uses sophisticated yet affordable dataviz tools to manage its business and to lay the foundation for future growth and functionality. While an exceptionally talented programmer, Jacobson is not independently wealthy. He and Haney did not spend millions of dollars on the core technologies that make Wedgies tick. No, Wedgies hasn't discovered the same types of things in its data as Netflix has, but make no mistake: the company is paving the way for future data discovery through its infrastructure and its culture. That is a hallmark of a Visual Organization.

On the future of Wedgies, Haney is optimistic. "Real-time content is really in its infancy. Viewers are tuning to Twitter instead of their TVs to find breaking news," he says. "Users are pulling more relevant content via social media than they are via traditional media. Social polling offers the ability to answer

---

*SOAP (Simple Object Access Protocol) is a simple XML-based protocol to let applications exchange information over HTTP. Put simply, SOAP is a means to easily access Web services.

questions in real time. It's just starting, and we're looking forward to powering the fastest, most elegant solution to this problem."

NEXT

In Chapter 5, we head to academia. We'll see how one institution of higher learning has embraced mobility, dataviz, and transparency.

NOTES

1. Vance, Ashlee, "Dropbox seeks valuation of more than $8 billion," November 24, 2013, http://www.sfgate.com/technology/article/Dropbox-seeks-valuation-of-more-than-8-billion-5008379.php, SFGate, Retrieved November 25, 2013.
2. Personal conversation with Jacobson, Monday, July 1, 2013.

CHAPTER 5

Transparency in Texas

> Knowledge is of no value unless you put it into practice.
>
> —Anton Chekhov

Academia is a funny place, an expensive amalgam of mind-bending innovation and mind-numbing tradition. On one hand, schools like MIT, Carnegie Mellon, Stanford, and others are pushing the boundaries of what's possible. Armed in some cases with massive endowments, curious students, and enthusiastic professors, they are pioneering essential research into an array of fields. On the other hand, many schools' stifling internal policies and politics drive faculty, administrators, and students to drink. Old habits die particularly hard in higher education, and many institutions have been loath to adapt to contemporary trends.

And let's not forget the elephant in the room: skyrocketing costs. College tuition rates have long been rising at twice the rate of inflation. The Project on Student Debt reported that, as of October 2012, the average amount of student loan debt for the Class of 2011 was $26,600, a five percent increase from 2010.*

Subsequently, total student debt in the United States now exceeds $1 trillion, according to the Consumer Finance Protection Bureau.[1] What's more, that

---

* To view the entire report, go to http://projectonstudentdebt.org/files/pub/classof2011.pdf.

debt is concentrated toward those least able to pay it. *Bloomberg Businessweek* reports that households whose net worth is under $8,500 hold over half of all student debt.[2]

Against this backdrop, something has to give. Education is ripe for disruption. In the past five years, we've seen the rise of Massive Open Online Courses (MOOCs), not to mention the colossal success of Kahn Academy and sites like Udemy and Coursera. And there's the controversial entrepreneur and venture capitalist Peter Thiel. The libertarian billionaire is paying 18-year-olds to pursue their start-ups. Each year, 20 Thiel Fellows receive $100,000 *not* to attend college.

Forget those on the outside looking in. Even many on the inside recognize that the status quo is untenable. "Universities are at a crossroads," says Terri Griffith, a professor at Santa Clara University and the author of *The Plugged-In Manager*. "They need to take a good look at how to create a new mix of students (lifelong learners), technologies (from online to the role of location), and methods. They need to answer the question: what is magical about a four-year degree or faculty from a single university? But universities shouldn't do this assessment alone or in a vacuum. We will provide the most value to our students and society if we work with employers to restructure when, how, and what education is offered."[3]

Griffith's attitude on the state of academia is progressive, refreshing, a tad irreverent, and anything but insular. Luckily, others share her viewpoint—*and are doing something about it*. Case in point: The University of Texas System.*

BACKGROUND

For more than century, the University of Texas System "has been committed to improving the lives of Texans and people all over the world through education, research, and health care."[4] UT is one of the nation's largest systems of higher education, with nine academic institutions and six health institutions. These are shown in Table 5.1.

As of this writing, UT educates more than 216,000 students and employs nearly 89,000 people, including nearly 70,000 faculty members. Its annual operating budget is roughly $14.6 billion. With so many students and employees, it is bound to generate a great deal of data. Unlike so many academic institutions, however, UT actually does something with that data.

---

* UT usually refers to the University of Texas at Austin. For the sake of brevity, UT will cover the entire 15-university system.

Table 5.1 UT Academic and Health Institutions

UT Academic Institutions	UT Health Institutions
The University of Texas at Arlington The University of Texas at Austin The University of Texas at Brownsville The University of Texas at Dallas The University of Texas at El Paso The University of Texas - Pan American The University of Texas of the Permian Basin The University of Texas at San Antonio The University of Texas at Tyler	The University of Texas Southwestern Medical Center The University of Texas Medical Branch at Galveston The University of Texas Health Science Center at Houston The University of Texas Health Science Center at San Antonio The University of Texas M.D. Anderson Cancer Center The University of Texas Health Science Center at Tyler

EARLY DATAVIZ EFFORTS

From 2004 through 2010, UT released an annual accountability report on the state of the system. These reports presented snapshots of system, school, and student data in charts, graphs, and raw numbers. These were insightful, but they were available only in static PDF formats. Figure 5.1 presents some sample data from the noninteractive, 200-page documents.

Evaluation of entire education experience at this institution: percent responding good or excellent

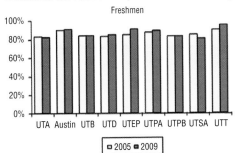

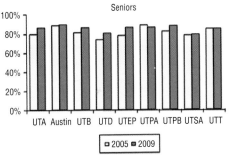

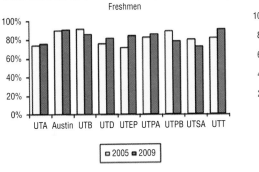

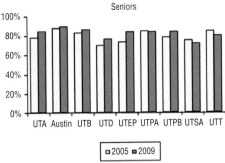

Figure 5.1 Data from UT 2009–10 Accountability Report*
Source: The University of Texas System Productivity Dashboard © 2013

*To view the entire report (or that report from other years), go to http://tinyurl.com/tx-accountability.

To be sure, not every school provides even this level of transparency. (Scroll through one of the accountability reports, and you may be surprised at the data that UT made available back then.) Rather than rest on its laurels, though, UT did what many Visual Organizations do: it took visibility and transparency to the next level via data visualization. Specifically, it deployed sophisticated dataviz applications from SAS, but not just to its own employees. Anyone with an Internet connection can play with UT data.

EMBRACING TRADITIONAL BI

In May 2011, Chancellor Francisco G. Cigarroa, M.D., and UT regents unveiled the UT Framework for Excellence,* an ambitious plan to transform education and health care in Texas. Here's a window into Cigarroa's vision for the future:

> The futures of our children and our grandchildren are at stake. How do we make higher education more accessible and affordable to an increasing number of students? How do we produce more doctors, nurses, and health professionals, and improve the quality of healthcare in Texas?

The goals are nothing if not lofty. Making them happen would require improved access to data, new dataviz applications, and a different organizational mind-set. To this end, in December 2011, UT launched the System Productivity Dashboard, a public portal that provides an open view into the performance of UT's administration and its individual campuses. At the time of the launch, *anyone* could explore UT student and administrative data, including Texas employees, legislators, the media, and the public at large. "The regents, legislators, and constituents were asking tough questions," explained Stephanie Huie, vice chancellor for UT's Office of Strategic Initiatives. "They really wanted to look at different aspects of the data, and they didn't want just one year. They might want to look at data over time, by gender, race, or ethnicity, for example."

And the UT dashboard allows anyone to do just that. Figure 5.2 provides an example of the kinds of views that UT makes available. At its core, the dashboard lets users view a wide range of indicators and explore a great deal of data. These include student success, faculty productivity, research and technology transfer, and finance and productivity. "It's one way that we can chart our institution's progress on achieving the chancellor's goals," explained Huie.

The dashboard also lets users download whatever they want for further analysis in Excel and other applications. In other words, UT realized that creating its dashboard and publicizing its data were important objectives, but

---

* Read the Framework here if you'd like: http://www.utsystem.edu/chancellor/framework.

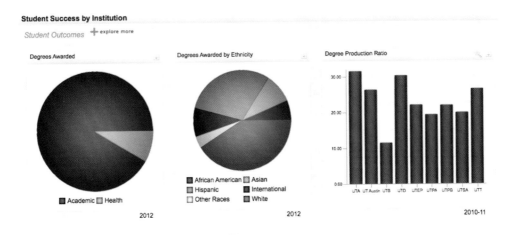

Student Success by Institution

Student Outcomes ➕ explore more

Degrees Awarded

Degrees Awarded by Ethnicity

Degree Production Ratio

■ Academic ■ Health

■ African American ■ Asian
■ Hispanic ■ International
☐ Other Races ■ White

2012

2012

2010-11

Figure 5.2 Student Success Dashboard
Source: The University of Texas System Productivity Dashboard © 2013

they represented means to more ambitious ends. Put differently, they ideally would lead to further questions and data exploration. Making the data more open can inhere tremendous benefits. As Huie says, "The dashboard gives users the freedom to let their ideas guide them wherever they want to go."

DATA DISCOVERY

In the years since its launch, the dashboard has been positively received. Still, UT hasn't rested on its laurels. Visual Organizations know that increasing access to data is always possible and advisable. This is especially true after initial successes, lessons learned, and user feedback. Early efforts yielded some interesting findings and results, but UT knew that it could—and must—do more. That is, contemporary dataviz isn't an "IT project" in the traditional sense.

For all of its insights and positive press, the dashboard was designed to work on PCs. It simply wasn't portable. To keep up with our increasingly mobile times and make its data more accessible, UT would have to adapt.

In January 2013, UT launched SAS Visual Analytics (VA), a much more mobile-friendly means of viewing data. Through VA, UT data is now available anywhere on any device. That is, employees and the public need not be tethered to proper computers to access UT data. From an iPad, users can view data visualizations using the SAS Mobile BI app. While they can take insights with them wherever they are, the app's exporting capabilities aren't as powerful as those of the dashboard. As a result, UT continues to support both the dashboard and the VA. The result: the tools provide nearly unprecedented visibility into the UT system.

Better Visibility into Student Life

Compared to even three years ago, VA and new data sources collectively provide UT with superior insights into academics. Employees today can easily see a wide array of academic measures by institution, department, and program levels. And

Visual Organizations understand that often one size does not fit all. Meeting employees, customers, and users wherever they are is invaluable.

this information has helped UT make better decisions and identify issues that may have remained unseen and unaddressed. For instance, consider average time-to-degree (TTD) for doctoral graduates. UT previously stored data only at the institutional level. In other words, administrators had previously been able to see only the average time for all Ph.D. graduates. They could not drill down on individual fields.

With VA, UT has armed itself with a powerful dataviz application that can access robust datasets. As a result, employees can now view performance at much more granular levels. Specifically, UT can now take full advantage of two- and six-digit Classification of Instructional Programs (CIP 2000) codes.* Today, UT staff members look at both broad fields, like the biological and biomedical sciences, and very specific programs within those fields like pathology. An example is shown in Figure 5.3.

Like others in the UT Office of Academic Affairs, Executive Vice Chancellor Pedro Reyes has used this new data in many different ways. For example, Reyes viewed the median TTD of one university's mechanical engineering program in the two most recent academic years. As part of the regular program review, he compared that TTD to that of other Ph.D. programs within the engineering field. Reyes found that the Ph.D. program under review performed better than most other programs. Reyes concluded that this program's TTD satisfied the UT standard. As a result, no further action was required.

However, as the staff continued to explore and visualize newly available data, other interesting patterns and anomalies began to emerge. Two of the outliers are shown in Figure 5.4: aeronautical engineering (the dark

▶ **NOTE**

The tree maps in Figures 5.3 and 5.4 use bigger boxes to represent larger cohort sizes. Colors correspond to median years enrolled by field of study. (See the scales at the bottoms of each figure.) For the sake of clarity, the individual labels that the VA application natively shows have been removed.

---

*The Classification of Instructional Programs (CIP) provides a taxonomic scheme that will support the accurate tracking, assessment, and reporting of fields of study and program completions activity. CIP was originally developed by the U.S. Department of Education in 1980. The 2000 edition (CIP-2000) is the third revision of the taxonomy and updates the existing instructional program classifications and descriptions. For more, see http://nces.ed.gov/pubs2002/cip2000.

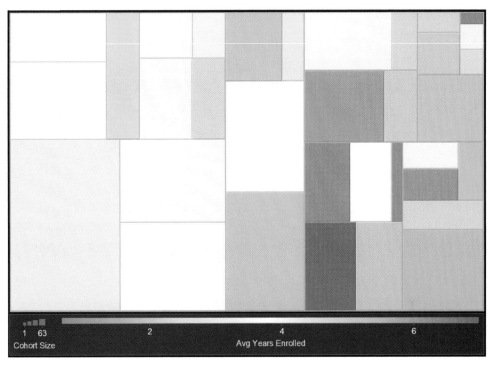

Figure 5.3 UT Time-to-Ph.D. (Subset of Programs)
Source: The University of Texas System Productivity Dashboard © 2013

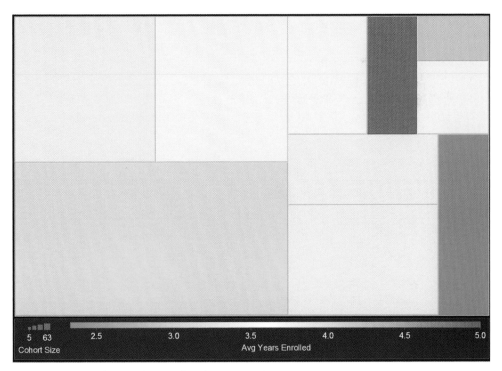

Figure 5.4 UT Time-to-Ph.D. (Engineering Programs)
Source: The University of Texas System Productivity Dashboard © 2013

brown) and materials engineering (the dark blue). This prompted a couple of questions:

- What was occurring in these programs and why?

- With only two years' worth of data, was this an actual pattern?

The visualization revealed something in the data that UT users might easily have missed. Data and dataviz at UT are collectively serving as the starting point for more questions and discussion.

Soon after launching VA, UT enhanced its dashboard by including a new section with more robust data visualizations. This section allowed users to create more advanced views of the data. Collectively, these provide the requisite context around data, helping employees understand it and make better decisions. Consider that student debt, in the opinion of Huie and many others, is one of the most critical issues facing higher education. "We're not just saying, 'Here's the data on student debt.' We're saying, 'Here's some contextual information on our student debt compared to statewide and national student debt.'" Context allows users to ask more intelligent questions.

UT has consistently started relatively small with dataviz and built upon those successes. In other words, it has not attempted to boil the ocean. Like most higher education shops, UT focuses primarily on its academic mission. Not surprisingly, its Academic Affairs office was one of the first in the Association for Institutional Research* to embrace transparency, visual analytics, and data discovery.

Over the years, UT had collected a great deal of student data, an amount that has grown considerably over the past five years. Examples include enrollment and degree data, student financial aid data, and course-level data. As of late, UT has started collecting data on faculty productivity, including research expenditures and scholarly productivity.

Visual Organizations understand that context is king.

Expansion: Spreading Dataviz Throughout the System

We have seen thus far that UT's academic side has routinely and successfully used data to make better decisions. Because of the way that it communicates through the system, different UT operational departments have started to take notice. They want in. Based on these successes, UT plans to roll out dataviz and data discovery tools to other pockets of the system. Groups like Shared Services, Endowment Compliance, Facilities, Risk Management, and even its Office of the Police are eager to start visualizing their data, asking better questions, and making better decisions. What's more, they present new data

---

* AIR is the world's largest professional organization for institutional researchers.

and opportunities to discover meaningful connections and patterns—not just within individual areas, *but throughout UT.*

First up is Shared Services. In 2013, Huie and her team began working with the arm of UT that attempts to consolidate redundant IT and business services.* Also on the docket is the Supply Chain Alliance (SCA), a group within UT created to expand the use of joint purchasing. SCA explores new opportunities to leverage the collective size and strength of UT institutions. The Alliance aims to provide reliable, sustainable solutions for the purchase and delivery of equipment, services, and supplies. In so doing, it hopes to improve customer satisfaction and reduce cost. By working across UT, the Alliance fosters the system-wide adoption of best practices.

Up until recently, the Alliance lacked real visibility into its data. Reporting was a manually intensive process. In the words of Richard St. Onge, associate vice chancellor for shared services:

> We plan to make these dashboards available to our chief business officers and chief purchasing officers. If they find them valuable, then we plan to go both deeper and wider. We want to look at transactional analytics for purchasing activities across all fifteen campuses. Additionally, we envision making these dashboards and analytical capabilities available for all projects under UT Shared Services. So, for a relatively minimal investment in time, we can grow the data culture and the demand for data.

RESULTS

Equipped with the right tools and organizational mind-set, UT hopes that significant discoveries, changes, and savings will stem from these new data sources. With so much data and so many different pockets of the system, the potential is considerable. Yet, so is the amount of work involved. UT is again starting small and learning as it goes.

To help the Alliance access and analyze data better, the Office of Strategic Initiatives built simple yet telling dashboards and interactive reports. An example of the former is presented in Figure 5.5.

Figure 5.5 shows the amount of money that UT was committed to spending in the 2012 fiscal year. In 2012 (its sixth year), the Alliance executed 50 contracts worth $150 million annually. These contracts decreased costs by 15 percent while concurrently improving the quality of UT services. The cumulative value to UT exceeds $100 million. UT employees can view "drill down" and see specific savings by contract and area.

---

* From the UT website: "Shared Services is distinct from mere centralization of services in that it encompasses the concept of shared governance and permits greater flexibility and responsiveness. It creates incentives for participation and is overseen not just by UT personnel, but also by representatives of the participating campuses."

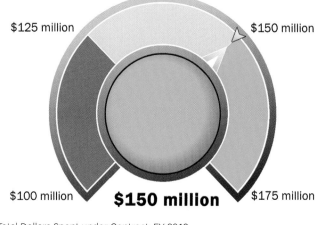

Figure 5.5 Total Dollars Spent under Contract, FY 2012
Source: The University of Texas System Productivity Dashboard © 2013

As a public institution of higher learning, UT aims to be progressive and socially conscious. To that end, meeting internal Historically Underutilized Businesses performance goals is an important system-wide goal.* Figure 5.6 shows the amount of money that the Alliance spent on HUBs in 2012. Dials like the one in Figure 5.6 allow UT employees to see the progress that individual institutions are making.

The Alliance refunds two-thirds of the fees it collects back to individual campuses based upon their spending levels. To each UT school, this represents extra money and an incentive to use contracted vendors. St. Onge plans to use this data to, among other things, evaluate where institutions are taking advantage of contracts and to find out, if they are not, why not. What is *not* being provided? Again, Visual Organizations understand that dataviz leads to better questions.

In April 2013, SAS named UT as the annual winner of its Excellence in Education award. The honor is meant to spotlight "an educational organization using SAS to improve operations, empower leaders, prepare students for today's workforce, spark innovation, and/or expand educational opportunities," SAS explained in its announcement.†

UT is fielding inquiries from other academic institutions both within and outside of Texas. Educause, an association that uses IT to advance higher education, has also taken notice. "This is the way higher ed is going, with more data being made available to the public," Huie noted. "But then the big questions

---

* A HUB is a small, for-profit entity with its principal place of business in Texas. It is at least 51% owned by an Asian Pacific American, Black American, Hispanic American, Native American, American woman, and/or Service Disabled Veteran. For more, http://tinyurl.com/5va4tuv.

† Read the entire announcement here: http://tinyurl.com/oa7dvh2.

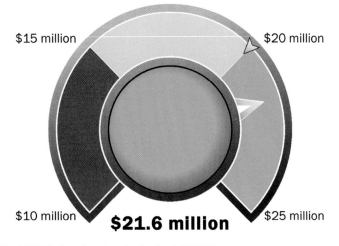

Figure 5.6 Total HUB Dollars Spent under Contract, FY 2012
Source: The University of Texas System Productivity Dashboard © 2013

are, 'How do you organize the data? How do you go about getting the data? How do you store it, and present it?' That's a long, complicated process."

LESSONS

UT is instructive on a number of levels. First, by embracing new sources of data and new dataviz tools, the system and its members have done much more than find the low-hanging fruit. They have laid the foundation for future data discovery. Second, UT demonstrates the importance of executive buy-in. Yes, a great deal can happen organically through the toil of individual employees, groups, and departments. In large enterprises, though, it's impossible to over-state the importance of senior-level commitment to transparency, data visualization, and exploration.

Finally, it's not necessary or even advisable to try to do everything at once, even with Small Data. Depending on an organization's culture, resources, other priorities, and the like, it may well be wise to start in a relatively conservative manner. Recognizing early successes and mistakes is a perfectly viable strategy for deploying dataviz tools. Lessons learned can then be passed to others, saving the organization considerable time and expense.

NEXT

Chapter 6 extrapolates the lessons to be gleaned from the case studies in Part II. It presents a simple model to understand the four different levels of Visual Organizations. What's more, it asks a key question that all organizations ought to be asking.

NOTES

1. Chopra, Rohit, "Too Big to Fail: Student Debt Hits a Trillion," Consumer Financial Protection Bureau website, March 21, 2012, http://www.consumerfinance.gov/blog/too-big-to-fail-student-debt-hits-a-trillion, Retrieved July 23, 2013.

2. Applegate, Evan, "Correlations: Student Debt Explodes," Bloomberg Businessweek: Global Economics, June 27, 2013, http://www.businessweek.com/articles/2013–06–27/correlations-student-debt-explodes, Retrieved July 23, 2013.

3. Personal conversation with Griffith, July 23, 2013.

4. The University of Texas System, "About the University of Texas System," http://www.utsystem.edu/about.

PART Three

Getting Started: Becoming a Visual Organization

In Part II, we saw how dynamic organizations like Netflix, Wedgies, and UT have embraced dataviz and seen spectacular results. We saw that Visual Organizations recognize the uncertainty inherent in today's business environment. Along with a wide variety of data types and sources, they are increasingly using data visualization to mitigate risks and make informed business decisions.

Part III takes a step back. What can we learn from Netflix, Wedgies, and UT? What lessons, myths, and mistakes can be extrapolated from Part II? No, the next chapters should *not* be considered a step-by-step checklist for becoming a Visual Organization. Rather, my goal is to present sage advice for readers interested in reaping the benefits of dataviz at work—and avoiding common pitfalls.

Chapters include:

- ▦ Chapter 6: The Four-Level Visual Organization Framework

- ▦ Chapter 7: WWVOD?

- ▦ Chapter 8: Building the Visual Organization

- ▦ Chapter 9: The Inhibitors: Mistakes, Myths, and Challenges

The Four-Level Visual Organization Framework

> Essentially, all models are wrong, but some are useful.
>
> —George E. P. Box

Introduced in the early 1960s, Bizarro World (aka *Htrae*) is a fictional planet in the DC Comics's universe. Comedian and *Superman* über-fan Jerry Seinfeld used Htrae as the inspiration for one of my favorite episodes of his eponymous TV show. In "The Bizarro Jerry," Elaine befriends a group of people who are both eerily similar to—and remarkably different from—George, Elaine, and Kramer.* (There's even a portly character named Vargas, a much friendlier version of *Seinfeld's* diabolical mailman Newman.) I'll leave it at that. Explaining any episode of the series is never a short exercise.

Let me take you for a moment to another fantastic place: Data Bizarro World (DBW). On this mystical planet, data quality issues don't exist. Interpretation is universal, and all data sources, types, and velocities are equal. In short, all data is perfect. Because of this, all data visualizations are equally effective and understood by all. Everyone looks at the same charts, graphs, and tree maps and instantly knows exactly what's going on and, even better, why.

---

* Brilliantly, the signature *Seinfeld* theme song is played backward in one scene of the episode.

117

So what do you think? Would you like to live on DBW? Things certainly seem simpler there. Data isn't nearly as messy as it is on Earth. There are fewer arguments since everyone's on the same page. Maybe work is more pleasant, if a little boring.

Enjoy yourself while this trip lasts, because we're going back to reality now.

As we saw in Part II, different organizations use different types of tools to visualize data. There's no one universally accepted or "right" way for an enterprise to visualize data. This shouldn't be surprising. After all, the business needs, objectives, and budgets of UT, Netflix, and Wedgies aren't exactly one and the same. Improving the quality of health care in Texas is hardly the same as serving up billions of hours of video across the world each month or conducting quick polls over the Web. As a result, the ways that each organization uses to visualize data aren't the same. In other words, Netflix reaches a higher level than UT and Wedgies.

Visual Organizations use the dataviz tools referenced in Chapter 2 to do the following things:

- Help employees understand what has happened—and possibly why.
- Help employees understand what's currently happening—and possibly why.
- Help employees understand what's about to happen—and possibly why.
- Discover new insights from existing datasets and sources.
- Make better business decisions.
- Diagnose and address nascent issues.
- Ask better questions of their data.

This brief chapter looks at the four levels of Visual Organizations, the value that each level can yield, and the logistics of moving among the levels. It uses as its basis the case studies from Part II.

BIG DISCLAIMERS

Before continuing, a few disclaimers are in order. First, this chapter presents a framework that is simple by design. Of course, data and dataviz are important. You'll never hear me say otherwise. By themselves, though, they do not and cannot *exclusively* drive revenue or profits. Neither data nor dataviz exists in a vacuum. In any enterprise, many other independent variables are at play. Success is always a combination of leadership, industry, company size, competitive landscape, organizational culture, patents, access to capital, human resources, and plain old dumb luck.

In addition, by no means does the forthcoming framework take into account all the technologies and tools necessary to successfully operationalize

Big Data. Allow me to make the following distinction. Data-visualization applications collectively represent the *front end* (read: the ones with the vast majority of employees directly interact). However, behind the scenes, Big Data requires organizations to deploy some very different *back-end* tools. These are not the same data warehouses and relational databases traditionally used to manage structured data. In *Too Big to Ignore*, I devote an entire chapter to data filesystems like Hadoop, Google BigTable, NoSQL, NewSQL, and other ways to handle nonrelational data. Making Big Data dance requires much more than just rolling out snazzy dataviz programs on top of the same infrastructure.

In short, the basic framework aspires to be useful, not "right." The late British mathematician and statistician George E. P. Box (quoted at the beginning of this chapter) would be proud.

A SIMPLE MODEL

There was a method to my madness in Part II. I chose to profile those organizations for a specific reason. I wanted to illustrate the fact that, like the use of data, the notion of a Visual Organization is not binary. It's not all or nothing; there are degrees.

We learned in Chapter 4 that start-up Wedgies and behemoth Netflix are in many ways polar opposites. The vast differences include the amount of data generated, not to mention headcount and financial resources. As such, Netflix discovers a great deal more about its subscribers than Wedgies can. (To be fair, though, most companies can't hold a candle to Netflix when it comes to knowing their customers.) It's like comparing grade-school T-ball to the New York Yankees.

At the same time, though, the two companies share some strong philosophical and technological similarities. Both understand the importance of Big Data and interactive dataviz. And, most important to this book, both are Visual Organizations; Netflix is just "more advanced." It benefits from types of data and dataviz tools that Wedgies currently cannot.

Put differently, Netflix is a Level-4 Visual Organization, which is the most sophisticated type. The four levels are displayed in Table 6.1.

Table 6.1 The Four-Level Visual Organization Framework (in Order of Descending Sophistication)

Level	Type of Data Used	Type of Dataviz Used
4	Big Data	Interactive
3	Big Data	Static
2	Small Data	Interactive
1	Small Data	Static
0	*Neither*	*Neither*

▶ **NOTE**

I have come across my fair share of dataphobic individuals, groups, and departments, but I have never seen an entire *organization* that summarily rejects the idea of data (in other words, a Level-0 Visual Organization.) Perhaps one is out there somewhere. For the sake of simplicity, however, I'll proceed as if such enterprises do not exist.

Inasmuch as this is a book about Visual Organizations, I would be remiss if I did not display a few graphical representations of this framework, the first of which is shown in Figure 6.1.

Figure 6.1 reveals a number of things worthy of additional discussion. First, let me explain the nature of the levels and why they increase in importance as they move "northwest." In English, this simply means that organizations can get away with using static dataviz tools on even large sets of Small Data. (As I know from experience, it's not hard to create standard reports on tables with tens of millions of records.) Big Data, however, is an entirely different ballgame. Deriving insights and value from petabytes of unstructured data usually requires using new, interactive dataviz tools—and building them from scratch when necessary. As we saw in Chapter 3, Netflix builds tools like Lipstick because they're needed and they just don't exist yet.

Limits and Clarifications

It's best not to get bogged down in the precise location of each level's maximum in Figure 6.1. For now, suffice it to say that these ceilings do indeed exist. The

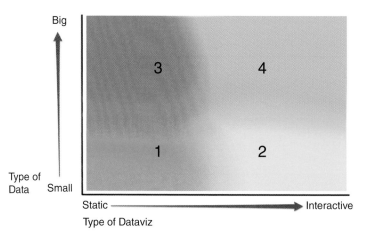

Figure 6.1 The Four-Level Visual Organization Framework

Sources: Concept by Phil Simon and Melinda Thielbar*

---

* A friend of mine pointed out to me that this image vaguely resembles the new Microsoft Windows logo. This is merely coincidental.

value that organizations can glean from *any* type of data is hardly infinite. Big Data is yielding better predictions, but it certainly can't project *everything*—and that day may very well never come. Still, only an ingénue fails to understand that Big Data can provide insights and answers that Small Data simply cannot. Whatever theoretical limits of Big Data and interactive dataviz exist today, they are best discussed over beers sometime, not here. This isn't an academic book. I would argue, though, that those ceilings are constantly rising. Amazon, Apple, Facebook, Google, Twitter, and Netflix are using Big Data today to do things that were impossible even five years ago.

Next, organizations can expect to realize greater benefits as they embrace interactive dataviz and Big Data. (Some benefits may occur gradually, others immediately.) Put differently, there's only so much that any enterprise can do with Small Data, irrespective of its dataviz tools (Level 2). The same is true for Big Data and static dataviz (Level 3). An enterprise can do *exponentially* more by using both Big Data and interactive tools. The potential benefits of Level 4 are shown in Figure 6.2.

Again, the four-level framework emphasizes potential value, not actual or even expected value. An organization that successfully visualizes Big Data and deploys interactive tools may never realize the (full) value of either one. Plenty of factors could stymie its efforts, including some type of scandal, a dysfunctional culture, and bad leadership.

Figures 6.1 and 6.2 imply that somewhat defined limits exist on each axis (read: type of dataviz and data). Remember that the framework is designed to be a simple construct. In reality, things are never that clean. That is, the *number* of data-driven discoveries and insights does not suddenly cease once organizations reach the highest point of Level 1. As we saw in Chapter 2, even visualizing Small Data in static but interesting ways can provide valuable insights into a business. (See the extracts from the Lemonly 2012 annual report in Figures 2.1 and 2.2.) Generally speaking, though, the *value* of insights tends to rise as organizations reach higher levels. Figure 6.3 displays this notion via a heat map.

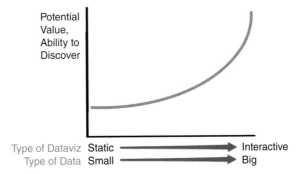

Figure 6.2 Potential Value and Insights from the Four-Level Visual Organization Framework

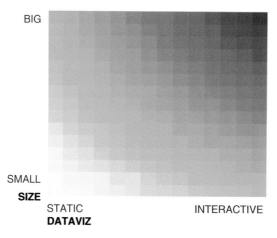

BIG

SMALL

SIZE

STATIC   INTERACTIVE

DATAVIZ

Figure 6.3 Heat Map of the Four-Level Visual Organization Framework
Sources: Concept by Phil Simon; heat map created by Melinda Thielbar in JMP Software, a business unit of SAS

The remainder of this chapter explains the nuances and ramifications of the Four-Level Visual Organization Framework.

Progression

How does an organization move from one level to another? In short, it takes time. We saw in Chapter 5 how UT moved from Level 1 to Level 2 over the course of nearly three years. That is, it "graduated" via a combination

A TALE OF TWO (FICTITIOUS) ORGANIZATIONS

Organizations are more likely to glean greater insights and value by ascending to higher levels in the framework. For instance, consider two fictitious organizations, Hogarth, Inc. and Mosley Industries. Both are stuck with static, standard reports. Neither does very much with Small Data, never mind the big stuff.

Here's where the two stories diverge.

Hogarth's CEO reads this book. She is inspired but, at the same time, she realizes that her company is just not ready for Big Data yet. She authorizes the purchase and deployment of some of the interactive tools discussed in Chapter 2. She knows that Hogarth's culture first needs to change (read: become more data-oriented). To that end, she focuses on garnering insights from Small Data and encouraging employees to act upon them. In effect, Hogarth is building the foundation for successful data exploration.

Mosley is not; its CEO is old school. He does nothing, believing that everything is just fine as is.

Let's say that I know nothing else about the two companies. If I had to bet on which organization would be more successful from this point forward, I would choose Hogarth any day of the week and twice on Sunday.

of executive commitment, employee buy-in, and deploying SAS Visual Analytics. (Chapter 8 provides more advice for organizations to become more visual.)

The framework poses a spate of other questions. Let's address them.

Is Progression Always Linear?

An organization doesn't "complete" Level 1 before "advancing" to Level 2. Visual Organizations aren't playing video games here. Inherent in the framework is the notion that different parts of an organization can concurrently operate at different levels with different degrees of success. That is not to say, however, that these levels are completely independent. They're not. For instance, a company that on the whole struggles with Level 1 is probably not excelling at Level 4. I have never heard of a single department, much less an entire organization, that works magic with Big Data while it struggles with the basic blocking and tackling that is Small Data.

Can a Small Organization Best Position Itself to Reach Levels 3 and 4? If So, How?

Yes. This is exactly what Wedgies is doing. By establishing a Big Data–friendly architecture and fostering a data-oriented mind-set, Wedgies stands a far better chance of reaching Levels 3 and 4 than larger organizations with a great deal of technological and cultural baggage.

Can an Organization Start at Level 3 or 4 and Build from the Top Down?

Possible? Sure. However, it's unlikely that a Visual Organization excels at Levels 3 and 4 but struggles with Levels 1 and 2. Think about it. Compared to Big Data, Small Data is comparatively easy. While variations may exist among certain departments, *organizations* only begin working with Big Data after there's a reasonable level of proficiency with Levels 1 and 2.

Is Intralevel Progression Possible?

Yes. The framework is simple by design. Just as the concept of a Visual Organization is not a binary, nor is the concept of a level. A company can improve over time within a given level, as Netflix no doubt has done. It was a Level-4 organization four years ago. Today, Netflix is doing things about which others can only dream. It is a "higher 4" now than it was in 2010.

Are Intralevel and Interlevel Progression Inevitable?

No. To be blunt, some organizations remain mediocre or worse. Many have no desire to do more with data and dataviz.

Can Different Parts of the Organization Exist on Different Levels?

Yes. Not all pockets of an organization need to operate at the same level. What's more, it's unlikely that every department or group is at the same level—or even the same point within that level. Remember from Chapter 2 that today current dataviz tools are relatively inexpensive and democratic. Everyone does not need to be on board or even on the same page. I can't imagine a chief marketing officer waiting two years for HR or Legal to get up to speed on "data stuff" before launching a critical dataviz tool. For every Level-4 HR department, I would hazard to guess that at least 100,000 fall into Level 1. A much less disparate ratio exists with regard to R&D departments.

Should an Organization Struggling with Levels 1 and 2 Attempt to Move to Level 3 or 4?

Ask yourself if this sounds like an ideal scenario: we're analyzing petabytes of unstructured data and finding some amazing things, but we don't really know who our customers are.

Regression: Reversion to Lower Levels

AOL, HP, Microsoft, and Yahoo are just four high-profile companies that have recently fallen from grace. Each reached a certain level of success and then, for whatever reason, started to stagnate or slip. Even the mighty sometimes fall, to paraphrase the title of Jim Collins's follow-up book to his 2001 bestseller *Good to Great*.

The same principle holds true with the framework presented in this chapter. Reaching a level by no means guarantees that the organization will stay there. Regression can and does happen. For example, in my consulting career, I have helped several organizations reach Level 2. I have deployed new enterprise applications, trained employees on how to use them, preached the data gospel, and purified millions of suspect records. More than once, I have returned to those same clients only to find that key employees have left and the tools deployed were no longer being used. These were regressions to Level 1, but what about higher-level regressions?

As of this writing and as discussed in the Introduction, the adoption of Big Data is anything but widespread. I have yet to see any organization excel at it only to drop the ball—that is, reach Level 4 and subsequently fall to Level 3 or worse. (Perhaps those that have are justifiably keeping a lid on things.) Amazon, Apple, Facebook, Google, Twitter, Netflix, and the other Big Data exemplars seem to be staying there, at least for the foreseeable future. Each company knows and recognizes the importance of data, both big and small.

Complements, Not Substitutes

The framework's four levels are *not* mutually exclusive. In fact, it's best to think of them as complements, not substitutes. Although powerful, Big Data does not supplant the need for intelligent management of customer, product, and employee lists (read: Small Data). Amazon knows exactly who buys what, and the company augments this transactional knowledge with insights gleaned from product reviews, browsing habits, and other information.

Deploying Big Data solutions like Hadoop does not mean that organizations should ignore relational databases, ERP systems, and other Level-1 sources of data. Yes, Level 4 is important, but being oblivious to lower-level issues and data sources is ill advised.

Accumulated Advantage

Rooted in the Bible, the Matthew effect portends that the rich will get richer and the poor will get poorer.* In the context of this book, it means that the four levels are additive and exponential. What's more, they result in accumulated advantage. In this way, the levels operate much like a network effect. A site like Facebook is so popular because, reflexively, it is so popular.

Netflix succeeds at each of the four levels in the framework. As discussed in Chapter 3, data and dataviz are part of the company's DNA. Netflix's human and technological resources give it an enormous competitive advantage, one that dissuades many entrepreneurs, existing companies, and VC firms from tangling with it. Is it any coincidence that one of Netflix's few legitimate competitors is Amazon, another Level-4 Visual Organization?

The Limits of Lower Levels

Organizations unable or unwilling to "leave" Level 1 or Level 2 effectively impose ceilings on themselves. The lower the level, the lower the ceiling and the greater the opportunity cost of inaction. (These ceilings may be high, but they're still ceilings.) Faced with such severe restrictions, a Level-1 organization simply cannot unearth the same type of knowledge about its business, employees, and customers that its Level 2, 3, and 4 counterparts can.

Relativity and Sublevels

The framework also allows for interorganizational comparisons. For instance, some organizations "do" Big Data better than others. I would place Amazon, Apple, Facebook, Google, and Twitter higher in Level 4 than Microsoft, Yahoo,

---

* Sociologist Robert K. Merton first coined the term in 1968. It takes its name from a line in the biblical Gospel of Matthew.

Oracle, and Dell. That doesn't mean, though, that the latter four companies are objectively "bad" at Big Data. I would merely place each company in the former group higher up in Level 4.

Should Every Organization Aspire to Level 4?

Maybe not bagel shops and nail salons, but generally speaking, yes.

NEXT

Chapter 7 asks a simple question, but it's arguably the most important one in this book.

WWVOD?

If we have data, let's look at data. If all we have are
opinions, let's go with mine.

—Jim Barksdale

I've only lived in Las Vegas for a little over two years, but it's evident to
me that it differs from most U.S. cities in many regards. Zappos's CEO Tony
Hsieh's $350-million Downtown Project to revitalize the city and 24/7 gam-
bling most easily come to mind. In one way, however, Sin City is pretty pedes-
trian, especially these days. Like Austin, Seattle, San Jose, San Francisco, New
York, Washington, DC, Boston, Boulder, and scores of other major U.S. cities,
Vegas sports a vibrant start-up community. (Wedgies, profiled in Chapter 4,
is one such start-up.) Never before has it been cheaper to start a company
and, generally speaking, when anybody can do something so easily, just about
everybody does. Untold numbers of entrepreneurs are trying to change the
world as I write this, or at least trying to become the next Instagram, Waze,
or Tumblr. Few ultimately will, but that hasn't changed the fact that start-ups
abound these days.

Against this backdrop, it's easy to forget that companies like Wedgies
remain the exception, not the rule. Most businesses operating today are not
greenfield sites. In May 2012, the Small Business Association reported that
more than 28 million active small businesses operated in the United States.[1]
Yes, these enterprises fail frequently, and new ones start on a daily basis.*
However, it's safe to say that millions of organizations today are not starting
from scratch. They are functioning within the confines of existing cultures,

---

* For an insightful breakdown of failure rates by industry, see http://tinyurl.com/small-biz-failure.

structures, politics, baggage, and business models. Throughout my career, I have found that there's generally an inverse relationship between (a) the size and age of an organization, and (b) its willingness and ability to change.

Put differently, all else being equal, larger and more mature companies tend to adapt slower than newer, smaller ones. This isn't inherently good or bad; it's just true. (See "Revenge of the Laggards: The Current State of Dataviz" in the Introduction.)

Against this backdrop, organizations intent upon capitalizing on Big Data and dataviz would do well to keep one question in mind as they navigate what can be a confusing and overwhelming business environment: what would a Visual Organization do (WWVOD)?

This chapter asks that question within the context of two examples: one actual and one hypothetical.

VISUALIZING THE IMPACT OF A REORG

During my brief tenure in corporate HR, I became the go-to guy for analysis, data, and reports, something that continued during my consulting career. I would guess that I have written nearly 5,000 proper reports while on the clock, hundreds of which involved employee movement of one kind or another. Most were pretty simple to build. A few hurt my head.*

At a high level, movement reports would present numbers and percentages related to employee hires, promotions, demotions, transfers, and exits. Some would even categorize movement by motivation, at least to the extent that a simple reason code could. (*Does anyone really leave a job because of a single motivation? Usually it's a combination of factors.*) The goals were generally twofold:

1. To determine which employees are moving up, sideways, and out.

2. To help recruiters and hiring managers staff accordingly.

Of course, unlike a profit and loss statement (P&L) or a trial balance, tracking employee movement is hardly an across-the-board requirement. For instance, at larger organizations, tracking employee movement is important. As Mark Wilson of *Fast Company* writes, "Unless you're self-employed, we're all cogs in a larger machine."[2] But start-ups and small businesses don't care about such things. They tend to have more important fish to fry. At smaller outfits, seemingly everyone knows when someone is hired, demoted, transferred, or leaves the company.† I certainly found this to be the case while researching and writing *The New Small*.

---

* I learned pretty quickly that the hardest part of the report-writing process is typically getting end users to explain what they want.

† There's usually plenty of water-cooler chat about these things.

Decision-making in most HR departments tends to rely almost exclusively upon things like intuition, corporate policy, occasional surveys, and maybe a few rudimentary standard reports. (Google is one exception that proves the rule.*) Whether these levers are helpful is dubious. Be that as it may, standard reports don't gauge an organization's true anatomy and pulse, and even surveys suffer from limitations. They don't provide meaningful insights into what an acquisition or restructuring *really* looks like. Yes, org charts and reporting relationships change, but so what? What's the *real* impact on employees, departments, and the organization? Even adept report writers like me can only begin to answer these critical questions with traditional tools.

Visualizing Employee Movement

Justin Matejka was thinking of these very questions on January 10, 2006. On that day, his professional life unexpectedly changed.

By way of background, Matejka had been working as a software engineer[†] at Alias, a leading developer of 3D graphics technology located in Toronto, Canada. Like just about every other Alias employee that January morning, Matejka arrived at work shocked to discover that Autodesk had acquired his company in a deal worth a reported $182 million. Although this is unexpected, the move made sense for Autodesk, a designer of three-dimensional software for industries as diverse as entertainment, natural resources, manufacturing, engineering, construction, and civil infrastructure.

In one fell swoop, Matejka went from working for a medium-sized, private company to a massive, publicly traded one worth more than $8 billion as of this writing. At the time of the acquisition, Autodesk was already a big company, employing thousands of people. Even if he kept the same title, Matejka knew that his job would change, but how? And, more broadly, how would the jobs of other people change?

Starting Down the Dataviz Path

Curious, affable, intelligent, and incredibly talented, Matejka began gathering internal Autodesk HR data in March 2007 and playing around. After a few months, he had built a prototype of what would ultimately become the Organic Organization Chart, a remarkable and animated dataviz that illustrates intraorganizational

---

* For a fascinating inside look at Google's HR department, see http://tinyurl.com/google-new-hr. At Google, HR rarely dictates; it convinces others with and through data.

† Matejka had been working for Alias as an intern but was rehired just after Autodesk acquired Alias. He was essentially part of the acquisition.

employee movement.* OrgOrgChart tracks *every* employee, manager, and departmental shift at Autodesk from May 2007 to April 2011. More specifically, it shows Autodesk's new hires, exits, and manager changes over a four-year period. Each second represents a week of activity for the company's growing staff. (Autodesk expanded from 6,500 to 7,500 full-time employees, temps, and contractors during this time.)

"When we joined this much larger company, it was difficult to understand where in the organization other people you met worked," Matejka told Mark Wilson. "So I started collecting the data initially to help us orient ourselves within our new company. After collecting the data on a daily basis for a little while, I figured it might be nice to look at the changes over time, and that is when the OrgOrgChart animation began." Matejka built OrgOrgChart with Java, Processing,[3] and GraphViz, an open-source graph (network) visualization tool. These tools allow for quick data processing and rendering and a visually appealing layout.

While researching this book, I discovered OrgOrgChart very quickly. In a word, I was amazed, perhaps because of my own background in reporting. Judging by his *Fast Company* article, Wilson was as well. He writes:

> Matejka ultimately created an ornate cell of trees and nodes, mutating and rearranging so quickly that your brain can barely process the facts. Yet it's completely logical. Autodesk president and CEO Carl Bass lies at the center of the circle, surrounded by upper management. Their departments project out like spokes, labeled by color.[4]

Let's say that Autodesk hires a new division VP. The meaningful areas light up "like a game of Simon." In other words, OrgOrgChart lets Autodesk employees easily appreciate the intricate ballet of a corporate structuring or a day's worth of resignations. Acquisitions become more than rows on a spreadsheet. They morph into vibrant blossoms of color that invite people to ask, "What's going on here?"

Nine sequential images from OrgOrgChart are presented in Figure 7.1. In early 2008, Autodesk's previous organization structure did not match its actual structure. The movement accurately reflects convergence of the two.

With approximately 6,000 employees, employee movement is taking place every day at Autodesk. To be sure, some days are busier than others, and not all movement stems from the decisions of individual employees. For instance, on March 17, 2009, Autodesk announced a corporate reorganization that is represented in Figure 7.2. The figure reflects Autodesk's shift from a product-focused organization to an industry-focused one.

---

* To see the whole project page, go to http://www.tinyurl.com/tvo-orgorg. The mesmerizing YouTube video can be seen at http://tinyurl.com/phil-orgorgchart.

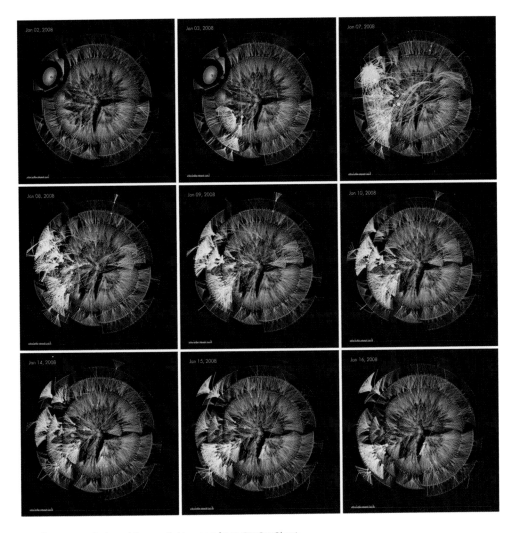

Figure 7.1 Series of Sequential Images from OrgOrgChart
Source: Justin Matejka

Figure 7.2 manifests that the reorg did not affect all Autodesk employees equally. Certain parts of the organization were affected more than others. (The bright green nodes on the left stand out the most.) Also, there was a great deal of movement on the right, cropped, expanded, and presented in turquoise in Figure 7.3.

I have never seen a reorg represented in this manner before, and I'll bet that you haven't either. OrgOrgChart is not a tool to answer a simple question. It does not evoke a clear answer to the question, "What do we do next?"

And that's not a bad thing. Visual Organizations like Autodesk create and use tools like OrgOrgChart to help them understand what's going on. Data-viz lets employees ask different—and, I'd argue, frequently better—questions

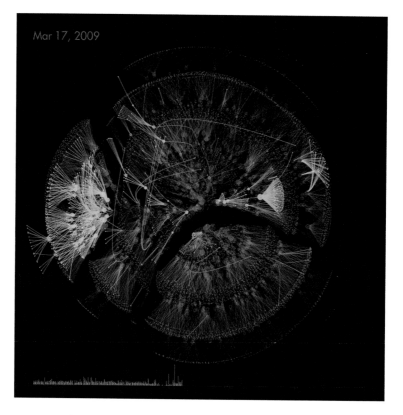

Figure 7.2 OrgOrgChart Overview of March 17, 2009
Source: Justin Matejka

New ways to represent and interpret data complement existing sources of information. In this case, anecdotal information from exit interviews would confirm what OrgOrgChart suggests.

of their data. For instance, could an increase in transfers and attrition explain an underperforming division or department? Possibly. Is a large group of employees "moving away" from a particular director or manager? Is that indicative of some type of management issue?

Over Skype one July morning, Matejka and I discussed the exploratory nature of contemporary data visualization in general, and OrgOrgChart specifically. He explained to me that he doesn't think of dataviz as simply another means of producing standard reports, key performance indicators (KPIs), and traditional analytics.

Even on days in which there is not a great deal of movement, like January 20, 2011, OrgOrgChart allows users to see what's happening. Figure 7.4 shows a relatively boring day, at least in comparison to the reorg displayed in Figure 7.2.

At first, Figure 7.4 looks pretty uneventful—mundane even. Upon closer inspection, however, movement is still taking place within Autodesk, as shown in Figure 7.5.

Figure 7.3 OrgOrgChart Zoom-In of March 17, 2009
Source: Justin Matejka

This isn't entirely unexpected at a company with more than 6,000 employees. Even on quiet days, there's always something going on.

Results and Lessons

"The most striking thing we learned from OrgOrgChart is just how much activity is happening on a daily basis," Matejka says. "In your own little corner of the company, you typically aren't aware that there are many changes going on. When you step back and look at the entire organization, however, things change. It is really striking amazing to see that there is always some amount of activity occurring."

The current incarnation of OrgOrgChart has evolved over time. In Matejka's words, "I had plenty of informal chats with my manager George Fitzmaurice and other members of the Autodesk research group. Those discussions resulted in many small but valuable improvements that I was able to incorporate into the current version."

OrgOrgChart has generated considerable press. Based upon internal Autodesk reviews, OrgOrgChart is particularly useful. In the words of Stacey

Figure 7.4 OrgOrgChart Overview of January 20, 2011
Source: Justin Matejka

Redman, senior HR director at Autodesk, "With a 30-year history and growth through acquisitions both large and small, our structure is consistently evolving. Autodesk is a highly dynamic global company, and OrgOrgChart has given us the ability to visualize that evolution. It has provided us with an excellent perspective on our history. We are applying these new insights to our future development."[5]

At a high level, OrgOrgChart proves that new dataviz tools can do a great deal more than old standbys. Traditional turnover or employee movement reports can still be useful, but they cannot begin to tell the type of story that OrgOrgChart can. A little curiosity, initiative, and data can go a long way.

It's interesting to note that in many ways Matejka is *encouraged to fail.* OrgOrgChart didn't have to succeed for Matejka to keep his job at Autodesk. Visual Organizations like Autodesk understand that innovation and creative thinking court failure, particularly in a Big Data world. To this end, Autodesk internally promotes a concept known as *fail fast forward* or *3F.* When allowed and even urged to take chances, amazing things like OrgOrgChart can result.

Figure 7.5 OrgOrgChart Zoom-In of January 20, 2011
Source: Justin Matejka

Future

When asked about the future of OrgOrgChart, Matejka is optimistic. "I think that we'll keep doing some internal development," he told me. "I would like to eventually bring in all of the data back to the beginning of Autodesk. I want to try to show the evolution from the first couple of employees all the way up to the thousands we have now." Matejka here touches on a key tenet of Visual Organizations. Starting (relatively) small and expanding in different directions can yield successful outcomes. An organization can't visualize all data immediately, especially at the beginning.

While Autodesk has no immediate plans to commercialize OrgOrgChart to HR professionals, Matejka concedes that it is certainly a possibility. "For now and the foreseeable future, I'm looking for other companies that are interested in using a visualization like this for their HR data. I am really interested in doing this. Since OrgOrgChart is still in the 'research project' phase, I would do it for free. I think the biggest trick will be getting access to the necessary data."

A MARKETING EXAMPLE

These days, it's fairly common for companies of all sizes to send periodic newsletters. Services like AWeber and MailChimp have made this easy enough. But too many organizations send newsletters and do nothing afterward to assess their results, much less improve. They fail to look at numbers and delve deeper. They don't ask questions of their data, much less make changes based upon answers. Eventually, many abandon these campaigns because, in their view, they just don't work.

So, given the above, what would a Visual Organization do?

At Visual Organizations, employees regularly use data and data visualizations to do their jobs. They refine business processes based on data, feedback, and testing results. They iterate. For instance, from 2005 to 2009, a Visual Organization sent one e-mail blast to its 20,000 U.S. customers at 10 a.m. EST every Monday. That is, all registrants received the company's e-mail at once, irrespective of time zone. (Whether all opened the e-mail at the same time is a different question, but let's keep it simple here.)

A Visual Organization would question whether a single, geographic-agnostic e-mail blast approach is not optimal. Based upon historical data, an employee created a choropleth and swiftly saw that its customers were fragmented as follows:

- East Coasters were inclined to open and respond to e-mails sent at 10 a.m. EST.

- West coasters were inclined to open and respond to e-mails sent at 11 a.m. PST.

A Visual Organization would then take the obvious next step. It would split its mailing list into two sublists: East Coast and West Coast. Let's say that click-throughs improved. After a few months, however, employees begin to notice something strange. For some reason, Oregonians generally aren't acting like other west-coast customers. They prefer their e-mails earlier in the day. Based on this new information, the Visual Organization further segments its mailing list into three sublists: East Coast, non-Oregon West Coast, and Oregon.

As this example illustrates, a dataviz can often result in a single and very valuable discovery, but don't stop there. Customers change. Preferences change. The world changes. Data changes. Keep playing. Keep discovering.

Visual Organizations understand the dynamic nature of today's business world. What's true now may very well not be true in six months or even six weeks. As such, these organizations continually use data visualizations to confirm what they know and to discover new things about their business, customers, employees, and the like. They then make changes accordingly.

NEXT

Asking "What would a Visual Organization do?" is certainly a good starting point, but that query alone does not a Visual Organization make. Chapter 8 provides additional advice.

NOTES

1. Mills, Karen, "28 Million Businesses Strong and Growing: Welcome to SBA's National Small Business Week!", Small Business Association, May 20, 2012, http://www.sba.gov/community/blogs/28-million-businesses-strong-and-growing-welcome-sba's-national-small-business-week, Retrieved August 23, 2013.
2. Wilson, Mark, "Infographic: Watch a Company's Management Team Mutate Over 4 Years," *Fast Company* Design blog December 19, 2012, http://www.fastcodesign.com/1671506/infographic-watch-a-companys-management-team-mutate#1. Retrieved July 23, 2013.
3. Learn more about Processing in the Appendix.
4. Wilson, Mark, "Infographic: Watch a Company's Management Team Mutate Over 4 Years," December 19, 2012, http://www.fastcodesign.com/1671506/infographic-watch-a-companys-management-team-mutate#1. Retrieved July 23, 2013.
5. E-mail exchange with Redman, June 25, 2013.

CHAPTER 8

Building the Visual Organization

If you can't explain it simply, you don't understand it well enough.

—Albert Einstein

Visual Organizations realize that today you can pretty much visualize anything. These days, powerful dataviz tools (like those discussed in Chapter 2) make it easy for "technically challenged" folks to slice and dice data. They can add new dimensions, data sources, elements, and graphics without any apparent end.

Becoming a true Visual Organization, though, requires much more than just buying some software and deploying it, and this chapter explores what it takes. This chapter takes a step back and provides some key data, design, technology, and management lessons. It looks at Visual Organizations and extrapolates the data, design, technology, and management lessons they can teach us.

DATA TIPS AND BEST PRACTICES

Put simply, there can be no data visualization without data. To become a Visual Organization, consider the following data-related tips.

Data: The Primordial Soup

When building a dataviz, it's important to consider factors, such as design, corporate culture, and technology. But remember that it all starts with data.

"We often think of visualization as a design and programming task, but the process starts further back with the data," writes author Nathan Yau, Ph.D. "You have to understand the data—its trends and patterns, along with its flaws and imperfections—and the rest follows."[1]

Walk Before You Run . . . At Least for Now

Bestselling author Dan Ariely said, "Big Data is like teenage sex: everyone talks about it, nobody really knows how to do it, everyone thinks everyone else is doing it, so everyone claims they are doing it." No argument here. Put differently, there aren't too many Level-4 Visual Organizations.

Despite the Data Deluge (or perhaps *because* of it), data often confuses us as citizens, as consumers, and most apropos to this book, as employees. As we saw in Chapter 3, Netflix is doing amazing things with Big Data and dataviz, but make no mistake: Relatively few companies have embraced Big Data. (For more on this, see "Revenge of the Laggards: The Current State of Dataviz" in the Introduction.) For every Amazon, Apple, Facebook, and Google, there are thousands of organizations that treat data as a problem, not as the powerful business asset that it is—or at least, that it could be.

In a convoluted way, the lack of Big Data adoption makes sense and, if I'm honest, it's probably a good thing. Many organizations aren't remotely prepared to start the Big Data journey—and, as I wrote in *Too Big to Ignore*, it is indeed a journey, not a "project." Organizations should improve their own internal, Small Data efforts before trying to derive meaning from petabytes of unstructured data.

> Walk before you run. Just realize that you can only go so far so fast by walking.

A Dataviz Is Often Just the Starting Point

When dealing with Small Data, it's often not difficult to see what's going on. Traditional business intelligence (BI) and reporting tools that handled relatively small amounts of structured data can adequately explain what's going on.

With Big Data, though, things often aren't that simple. Depending on the data and what you're trying to do with it, "visuals cannot tell the whole story," writes Sinan Aral on the *Harvard Business Review* blog.* Aral is an assistant professor and a Microsoft Faculty Fellow at NYU's Stern School of Business and the Scholar-in-Residence at the *New York Times* R&D Lab. Visuals help us

---

* Aral here is referring to a project in which he is documenting every tweet, retweet, and click on every shortened URL from Twitter and Facebook that points back to *New York Times* content. Still, the general point applies to dataviz, especially with regard to Big Data.

"know where to look and what questions to ask of the data. That is, we can't build the more complex models until we know the most suitable places for building them. These visuals give us some of that insight."[2]

> Visual Organizations know that even a well-crafted dataviz might serve as the starting point for discussion, additional analysis, and even further data visualizations.

Visualize Both Small and Big Data

At this point, Wedgies, Autodesk, and UT don't handle the same type of data volumes as Netflix, Amazon, and eBay—and, to be fair, they probably never will. The latter three companies use Big Data to larger extents than just about every organization on the planet. That doesn't mean, though, that behemoths ignore Small Data. Although *Big Data* is the sexier term right now, Reed Hastings, Jeff Bezos, and John Donahoe know that there's enormous value to be gleaned from relational, transactional data.

Small Data is typically the purview of traditional BI, reporting, and data mining tools. Cubes and data warehouses could easily handle even fairly large amounts of structured, transactional, and relational data. Although the majority of the dataviz applications described in Chapter 2 can handle unstructured and semi-structured data, Visual Organizations recognize the importance of all forms of data.

Small Data in many cases enhances the insights and value to be gleaned from Big Data, and vice versa. The two are complements, not substitutes.

Don't Forget the Metadata

In June 2013, I was writing the manuscript for the book you are now holding. At that time, the National Security Agency (NSA) found itself embroiled in an international scandal over the outing of its PRISM program. It turns out that the NSA had compelled Apple, Facebook, Google, Microsoft, and other tech heavyweights to supply information related to their users and their online activity. The source of the leak: Edward Snowden, a 28-year-old former technical assistant for the CIA.

The imbroglio ignited a national debate about the trade-off between security and privacy. While that argument lies beyond the scope of this book, one aspect of PRISM warrants discussion here. Dataphiles like me watched PRISM-gate unfold and wondered, "Is the NSA collecting and analyzing data, metadata (data about data), or both?"

And information-management professionals were hardly alone in asking this admittedly esoteric question. Many in the mainstream media pressed Obama and government officials about the type of data being collected by the

NSA. William Saletan wrote on *Slate* about how the NSA has been compiling a database of billions of phone records:

> But don't worry. According to the Obama administration, it's just "metadata." "The information acquired does not include the content of any communications," says White House spokesman Josh Earnest. Analysts can only search "phone numbers and durations of calls," says President Obama. "They're not looking at content." James Clapper, the director of national intelligence, likens it to reading the Dewey Decimal number on the cover of a library book. You're not seeing what's inside the book.[3]

To some, the data-metadata distinction seems semantic. (Laypersons don't use the term *metadata* too often, and few people expected President Obama to ever publicly utter that word.) For those familiar with the notion of metadata, the difference between the two terms frequently becomes blurry. As is often repeated in data-management circles, one person's metadata is another person's data. As someone who has spent a great deal of time working with structured enterprise data, metadata can be invaluable in diagnosing all sorts of issues. I have solved many a problem for my clients by looking at not just the data, but the data behind the data. The time, date, and person or entity behind the entry often provided valuable clues about the source of the issue. As Fred Smith, FedEx founder and CEO, famously said in 1978, "The information about the package is just as important as the package itself."

But don't make the mistake of thinking that metadata only applies to structured data. On the contrary, metadata is as—if not more—valuable for understanding and interpreting unstructured data. Visualizing the inherent data in YouTube videos, tweets, Instagram photos, phone calls, and other forms of unstructured data is often difficult if not impossible—at least now. Yes, in our constantly connected world, we generate, consume, capture, and store a mind-boggling amount of data. However, not all that data is (completely) usable. Case in point: voice, image, and facial recognition continue to improve, but few would characterize these fields as perfect at present. Of course, as the 2013 Boston Marathon bombings proved, even incomplete data can be helpful. With enough photos, audio, and video, authorities can quickly apprehend suspected terrorists intent on doing even more harm.

As PRISM demonstrated, metadata allows organizations to better understand these forms and sources of data—and ultimately take action. In the case of PRISM, the stakes were particularly high. Army Gen. Keith Alexander, the director of the NSA, testified before the U.S. Senate on June 13, 2013, that the data and metadata gathered from the formerly surreptitious program helped the government prevent "dozens" of terrorist acts.

It's important to note that effective data visualizations often include not just source data, but metadata. For instance, a dataviz on photos may represent things like where and when each photo was taken, the subject or tags of the photos, where they were posted (read: Facebook, Instagram, and so on), and the like.

Look *Outside* of the Enterprise

Traditional BI applications have focused almost exclusively on data internal to enterprises. That is, for the most part, they have historically ignored valuable data sources from outside an organization's walls—and control. This insular thinking often results in suboptimal decisions, as Hjalmar Gislason, the founder and CEO of DataMarket, points out. As Gislason writes:

> Decision-makers in the enterprise spend a lot of their time looking at the dashboard—sometimes literally—but only have a blurry and fragmented view of their surroundings: the markets they operate in, the economies they belong to and the demographics they target.
>
> There is a lot of good data out there, from public and proprietary sources alike. Government databases are opening up and contain more valuable information than most people realize. Syndicated research—trackers, forecasts and surveys—is plentiful but hard to find and quickly gain insight from. And data from custom research, whether internal or from research vendors, is usually delivered in static formats. As a result, too much of it ends up sitting on hard drives somewhere with no good way to search, compare or access later—let alone to keep an eye on updates to the underlying data.[4]

Visual Organizations don't make the mistake of thinking that the only good data resides inside the organization. Look outward. You'll be amazed at what you'll find.

The Beginnings: All Data Is Not Required

Visual Organizations err on the side of inclusion, constantly looking at and for new sources of data. However, they realize the futility of gathering *all* available data, much less visualizing it. For instance, Justin Matejka created OrgOrgChart with only a subset of available Autodesk HR data. If he had waited to receive permission to use all of it, OrgOrgChart may very well never have come to fruition.

Yes, more is generally better than less, but what are the odds that an organization can cobble together every conceivable piece and source of

Metadata serves as a strong and increasingly important complement to both structured and unstructured data. Even if you can easily visualize and interpret primary source data, it behooves you to also collect, analyze, and visualize its metadata. Incorporating metadata may very well enhance your understanding of the source data.

information to answer a question? Sure, a comprehensive list of customers or sales may not be terribly hard to produce, but what about *every* tweet, e-mail, video, photo, blog post, and comment?

Visualize Good *and* Bad Data

For years, information-management professionals have stressed the importance of a simple maxim: "Garbage In, Garbage Out." GIGO still holds water in a Big-Data world. After all, no organization wants to pay its employees incorrectly or report incorrect financial results because of bogus records and sloppy data entry.

By the same token, though, data perfection is unattainable. Visual Organizations recognize that data visualizations may include bad, suspect, duplicate, or incomplete data, but that doesn't stop them from proceeding. In fact, a dataviz can help users identify fishy information and purify data faster than manual hunting and pecking.

Data quality is a continuum, not a binary. Use data visualization to improve data quality.

Enable Drill-Down

For privacy reasons, many open datasets generally do not include individually identifiable information like name and social security number. Sure, exceptions exist, like with sex offenders. For instance, Chicago makes this type of data available, along with name and address.* In this case, Chicago believes that the benefit to public safety exceeds the imposition on these individuals' privacy.

And then there are companies like Amazon that manage and protect their data exceptionally well. As an author, I would love to know which people and organizations have purchased my books, but Amazon won't help me in my quest—*and it shouldn't*. Its Author Central[†] dashboard allows authors to see sales of each title by region and date but not by entity (read: individually identifiable customer). Publishers lack the same capability. Rest assured, though, the right Amazon employees can easily determine which customers bought

▶ **NOTE**

Figure 8.1 only shows inflation-adjusted revenue growth for the 100 largest public software companies; it excludes the rest. Most software companies don't go public. They stay (relatively) small, fail, merge, or agree to be acquired.

---

* See https://data.cityofchicago.org/Public-Safety/Sex-Offenders/vc9r-bqvy.

[†] See https://authorcentral.amazon.com.

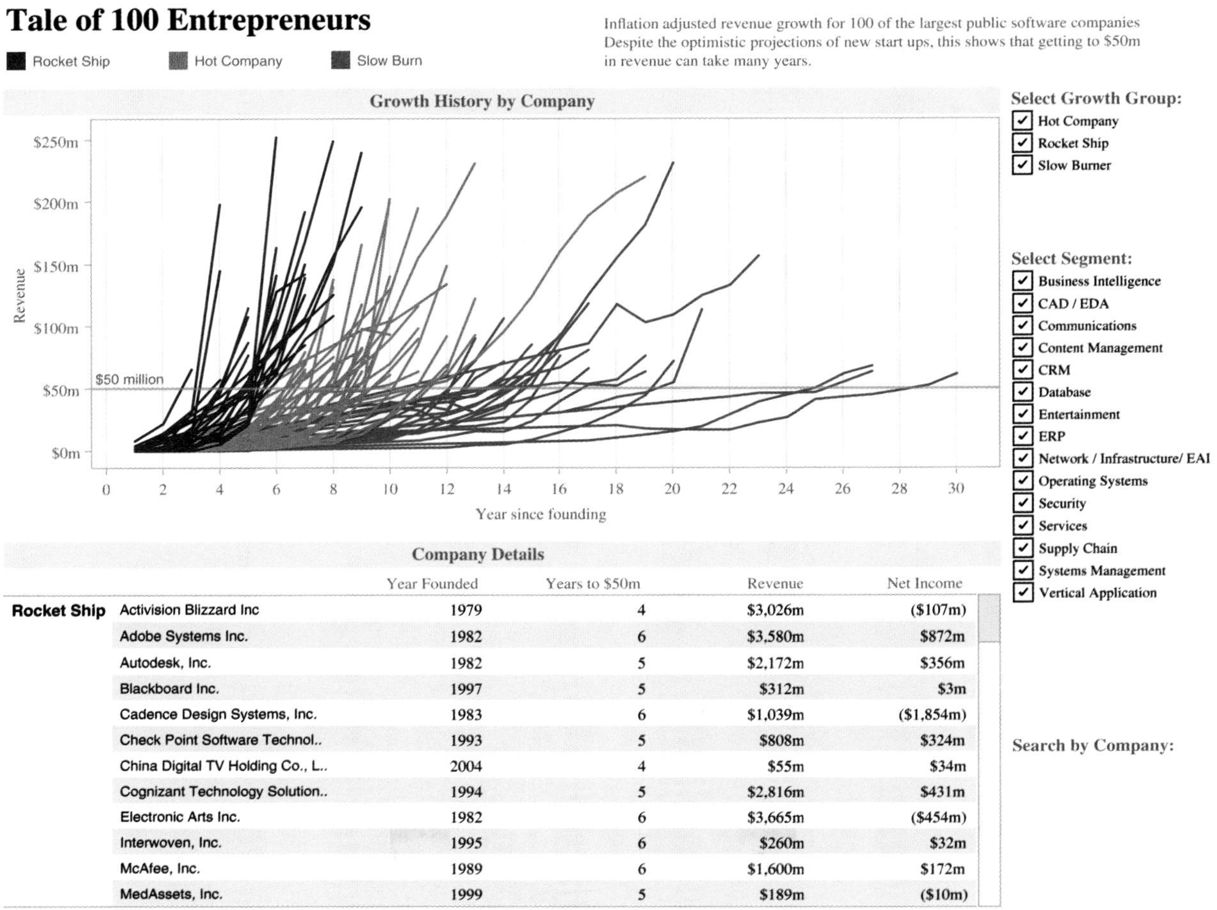

Tale of 100 Entrepreneurs

■ Rocket Ship ■ Hot Company ■ Slow Burn

Inflation adjusted revenue growth for 100 of the largest public software companies. Despite the optimistic projections of new start ups, this shows that getting to $50m in revenue can take many years.

Growth History by Company

Select Growth Group:
☑ Hot Company
☑ Rocket Ship
☑ Slow Burner

Select Segment:
☑ Business Intelligence
☑ CAD / EDA
☑ Communications
☑ Content Management
☑ CRM
☑ Database
☑ Entertainment
☑ ERP
☑ Network / Infrastructure / EAI
☑ Operating Systems
☑ Security
☑ Services
☑ Supply Chain
☑ Systems Management
☑ Vertical Application

Search by Company:

Company Details

		Year Founded	Years to $50m	Revenue	Net Income
Rocket Ship	Activision Blizzard Inc	1979	4	$3,026m	($107m)
	Adobe Systems Inc.	1982	6	$3,580m	$872m
	Autodesk, Inc.	1982	5	$2,172m	$356m
	Blackboard Inc.	1997	5	$312m	$3m
	Cadence Design Systems, Inc.	1983	6	$1,039m	($1,854m)
	Check Point Software Technol..	1993	5	$808m	$324m
	China Digital TV Holding Co., L..	2004	4	$55m	$34m
	Cognizant Technology Solution..	1994	5	$2,816m	$431m
	Electronic Arts Inc.	1982	6	$3,665m	($454m)
	Interwoven, Inc.	1995	6	$260m	$32m
	McAfee, Inc.	1989	6	$1,600m	$172m
	MedAssets, Inc.	1999	5	$189m	($10m)

Figure 8.1 Tale of 100 Entrepreneurs
Source: Tableau Software

which books. That data serves as the basis for its highly successful "If X Then Y" e-mail marketing program.

Visual Organizations understand that the ability to easily drill down is essential. (Going to a separate report or application is at best inefficient. Worse, it often results in to poor business decisions.) Aside from contacting a user or a customer with a specific question, providing detailed data often verifies questionable findings. It can answer the simple but indispensable question, "Really?" Visual Organizations understand that it's better to easily present supporting information if desired. It's better to have it and not need it than vice versa.

I began this book with the tale of Tableau and how, in my view, it may have signified the birth of the Visual Organization. Let's say that you work for a venture capital firm. You probably know that most entrepreneurs are very ambitious. I've met my fair share of them in my life, and few think that they *aren't* going to change the world. Let's say that an entrepreneur projects revenue of $50 million or more in the first five years. Of course, projections and reality often diverge, and this is a case in point. As Scott Austin writes in *The Wall Street Journal*, "Most tech giants come nowhere near those numbers in the first five years."[5] Figure 8.1 proves the point. Just look at the data.

> An effective and interactive dataviz typically includes the ability to drill down. Visual Organizations know that, generally speaking, supporting data matters.

WINDOWS INTO THE DATA

Data science is an iterative process. It starts with a hypothesis (or several hypotheses) about the system we're studying, and then we analyze the information. The results allow us to reject our initial hypotheses and refine our understanding of the data. When working with thousands of fields and millions of rows, it's important to develop intuitive ways to reject bad hypotheses quickly.

Just as data visualization can help an analyst communicate with a nontechnical audience, a dataviz can help the data communicate with the analyst. In my consulting projects, a great deal of my preliminary analysis involves building visualizations for my team and me. I called this process "Building Windows into the Data."

Figure 8.2 shows an example network from a hypothetical fraud detection analysis.

Note that documented relationships are shown in the same color. When multiple colors appear in the same graph, there are undocumented, and therefore potentially fraudulent, relationships. The use of color and scaled metrics allows analysts to quickly understand the relationships and the potential scope of the fraudulent activity.

WINDOWS INTO THE DATA *(Continued)*

Individuals and organizations often hide fraudulent activity by maintaining multiple identities. This makes fraud difficult to detect because it's often necessary for the same individual to appear in a database under different names or identification numbers. For instance, a married woman might appear under a maiden name and a married name. Two different businesses might be owned by the same person but operate under different legal names. Although there are many legitimate reasons for an organization or individual to have multiple records, those relationships should be documented within the data.

In Figure 8.2, each individual in the database is represented by a circle. Individuals with documented relationships share the same fill color. The lines represent activity between individuals, such as bank transactions, and the thickness of the line measures how much activity is occurring. In this application, we expect considerable activity between individuals with documented relationships and very little between individuals who do not have documented relationships. If two or more colors show on the same graph, we know it's a relationship that should be documented but isn't. This signals either a data problem or potential fraud.

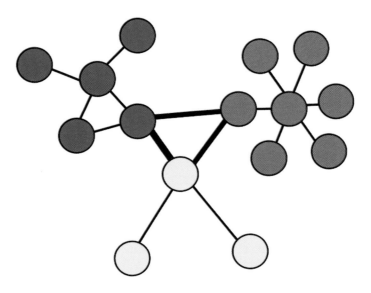

Figure 8.2 Potential Fraud Network
Source: Melinda Thielbar. The yellow circles are known subsidiaries of a company called Burnett Co. LLC. The blue circles are known subsidiaries of a company called Steve Corp. Inc. The magenta circles represent known subsidiaries of Steve Burnett and Company, LLC. The lines on the graph show employees who are working for both companies at the same time.

The network pictured is interesting because of both the number of different colors and the strength of the connections between the different-colored groups (represented by the thicker lines). My team and I were able to process hundreds of potential networks quickly using visualizations like the one shown.

(continued)

WINDOWS INTO THE DATA *(Continued)*

BEST PRACTICES FOR DATA EXPLORATION USING DATA VISUALIZATION

While visualization is an invaluable tool, particularly as the volume of data grows, there are potential pitfalls. The following best practices can help analyst teams avoid common mistakes:

- *Develop the visualizations at the beginning of the analysis.* Visualization is a great way to let the data tell a story. It's also a great way for analysts to fool themselves into believing the story they want to believe. Choose dataviz methods at the outset based on the kind of information you have and the relationships you're attempting to analyze. This allows the visualizations that really illustrate the story behind the data to stand out—no tweaking or lengthy selection process required.

- *Create visualizations that are independent of scale.* Scaling is one of the easiest mistakes to make in data analysis. Visualizations that don't consider scale can make something measured in inches look 12 times as important as the same thing measured in feet. Events that are only possible at the first of the month look rare compared to events that can happen every day. Basing visualizations on ratios, percentages, coefficients of variation, and other measures that are independent of scale keeps analysts from making this common mistake and keeps the visualization from tricking your eyes into seeing something that isn't there.

- *Automate, automate, automate.* Today's data analysis projects usually involve many different data sources and large volumes of data. Generating and tweaking individual visualizations is time consuming and (for the reasons noted in the first bullet) potentially misleading. Automation both speeds up the process of generating visualizations and allows the data to speak for itself.

Melinda Thielbar, Ph.D. is a statistician with 15 years of experience in software development and government contracting. She currently works for JMP, a business unit of SAS, as a research statistician developer.

DESIGN TIPS AND BEST PRACTICES

Although this is not a book on design, it behooves you to consider the design of data-visualization tools. After all, poorly designed dataviz applications are likely to be misunderstood. The result: bad business decisions.

Begin with the End in Mind (Sort of)

In his bestselling book *The 7 Habits of Highly Effective People*, the late Stephen R. Covey writes about the importance of "beginning with the end in mind." The catchy phrase has been repeated countless times and can be applied to virtually any scenario, including data visualization.

Visual Organizations recognize that there are more ways than ever to visualize data, and some are certainly better than others. Before beginning, it's wise to consider the suggestions in Figure 8.3 from Dr. Andrew Abela, founder of Extreme Presentation.

Chart Suggestions—A Thought-Starter

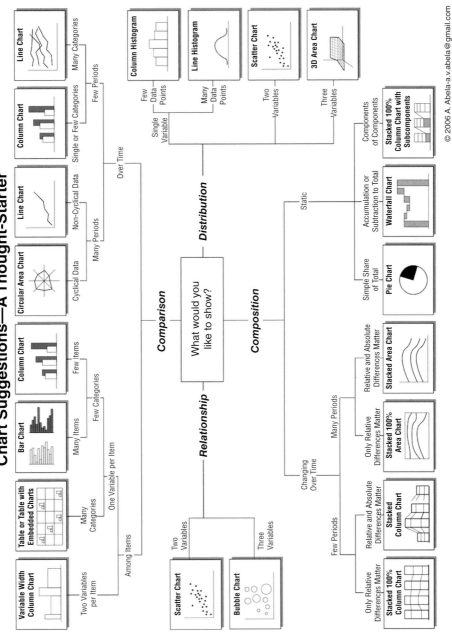

Figure 8.3 Chart Suggestions—A Thought-Starter

© 2010 A.V. Abela, http://www.extremerepresentation.com. Used with permission.

© 2006 A. Abela-a.v.abela@gmail.com

If a dataviz looks better in theory than in practice, junk it and try something else. If users can't easily use a data-visualization tool and act upon its results, go back to the drawing board. Data visualization should not be confused with art. Visual Organizations and their employees understand that clarity, utility, and user-friendliness are paramount to any design aesthetic.

Figure 8.3 should only serve as a starting point for representing data; it does *not* reflect every type of possible chart or dataviz, such as choropleths. These thematically displayed areas are shaded or patterned in proportion to the measurement of the statistical variable being displayed on a map. Examples include population density, unemployment rate, and per-capita income.

Subtract When Possible

In his book *The Laws of Subtraction: 6 Simple Rules for Winning in the Age of Excess Everything*, Matthew May writes about Italian design company Selle Italia. In 1998, the firm introduced an innovative kind of bike seat, the SLR SuperFlow Saddle. Selle Italia employed several subtractive strategies in its design, including a male-friendly "anatomic cutout" to promote comfort while cycling. May continues, "The original design was introduced in 1998 with the Trans Am saddle, which featured a slim opening in the seat middle to relieve pressure. Over time, weight and material have been removed through constant research and innovation."

And Selle Italia is hardly alone in including only what is needed. Less is often more. Many of Apple's products won design awards not for features included, but for *omissions*. 37signals builds software that, as a matter of principle, explicitly rejects feature creep and busy interfaces. The company attempts to create minimalist products based on the Pareto principle—aka, the familiar 80/20 rule. Eighty-percent of people use 20 percent of a product's functionality.*

Visual Organizations understand that the best data visualizations share a great deal in common with intelligent product design. Just because you can add more doesn't mean that you should. Busy visuals induce boredom, confusion, and bad decisions.

UX: Participation and Experimentation Are Paramount

Look around. It's not hard to find truly awful representations of data. There are others that are simply too busy; they confuse people more than they convey information, to paraphrase the late George Carlin. But what makes a great dataviz? Visual Organizations understand the design process is rarely a linear

---

*For more on the 37signals's design philosophy, check out founder Jason Fried's 2010 book *Rework*.

one. What looks good in theory or in wireframes might not work well in practice. Sometimes, it takes a few iterations to get it right.

Encourage Interactivity

There's little doubt that basic, static pie charts and even infographics can still tell a story. But Visual Organizations understand that contemporary dataviz tools (like those discussed in Chapter 2) allow for a high degree of interactivity, motion, and animation. Technological advancements allow users to play with data and discover new relationships among variables.

Generally speaking, some degree of failure is inevitable in an era of Big Data. It may take a few tries to get a data visualization right. Visual Organizations don't let a few missteps dissuade them. Not all visualizations are created equal, and the first dataviz will probably not be the last, nor should it be.

If at all possible, Visual Organizations create data visualizations with embedded interactivity. These types of tiiks allow users to easily and quickly ask and answer questions. In the end, better business decisions result.

Use Motion and Animation Carefully

Just because you can doesn't mean you should. It's one of my favorite bromides, and it applies to many areas of life, including dataviz. Funky treatments should not be added for the sake of doing so. Aside from confusing users, superfluous effects and elements may cause technical problems on different devices. Remember that data visualizations do not just need to render successfully on PCs running a version of Microsoft Windows. The number of devices, platforms, and operating systems continues to explode.

Andrew DeVigal is the director of content strategy at media production company Second Story. As he writes on the *Harvard Business Review* blog,

> Animation for the sake of animation is likely to detract from the overall aesthetic. Each element of a data visualization should [use] motion purposefully. Make sure that you're using it to convey meaning. Avoid using motion as a type and motion study, as in many college animation assignments. Use motion to show growth, demonstrate a shift over time, or to emphasize a piece of data.[6]

Use Relative—Not Absolute—Figures

Visual Organizations understand that data visualizations lacking context suffer as a result. They leave the user asking, "Compared to what?" David McCandless is a London-based author, data journalist, writer, and designer. In 2010, McCandless gave a fascinating TED talk in which he made this very point.*

---

* To watch it online, see http://tinyurl.com/dv-McCandless.

Visual Organizations know that a dataviz without context is not ideal. Don't make customers or employees infer meaning from missing design elements. The odds of a poor business decision increase.

A Wedgie with 50,000 responses would be enormous given the state of the company, but for Netflix, a blockbuster film with the same number of views one weekend would be considered small potatoes.

TECHNOLOGY TIPS AND BEST PRACTICES

Visual Organizations understand that data and design do not exist in a vacuum. Without contemporary technologies, employees face severe restrictions on what they can do.

Where Possible, Consider Using APIs

ETL (extract, transform, and load) may very well have jumped the shark. Yes, it still matters to countless organizations, but no longer is it the only game in town. For the foreseeable future, the majority of organizations will have to juggle multiple means of accessing data. Because of their power, speed, and flexibility, APIs (application programming interfaces) have grown in popularity. (See "The Relative Ease of Accessing Data" in Chapter 1 for more on this subject.) I loathe to claim that APIs are inherently "better" than ETL. However, let me say this: if an organization can build or use an API while concurrently addressing security, regulatory, or technology concerns, then it probably should. Netflix, Wedgies, and other Visual Organizations understand this all too well.

"APIs enable the encapsulation of specialized services, facilitating overall maintenance and usage," says Dalton Cervo, founder of Data Gap Consulting and coauthor of *Master Data Management in Practice*. "Well-written APIs can help decouple specific tasks, consequently increasing scalability and reusability. Data quality can also benefit since the intrinsic nature of APIs is to provide direct access to information typically developed and maintained by subject matter experts."

Embrace New Tools

As discussed in the Preface, the immediate success of the Tableau Software IPO is telling—and endemic of a much larger trend: the rise of the Visual Organization. Today organizations only do so much with applications designed to handle transactional, structured information (read: Small Data). Fortunately, options abound. Hadoop, NoSQL, Amazon Web Services (AWS), and their ilk are simply better equipped to handle petabytes of unstructured data. By the same token, most of the dataviz tools referenced in Chapter 2 lend themselves to insightful and interactive representations of this data.

Visual Organizations understand that complacency is the enemy of progress. No, they don't make it a habit of trying the latest and greatest dataviz tool every day. At some point, you have to live with your choices, at least in the short term. However, selecting a data-visualization application does not mean entering a technological bubble. Poking around the Web every so often isn't a bad idea, nor is attending dataviz conferences and talking to colleagues about what they're doing. Dataviz is a dynamic field these days, and the perils of a "set it and forget it" mind-set cannot be overstated.

At a high level, Visual Organizations recognize three critical things. First, the need to visualize data has never been more pronounced if, for no other reason, there's just so much of it. Second, generally speaking, contemporary dataviz tools are much easier and cheaper to deploy than the on-premise client-server systems and applications so prevalent in the 1990s. (See "Better Data Tools" in Chapter 1.) Third, these applications are user-friendly. They hardly are the sole purview of academics, statisticians, scientists, and others with years of specialized training.

> The geeks have inherited the earth. Fortunately, they have created many accessible dataviz tools for laypeople. Ignore them at your own peril.

Know the Limitations of Dataviz Tools

The dataviz applications described in Chapter 2 can do amazing things, but it's important to place dataviz in its appropriate business context. Visual Organizations realize that, by itself, no data-visualization application magically "solves the Big Data problem." Rather, data-visualization must work in conjunction with Big Data and other applications. Amazon, Apple, Facebook, eBay, Netflix, Google, Twitter, and other Big Data companies think cohesively and strategically about what they are doing—and how. They don't connect a best-of-breed dataviz tool to an outdated data repository that's about to break.

Becoming a Visual Organization requires much more than purchasing and deploying sophisticated tools. It's more about a mind-set, culture, and way of thinking about data.

Be Open

From 1998 to 2000, I worked for a prestigious Fortune 50 company. As one of my responsibilities, I needed to manage the compensation administration process for nearly 3,000 employees, most of whom worked outside of the United States. The company's homegrown application was, put mildly, weak even by late-1990s standards. The software and business process behind it effectively hamstrung the organization's HR department for five months every year.

Today, there are more ways than ever to improve upon a base application or, more generally, idea. Visual Organizations get this. Unfettered openness is probably not desirable, but the advantages of embracing ecosystems and communities usually outweigh their drawbacks.

For two years, I made suggestions on how to improve the application. I think that I set the unofficial company record for enhancement requests. Granted, these ideas (if implemented) would only apply a Band-Aid to a gushing wound. There was no way for me to make these changes myself. A cabal within the IT department strictly controlled that horrible application and, to be fair, I can think of many disadvantages of letting individual users fork an internal application.

By way of contrast, today many open-source projects allow for and even encourage external-driven innovation. Open APIs, datasets, mashups, and SDKs all fall under a more open and community-driven umbrella. Chaotic? It can be. However, as the Chinese say, there is opportunity in chaos.

MANAGEMENT TIPS AND BEST PRACTICES

Becoming a Visual Organization requires more than grabbing a bunch of data and then buying and deploying best-of-breed tools. Organizational culture and employee attitude are critical factors. In other words, don't neglect the management side of the equation.

Encourage Self-Service, Exploration, and Data Democracy

Chapters 2 and 3 described how eBay and Netflix both embrace an ethos of dataviz, self-service, discovery, and data democracy. This does not mean that Visual Organizations make all information available to everyone. I shudder to think of the utter chaos that would ensue. (*Saul makes how much more money than I do?*) Placing the IT department squarely in the middle of all data requests, however, is a surefire way to discourage innovation and exploration.

Just about any type or source of data can be visualized, but visualized data do not make business decisions by itself. *People do.* Yes, everyone brings biases to the table, but employees at Visual Organizations are generally more open to new interpretations than their counterparts. They explore. To paraphrase Swedish medical doctor, academic, and statistician Hans Rosling, "Let the data-set change your mind-set."

Visual Organizations err on the side of democracy. A little anarchy is preferable to a little too much bureaucracy.

Exhibit a Healthy Skepticism

Data visualizations are invaluable in an era of Big Data. That doesn't mean, though, that the data knows all. Employees at Visual Organizations don't check their brains at the door, and the ability to question findings has never been more essential. Ideally, a dataviz facilitates additional research, refined questions, and, ultimately, a more informed answer.

American writer and futurist Alvin Toffler once said, "You can use all the quantitative data you can get, but you still have to distrust it and use your own intelligence and judgment." You'll find this same critical mentality at Visual Organizations. Yes, dataviz tools can manifest previously unknown or obscured trends, but those trends might mask deeper trends or mislead people entirely.

In statistics, this phenomenon is known as *Simpson's Paradox* or *the Yule–Simpson effect*. As David Moore and George McCabe write in *Introduction to the Practice of Statistics,* it is the "reversal of the direction of a comparison or an association when data from several groups are combined to form a single group."

Even with a simple table or crosstab, it's easy for people to look at high-level data and reach mathematically incorrect conclusions and interpretations. (As Homer Simpson would say, "D'oh!")* Dataviz arguably makes this danger even more pronounced, as we tend to believe what we see. Sometimes it is advisable and even necessary to add additional (independent) variables to truly understand what's going on.† Again, the contemporary data-visualization tools discussed in Chapter 2 can help overcome this problem, as users can easily drag and drop in additional variables as needed.

> Visual Organizations realize that an original dataviz may ultimately suggest or "prove" something. There's nothing wrong with doubting what you see. A dataviz may naturally lead us to draw seemingly obvious conclusions; that doesn't mean that they are the *right* conclusions, though.

Trust the Process, Not the Result

Professional poker players are successful because of skill, not luck. "Bad beats "—miracle cards drawn by inferior players to defeat superior ones—tend to even out over time. When professionals lose hands in which they are huge statistical favorites, they rarely become upset. They trust the process, even if the outcome of any single hand hinges upon Lady Luck.

The same holds true for Visual Organizations. The outcome of any particular dataviz may not result in that one groundbreaking innovation, new product, or customer insight. So what? The process of visualizing information to find new trends must be respected. On the *Harvard Business Review* blog, Jer Thorp makes this very point. Thorp is the cofounder of the Office for Creative Research and an adjunct professor in New York University's ITP program. He

---

* Okay, that's a bad pun.

† For more on Simpson's Paradox, see http://tinyurl.com/simpsons-paradox.

writes, "Visualization…is a verbal noun. The word *visualization* encapsulates a process. And it's really that process that's the essential part, *not the thing that results*."[7] [Emphasis mine.]

Avoid the Perils of Silos and Specialization

In the Preface, I mentioned that forward-thinking organizations are hiring data-visualization specialists. Examples include the Massachusetts Institute of Technology and the *New York Times*.* This is a bit of a mixed blessing. Let me explain.

When progressive, respected, and tech-savvy establishments hire employees in a growing field, influential people are apt to pay attention. I know from personal experience that many other educational institutions, not to mention private-sector companies, have historically followed MIT's lead. This type of behavior is entirely reasonable. After all, MIT and their ilk are typically at the forefront of major technological trends. If MIT thinks that dataviz is important, it must be. *We should hire a bunch of dataviz specialists!*

On the other hand, creating and staffing a new position does not a Visual Organization make. Management guru Peter Drucker once famously said, "Culture eats strategy for lunch." Dataviz should *not* be confined to a single department or a group of highly skilled employees. Avoid that mistake. I shudder at the thought of someone saying, "No, that's the dataviz department's job." Silos and overspecialization have crippled many an organization, something I have seen firsthand during my consulting days. Microsoft, shown in Figure I.5 of the Introduction, is a particularly instructive case.†

> Your organization's CEO probably does not have the time or the skills to create cool and interactive choropleths. Ideally, however, every employee in your workplace should be at least mildly comfortable with data, and with viewing, creating, and interpreting basic data visualizations. Data is becoming the *lingua franca* of business. Get used to it.

If Possible, Visualize

Always creating a sophisticated dataviz isn't necessary or even advisable. At a high level, some things are obvious, even in an era of Big Data. For instance, the founding partner of a boutique consulting firm knows that 98 percent of her company's annual sales stems from a single client. She does not need a dataviz to tell her as much. (However, I'd be curious to see if the firm's sales have changed over time. Ditto for the types of consulting services provided.)

---

* Sites like Twitter and Dice make information like this easy to come by.

† For more on this, see http://tinyurl.com/ms-silos.

And what happens if an organization lacks the right data to effectively visualize? Yes, this does happen. Earlier in this chapter I mentioned Amazon Author Central, a tool that provides different cuts of book sales. Yet, Amazon intentionally does not provide authors and publishers with individually identifiable data and metadata. I'm talking about customer name, exact time and date of purchase, location, number of books, and so on. As such, there are limitations to what even the most dynamic and interactive dataviz can do. There's just not enough detail in the data behind it. (See "Data: The Primordial Soup" earlier in this chapter.)

But these types of scenarios are increasingly becoming the exception to the rule. On just about any topic these days, a swath of data is out there. When trying to understand what's going on and why, Visual Organizations try to visualize as much of their data as possible, especially if the trend or issue is of an ongoing concern. UT and Wedgies were cases in point.

Seek Hybrids When Hiring

Visual Organizations understand that just about all employees ought to routinely use data as part of their jobs. As a corollary, data visualizations should be widely deployed and available. Employees should not have to submit a support ticket to IT or "the Data Department." Dataviz tools and their results should generally be democratic.

You should not confuse *using* tools with *designing* them. Sure, products from Tableau and QlikView are powerful and user-friendly. They have raised the bar for everyone, in many cases obviating the need for proper coding skills. However, it would be folly to claim that they completely level the playing field. That is, dataviz superusers and designers can still do things that everyday users cannot.

The "ideal" designer should possess a hybrid background that may include computer programming, technology, design, general business, mathematics, data modeling, and statistics. Yes, formal degrees are useful, but you're unlikely to find someone with such a pedigree today. People with natural curiosity, intelligence, and practical experience can generally hit the ground running.

Think Direction First, Precision Later

"When decisions need to be made in real time, it is often more important to be directionally correct than it is to be precise," Patrick Martin, marketing analytics manager at Zappos told me over lunch one sweltering summer day in Las Vegas. "Do not get caught in analysis paralysis."

Martin told me of several instances in his role at Zappos in which an interactive dataviz shed light on a particularly thorny issue. In one, a data visualization—

and the data behind it—strongly supported increasing marketing spend in a few areas. So Martin did just that. Only over the course of a few months, however, did he determine the optimal amount of the increase. Martin first proceeded cautiously with a small bump before homing in on the optimal number.

"Measure twice, cut once" doesn't typically play in Visual Organizations. They recognize that, today more than ever, the costs of inaction often dwarf the costs of action. What's more, decisive action should not hinge upon exactitude. To quote hockey legend Wayne Gretzky, "You miss 100 percent of the shots you don't take."

NEXT

Today employees are bombarded with more data than ever, and there have never been more ways to represent that data. For these reasons, becoming a Visual Organization can be a little daunting. Besides following the best practices described in this chapter, it's important to avoid making key mistakes. That's the goal of the following chapter.

NOTES

1. "Wiley Announces Nathan Yau's Latest Book *Data Points: Visualization That Means Something*,"press release, May 21, 2013, http://www.business-wire.com/news/home/20130521006105/en/Wiley-Announces-Nathan-Yau%E2%80%99s-Latest-Book-Data, Retrieved June 11, 2013.
2. Aral, Sinan. "To Go From Big Data to Big Insight, Start With a Visual ," *Harvard Business Review* blog, August 27, 2013, blogs.hbr.org/cs/2013/08/visualizing_how_online_word-of.html. Retrieved August 27, 2013.
3. Saletan, William, "Meta Man," Slate, June 13, 2013, http://www.slate.com/articles/news_and_politics/frame_game/2013/06/nsa_metadata_obama_s_non_answers_to_questions_about_government_surveillance.html, Retrieved June 16, 2013.
4. Gislason, Hjalmar, "Data-Driven Decision Making: Beyond Today's BI," DailyTekk, May 21, 2013, www.dailytekk.com/2013/05/21/data-driven-decision-making-beyond-todays-bi, Retrieved June 17, 2013.
5. Austin, Scott, "How Long Does It Take To Build A Technology Empire?," *Wall Street Journal* Venture Capital Dispatch, August 25, 2009, blogs.wsj.com/venturecapital/2009/08/25/how-long-does-it-take-to-build-a-technology-empire, Retrieved June 11, 2013.
6. DeVigal, Andrew, "Tell Better Data Stories with Motion and Interactivity," *Harvard Business Review* blog, April 10, 2013, http://blogs.hbr.org/cs/2013/04/tell_better_data_stories_with.html, Retrieved June 17, 2013.
7. Thorp, Jer, "Visualization as Process, Not Output," April 3, 2013, *Harvard Business Review* blog, blogs.hbr.org/cs/2013/04/visualization_as_process.html, Retrieved June 12, 2013.

CHAPTER 9

The Inhibitors: Mistakes, Myths, and Challenges

Beware of false knowledge; it is more dangerous than ignorance.

—George Bernard Shaw

U.S. Marine Corps Joint Forces commander James N. Mattis is not one to mince words. "PowerPoint makes us stupid," he told attendees at a military conference in North Carolina in April 2010. (In case you were wondering, he was speaking *without* the aid of Microsoft's popular presentation program.)

And Mattis is certainly not the only military man with contempt for PowerPoint. Brigadier General Herbert Raymond McMaster goes even further. He believes that the program is nothing short of an internal threat. "It's dangerous because it can create the illusion of understanding and the illusion of control," McMaster told the *New York Times* in a telephone interview after the same conference.[1] "Some problems in the world are not bullet-izable."

Now, I know absolutely nothing about military combat. I have never served in any branch of the armed forces. Fortunately, I have no personal experience dodging enemy bullets, and I have never had to disable a bomb. I do, however, know a great deal about giving presentations that interpret and represent data. As a public speaker, I frequently use PowerPoint. Despite the popular phrase "death by PowerPoint," there's nothing inherently wrong or evil about the program or competing products like Keynote and Prezi. The problem is not the tool itself; it's how people use (read: abuse) it. And some venues and forums just don't lend themselves to slides, no matter how pretty fonts and images on the latter are.

General Stanley A. McChrystal certainly agrees with me here. McChrystal served as the leader of American and NATO forces until June 2010. When shown one particularly complex visual that was supposed to portray the complexity of American military strategy in Afghanistan, McChrystal (now retired) remarked, "When we understand that slide, we'll have won the war."*

No matter how long I stare at that diagram, I don't understand any part of it. Take a look at it and see if you agree. Of course, whether John Q. Public gets it doesn't really matter. Its target audience was senior U.S. and NATO military personnel, not the general public.

Reasonably informed and intelligent civilians like me can recognize the obvious: representing the American military strategy in Afghanistan is not an easy task. It's not a game of Risk. Be that as it may, Mattis, McMaster, and McChrystal are completely right. As a communications tool, PowerPoint and its ilk are often grossly misused, and this is a case in point. Someone in the U.S. military created that overly complicated visual—*and honestly expected others to understand it.* (The lime-green font against the white background is particularly indecipherable.) No doubt, the creator thought that he was conveying information, not confusing people. It clearly didn't work, and McMaster subsequently banned PowerPoint when he led the successful effort to secure the northern Iraqi city of Tal Afar in 2005.[†]

It turns out that the U.S. military is far from the only organization to rely too much and too often on PowerPoint. Many organizations depend exclusively on these old standbys when presenting and representing data. This chapter covers other mistakes and myths that inhibit potential Visual Organizations.

MISTAKES

The preceding story illustrates one of many classic dataviz blunders, but it's far from the only mistake that Visual Organizations avoid making.

Falling into the Traditional ROI Trap

Historically, most large organizations have assessed major technology purchases in methodological manners. With the help of consulting firms and software vendors, they attempt to determine the expected return on investment (ROI) before signing contracts.

---

[*] To see the actual monstrosity of a figure, go to http://tinyurl.com/bad-figure-1. Not surprisingly, I was unable to get permission to use it for this book.

[†] Other organizations frown upon PowerPoint. Executives at Amazon read six-page essays *before* meetings. In researching this book, I came across a few companies that ban the application.

For two reasons, this type of thinking used to be entirely logical but isn't anymore. First, 15 years ago, open-source software, cloud computing, and software as a service (SaaS) were not the transformative technological forces they are today. Back then, organizations could not test the waters like they can now.

Today's IT world could not be more different. No longer do organizations have to spend years and invest millions of dollars before their employees can use formidable new applications. It has never been easier to kick the tires of new tools sans massive investments. Despite this, far too many organizations attempt to justify these purchases with tried-and-true ROI calculations. They remain hesitant about deploying new and much-needed tools.

Second, ERP and CRM applications typically lend themselves to at least rough ROI approximations because they automate largely manual business processes. Yes, they sometimes manifest business issues and result in interesting findings. However, by and large, these types of systems are not predicated on data discovery and exploration.

Visual Organizations don't fall into the traditional ROI trap. They recognize that all ROI calculations are extremely subjective. They are much more art than science. Beyond this classic criticism, though, contemporary dataviz tools allow organizations to see things that would otherwise have gone unnoticed. (The Netflix cover color analysis is just one example from Part II.) New customer and employee insights *may* ultimately result in entirely unexpected products and lines of business, but those types of findings are not guaranteed. To that end, how can anyone attempt to precisely quantify the ROI of a new dataviz application? Finally, most organizations have focused on the ROI of action. But what happens if an organization misses the opportunities that a dataviz would have manifested? Phrased differently, what's the potential cost of *inaction*? In many cases, it might be irrelevance or eventual extinction.

No, budgets are not unlimited, but Visual Organizations know that any Big Data or dataviz ROI calculation is at best a SWAG.*

Always—and Blindly—Trusting a Dataviz

As we saw in Part II many employees at Visual Organizations are inherently curious and skeptical, and those traits don't disappear once a dataviz has been created and shared with others. Newsflash: mistakes happen at every enterprise. After all, employees at every organization operate in an era of Big Data, and certainty is far from guaranteed.

Beyond true accidents, the *intentional* manipulation of data can accentuate certain parts of a story and minimize others. Regardless of benign or malicious intent, data visualizations don't guarantee successful outcomes and shouldn't

---

* Strategic wild-ass guess.

Just because data is visualized doesn't necessarily mean that it is accurate, complete, or indicative of the right course of action. Exhibiting a healthy skepticism is almost always a good thing.

always be trusted, even at Visual Organizations. In the words of data journalist John Burn-Murdoch of *The Guardian*, "Even something as simple as color scheme can have a marked impact on the perceived credibility of information presented visually—often a considerably more marked impact than the actual authority of the data source."[2]

Ignoring the Audience

Chapter 1 discussed how today's employee is more tech- and data-savvy than ever—and this is doubly true for Millennials. But it's folly to assume that everyone speaks the language of data with the same fluency. A true data scientist brings a different, more technical skillset to the table than a CEO, even one from Netflix or eBay. Not all data visualizations are meant for the same audiences. What works for one group may not work for another.

Visual Organizations don't assume that all employees possess the same backgrounds and technical proficiency. One size never fits all.

Developing in a Cathedral

Eric S. Raymond's classic text *The Cathedral & The Bazaar* examines the tension between top-down and bottom-up software development. In a nutshell, there are two options: the cathedral (top-down) and the bazaar (bottom-up).

Now, let me be clear: there's no one right way to develop software; there are benefits and drawbacks to both approaches. It's possible to combine elements from each approach. Still, Visual Organizations understand that data visualizations need to be used by the masses, not just a few select employees.

Think more bazaar than cathedral.

To that end, incorporating new features and data is paramount. We saw this in Chapter 7 with Justin Matejka and OrgOrgChart. Dataviz development generally should not take place in a vacuum.

Set It and Forget It

In 2002, I consulted for a large utility company in New Jersey. I built many reports and a few extract, transform, and load (ETL) tools during my time there. Five years later, the company called me back to assist with a major enterprise resource planning (ERP) system upgrade. Soon after walking in the door, I noticed a familiar face. A woman was looking at a Microsoft Access database eerily like something I would design. (I'm either a very consistent or prosaic developer, depending on your point of view.) I went over to her, smiled, and introduced myself. I complimented her on her design style and remarked that I used a similar method. She chuckled and reminded me that five years ago I had built the very data conversion tool that she was still using. When I asked her if she had made any changes since I was first there, she said no.

> It's a mistake to think of data and data visualizations as static terms. They are the very antitheses of stasis.

I get it. It ain't broke; don't fix it. But employees from eBay, Netflix, Amazon, Google, and Twitter don't build dataviz tools and mechanically follow their recommendations for five years without ever wondering if those tools need to be tweaked. Part II showed how Visual Organizations are continuously revisiting and improving data visualizations—and augmenting the data behind them.

Bad Dataviz

In the Introduction, I cited the work of dataviz pioneers like Few, Tufte, Yau, and others. In their texts and research, they describe the best ways to visually represent different types of information. I won't repeat all of them here. I will, however, describe a few particularly egregious practices that hinder organizations from becoming (more) visual.

TMI

Bad, messy, and overly crowded design can foil even powerful dataviz tools. Consider the story of the Higher Education Funding Council for England (HEFCE), an institution that "promotes and funds teaching and research in higher education institutions. Includes general information and sections on finance, good practice, and research."*

HEFCE has shown that, from 2005 to 2011, the participation of young people from disadvantaged backgrounds in higher education has increased. Now, it is important to keep this in perspective. HEFCE studied the percentage of young people from historically low participation areas who attend college. That number rose approximately 30 percent since 2005, but so did that of the base population. As a result, the overall proportion of young people in higher education from low participation areas remained virtually unchanged over this period. Figure 9.1 breaks down participation by 21 elite U.K. schools.

Put simply, Figure 9.1 is a mess. Employees that represent data in this manner don't do their colleagues any favors.

Using Tiny Graphics

No one likes to squint. Trying to cram too much information onto a single dataviz is unlikely to convey meaning, much less *the right meaning*. Rather,

---

* See http://www.hefce.ac.uk.

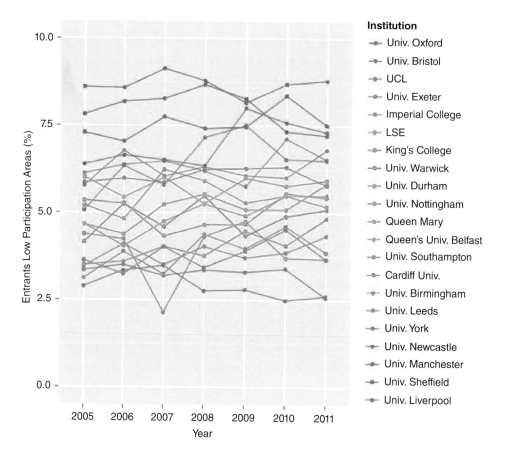

Institution

- Univ. Oxford
- Univ. Bristol
- UCL
- Univ. Exeter
- Imperial College
- LSE
- King's College
- Univ. Warwick
- Univ. Durham
- Univ. Nottingham
- Queen Mary
- Queen's Univ. Belfast
- Univ. Southampton
- Cardiff Univ.
- Univ. Birmingham
- Univ. Leeds
- Univ. York
- Univ. Newcastle
- Univ. Manchester
- Univ. Sheffield
- Univ. Liverpool

Figure 9.1 Percentage Change in Enrollment by Disadvantaged Students in Russell Group Schools, 2005 to 2011
Source: Significance Magazine, Published by Blackwell Publishing Ltd, a company of John Wiley & Sons, Inc. http://bit.ly/19zT9A1

it will confuse users. Three-dimensional tools (like Autodesk's OrgOrgChart) allow for innovative ways to display information. That is, Visual Organizations can move beyond x- and y-axes.

Tiny graphics can especially frustrate users on tablets and mobile devices, and they certainly aren't optimal for data discovery. (This is one of the reasons that UT deployed a mobile-friendly dataviz application.) Imagine trying to touch an icon or data point but consistently hitting the wrong one because it's smaller than your index finger. Remember that the world is going mobile. PC sales have been consistently declining with no end in sight.* Smaller screens pose their own set of challenges. Just because a dataviz looks great on a 22-inch monitor doesn't mean that it will represent well on a smartphone or iPad.

---

* For more here, see http://www.bbc.co.uk/news/business-23251285.

There are plenty of ways to bastardize data and confuse users.* While good design is easier said than done, a good rule of thumb is to never forget the audience.

MYTHS

Visual Organizations understand the pernicious nature of the dataviz myths described in this section.

Data Visualizations Guarantee Certainty and Success

There has never been such a thing as complete certainty, and Big Data doesn't change that. Visual Organizations understand that a dataviz usually does not *immediately* solve a problem or answer a question. A data visualization often merely leads to a greater understanding of the problem—*and that's still very valuable*. Perhaps interacting with different types of data causes users to ask better questions—or refine existing ones. Visual Organizations understand that errors are inevitable. At the same time, though, to quote English mathematician and inventor Charles Babbage, "Errors using inadequate data are much less than those using no data at all."

Visual Organizations realize that dataviz and Big Data only increase the chances of making optimal decisions and realizing successful outcomes. What's more, visualizations don't represent some "absolute" and "permanent" truth. Data can still manipulate us, confuse us, and cause poor decisions. Mark Twain's legendary quote still rings true: "There are three kinds of lies: lies, damned lies, and statistics."

> The notion that a dataviz—no matter how good—guarantees a successful outcome is simply ludicrous.

Data Visualization Is Easy

Although the tools have inarguably become more user-friendly, doing dataviz right remains elusive for many organizations. In this vein, data visualization is much like creating videos, launching a website, writing a book, or making music. Doing it and doing it well/right are two different things.

As author and data journalist David McCandless wrote in an e-mail to *InformationWeek* in September 2013:

> The biggest thing to know is that data visualization is hard. Really difficult to pull off well. It requires harmonization of several skills sets and ways of thinking: conceptual, analytic, statistical, graphic design, programmatic, interface-design, story-telling, journalism—plus a bit of 'gut feel.' The end result is often simple and beautiful, but the process itself is usually challenging and messy.[3]

---

* For some real dataviz atrocities, check out http://wtfviz.net.

Data Visualizations Are Projects

At some point during my career, the word *project* began to take on a negative connotation with me. Perhaps the tipping point occurred during one of the poorly run IT projects on which I was consulting, many of which informed my first book *Why New Systems Fail*. Through all my conversations with data-viz professionals researching this text, I can't recall hearing the word *project* a single time. Perhaps that's because Visual Organizations don't think of the deployment of data-visualization tools as projects, at least in the traditional sense. Thinking of them as *IT projects* is particularly dangerous, as it reinforces the apocryphal role of IT as primarily responsible for data-related matters. What's more, this mind-set contravenes the notions of data democracy and ownership.

IT projects imply the following:

- Definitive start dates and deadlines

- Detailed project plans and Gantt charts

- Meetings

- Testing

- Training

- Temporary roles

- Consultants hired to assist the enterprise in getting from Point A to Point B

Visual Organizations recognize that data visualization is too important to be associated with traditional deadlines and end dates. Dataviz serves as one of the fulcrums upon which a Visual Organization is built. It should represent *ongoing* efforts to understand what is happening and why.

There Is One "Right" Visualization

Figure 9.1 proves that bad data visualizations usually confuse the very people attempting to understand them. (Again, the books of Few, Tufte, Yau, and others offer much more guidance about the mechanics of creating a compelling dataviz).

At Visualization Organizations, employees don't search for months or years for the one "right" or "perfect" dataviz. As Voltaire said, "The perfect is the enemy of the good," and that applies to the dataviz world as well. And a functional and even insightful dataviz may need to be retired or transformed as data volumes and sources increase. What looks good with four data sources may very well appear perplexing with 40.

Excel Is Sufficient

It might seem that I despise Microsoft Excel. Actually, nothing could be further from the truth. I love Excel. I have spent more than 10,000 hours using it in my career. To this day, it remains an indispensable application *for certain things*. This has been the case for a very long time with respect to dataviz. Back in 1996, basic pie charts and bar graphs were usually sufficient when visually representing data. After all, Big Data didn't really exist back then, certainly by today's standards.

Has Excel improved over the past two decades? Unquestionably. (See "LESVs: The Case For" in Chapter 2.) Considerable advances have been made on a number of levels. However, we have already established that today there are many other (better) means to visualize data. At its core, "Excel …is fundamentally a piece of accounting software," says Daniel Nadler, CEO of Kensh ō Technologies.[4] (Nadler is also currently a Ph.D. candidate at Harvard University and a visiting scholar at the U.S. Federal Reserve.) Just because we're accustomed to Excel—and know how to use it well—doesn't mean that it's adequate for today's data types and streams.

These mature reporting tools have worked well with large structured and transactional datasets, and this continues to be the case. They allow users to create simple data visualizations from spreadsheets or databases. But they were unquestionably not built to handle the petabytes of unstructured and semi-structured information that confront us today. As a result, they often suffer from significant limitations.

> Visual Organizations realize that antiquated tools aren't suited for contemporary dataviz. They use new dataviz applications that are orders of magnitude more advanced than their processors.

CHALLENGES

As we saw in Part II, Visual Organizations aren't an entirely different breed of cat. They are not conjured out of air or transformed because a CEO signs off on Tableau. They do, however, tend to avoid the challenges in the following section that plague other kinds of enterprises.

The Quarterly Visualization Mentality

We've all been in PowerPoint Hell at one time or another. Everyone has endured god-awful presentations rife with downright inscrutable slides. We're talking about 10-point fonts, slides with 12 bullet points and a few subbullets to boot, and opaque graphics. And it didn't help that the presenter kept using horrible buzzwords like "synergy."

Like Excel, Visual Organizations don't prohibit PowerPoint. The program has its place. Relying too much upon any one application, however, is typically a problem. As Abraham Maslow once famously said, "If you only have a hammer, you tend to see every problem as a nail."

PowerPoint dependence is not the disease. It is a symptom of a larger and more dangerous malady, one that I call *the quarterly visualization mentality*. Visual Organizations do not suffer from this disease. Rather, employees at these progressive workplaces think about ways to *routinely* visualize data, not only in the context of periodic presentations. And it goes way beyond thinking and into the far more important realm of doing.

Data Defiance

You'll get no argument from me about the astonishing amount of hype surrounding Big Data. Yet, beneath all the exhortations and grand promises, there lies more than a kernel of truth. Big Data doesn't just matter; it is a game-changer. As I wrote in my last book, it has become too big to ignore.

Within an organization, skepticism usually isn't confined to one type of technology or change. Employees who doubt the import of Big Data are likely to adopt a commensurate mentality with respect to new dataviz tools—and the need to become a (more) Visual Organization. At best, these employees and organizations are stuck in Level 2 of the framework laid out in Chapter 6. They believe that only structured data matters (read: orderly, transactional, table-friendly information). As a result, they think that their current applications sufficiently address their needs.

> Employees at Visual Organizations understand the transformative power of Big Data, even if they're not doing much with it at the moment.

Unlearning History: Overcoming the Disappointments of Prior Tools

Starting a new venture is never easy, but greenfield sites have at least one thing going for them. Newly formed start-ups and small businesses generally don't face the same technological baggage of larger, more mature organizations. As I wrote in *The New Small*, often employees at small businesses are usually happy to use *any* application that makes their lives easier. The new tool doesn't supplant an existing favorite. Employees don't have to "unlearn" habits, both good and bad. More important, significant cultural barriers don't stand in their way. Technology is much less political.

Unfortunately, in my experience, more often than not the same sense of openness is noticeably lacking in many mature, big organizations. In these cases, often a new application has been hailed as the next great thing. During the selection process, internal politics can be intense, as different executives lobby for their pet reporting applications. Perhaps a VP has a prior relationship with the head of sales at Software Vendor X. Things can get chippy, and VPs who lose internal battles aren't above acting like children. (Once I heard a senior executive say in a meeting that he would "make sure that [the new system] fails." And some of the actions I've seen behind closed doors would qualify as insubordination and grounds for termination at lower levels.)

When this type of politicking occurs, many users ignore shiny new toys and revert to old standbys, minimizing the impact of new applications. Because of organizations' less-than-stellar track record deploying new technologies, there's often a great deal of resistance to purchasing new data-discovery and reporting applications. What's the point if employees aren't going to adopt it?

At least there's hope. As mentioned in Chapter 2, no longer is deploying a new application necessarily an enterprise-wide endeavor. The arrival of open-source software, cloud computing, and SaaS collectively is a godsend to more forward-thinking pockets of the organization. They can operate in relatively autonomous manners, especially if hidebound departments hem and haw. Perhaps a VP of sales will have the moxie to move ahead while the rest of her company gets its act together.

NEXT

This book concludes with a summary chapter and a brief look at the future of dataviz.

NOTES

1. Elisabeth Bumiller, "We Have Met the Enemy and He Is PowerPoint," *New York Times,* April 26, 2010, http://www.nytimes.com/2010/04/27/world/27powerpoint.html?hp&_r=0, Retrieved June 10, 2013.

2. Burn-Murdoch, John, "Why You Should Never Trust a Data Visualisation," *The Guardian,* July 24, 2013, http://www.guardian.co.uk/news/datablog/2013/jul/24/why-you-should-never-trust-a-data-visualisation, Retrieved July 24, 2013.

3. Booker, Ellis, "How Data Visualization Experts See the Future," InformationWeek, September 11, 2013, http://www.informationweek.com/big-data/news/big-data-analytics/how-data-visualization-experts-see-the-f/240161003, Retrieved September 14, 2013.

4. Boesler, Matthew, "Wall Street's Biggest Institutions Are Testing Software That Will End the Era of the Quants," Business Insider, July 15, 2013, http://www.businessinsider.com/kensho-brings-the-cloud-to-wall-street-2013–7#ixzz2dH0JkLE7, Retrieved August 28, 2013.

PART
FOUR

Conclusion and the Future of Dataviz

P art IV starts with a Coda, presenting some cautious predictions about the future. We'll see that Big Data is only getting bigger, increasing the need for dataviz tools and mind-sets predicated on data discovery. In short, the future augurs well for Visual Organizations. This book concludes with a short Afterword that offers a few personal reflections.

This Part includes the following:

- Coda
- Afterword

Coda: We're Just Getting Started

It's tough to make predictions, especially about the future.

—Yogi Berra

I t has *never* been easy to predict the future, not that that fact stops many "experts" from claiming that they know where technology, the stock market, or the body politic is going. The political, business, and technology landscapes are littered with centuries of prognostications from famous experts that turned out to be spectacularly wrong. Many of these are laughable now. Perhaps my favorite comes from Ken Olson in 1977. At the time, Olson was the president, chairman, and founder of Digital Equipment Corporation, then computer industry powerhouse. He confidently stated, "There is no reason anyone would want a computer in their home."

Whoops.

Experts like me may be able to proffer a decent explanation of what's happening *now* and maybe even why. When it comes to what will happen *tomorrow*, however, our batting averages plummet. Scores of books and studies have confirmed as much. *Wrong* by David Freedman and *The Signal and the Noise* by Nate Silver are particularly good ones.

In June 2013, I spoke to a few hundred people at a TechCocktail event in Las Vegas, Nevada. The talk, titled "I'm an Expert. Don't Trust Me," concerned how and why experts have historically had a pretty terrible track record in making accurate predictions.* (My talk touched upon a wide array of

---

* Watch the 26-minute talk here: http://tinyurl.com/phil-trust.

businesses, popular TV shows, musicians, and books.) If anything, prognosticating is even more difficult today, especially on technology-related topics. Our world is changing faster than ever.

This realization is tough for most experts to swallow, and I'm including myself in that. I like to think that my own predictions will be valid. After all, I pay attention to current and future trends. And my books have been on target, especially the ones on platforms and Big Data. As I wrote them, I believed that they covered game-changing trends. Nothing has happened since to make me think otherwise. In fact, I'd argue that each subject has become more important, not less.

Barring some calamity, all the trends discussed in Chapter 1 should only intensify. Data will become bigger and more open, and organizations will find new uses for it. Innovative products and services based upon new forms of data are coming, as are improvements to existing offerings. Technology will reach more people and profoundly change our lives in ways that we haven't yet begun to understand.

Pressure to visualize data will not merely emanate from tech-savvy twenty-somethings. In the words of Simon Samuel, Head of Value Solutions at the U.K. bank, Lloyds TSB:

> Being able to visualize data is important today, and it's going to be even more important going forward. Executives are demanding more visualization tools to help them support their insight and analysis, and also to accelerate their understanding of key business drivers.
>
> And data visualization is going to change the way our analysts work with data. They're going to be expected to respond to issues more rapidly. And they'll need to be able to dig for more insights— look at data differently, more imaginatively. Data visualization will promote that creative data exploration.[1]

Visual Organizations are benefitting from a combination of top-down and bottom-up forces. While I have no crystal ball, of this much I am relatively sure: the concept of a Visual Organization is here to stay. Organizations and their employees will continue to push the envelope. They will use Big Data and existing dataviz tools in innovative ways. And they will create new, more formidable, and more user-friendly tools to help them manage, understand, and act upon the Data Deluge.

ON BEING AN EXPERT

I'm not the most circumspect man on the planet, but sometimes I reflect on where I've been, where I am, and where I'm heading. At the risk of being immodest, I'm pleased with my career's progression. I enjoy my work, and my boss is pretty cool. I'm no rock star, but I've attained a certain status. In fact, before I take the stage to give a keynote speech, I am usually introduced as an *expert* of some sort.

To be sure, there's nothing inherently wrong with the word *expert*. I have been called much worse in a professional setting. Consultants regularly enter highly politicized and contentious environments. Technology is inherently political, and I learned early on that it was nearly impossible to make everyone happy. Even the most polite and tactful tech consultant has offended someone at some point.

Maybe it's just me, but people seem to be throwing around the term *expert* pretty loosely these days. Even though I have written what I hope is an informative and cogent book, I struggle with the term *expert*. I just can't see calling myself a true *data-visualization expert*. (Trust me: you'll meet a bunch of them in the following pages, and even a few data artists.) I sport no formal bona fides on the subject. And I doubt that I would pass the 10,000-hour test proposed by Malcolm Gladwell in his bestselling book *Outliers: The Story of Success*. Or perhaps I'm just too persnickety about that particular word.

Of course, that is all neither here nor there. As I've argued over the course of this book, it doesn't take an expert to see that today data is informing more and more business decisions. The Visual Organization is here to stay.

FOUR CRITICAL DATA-CENTRIC TRENDS

Organizations have always had to balance short- and long-term needs. All else being equal, the most successful companies of the day allocate sufficient resources not only for tomorrow, but also for what is likely to happen five or ten years down the road. (Or, in the case of visionaries like Jeff Bezos, the next quarter-century.*) Yes, the volume, variety, and velocity of data will continue to increase. But four other inexorable trends are also driving the Visual Employee and, by extension, Visual Organizations. This chapter closes by looking at them.

Wearable Technology and the Quantified Self

The 2004 film *The Final Cut* is set in a futuristic world in which people walk around with implanted devices that record their entire lives. Robin Williams plays Alan Hakman, a "cutter" who curates movies of his clients' lives played during their funerals. Williams's movies are always hit or miss. I enjoyed this one, although the movie seemed a bit far-fetched to me when it was released. As I reflect on that movie a decade later, the reality that it portended is arriving—and fast.

Over the past few years, we've seen remarkable strides in wearable technology. To be sure, this isn't a new phenomenon. The Sony Walkman debuted in 1979, and Casio introduced the first electronic wristwatch back in 1974. Apple's iPod changed the game for good in 2001.

---

* According to a 2012 Apps Run the World vendor survey, Amazon spent $4.5 billion on research and development (R&D). This equates to an astonishing 7.5 percent of sales. This is why Jeff Bezos can entertain crazy ideas like delivery drones.

By comparison, each of these digital devices is primitive compared to more contemporary products like FitBit, the Nike+ Fuelband, Jawbone UP, and Striiv. Samsung released its first smartwatch in 2013, and Apple, Microsoft, and other tech heavyweights are rumored to be working them as well. Smartphones will only continue to evolve and improve. Augmented reality is coming.

Wearable tech is getting a great deal smarter, and we ain't seen nothin' yet. More revolutionary and data-powered products will be arriving sooner than you think, and not just Google Glass.* Start-up Scanadu is building a small, pocket-sized device that reads body temperature, oxygen levels, and heartbeat. Future versions will include EKG, EEG, and blood-pressure measurements. And the market for brainwave technology is starting to take off, buoyed by players like Muse by Interaxon, ZenTunes, and MindWave. Each of these devices captures and responds to enormous amounts of data, much of it *contextual*. That is, the device will know exactly *where* it is and can take actions and respond appropriately.

We will without question hear more about terms like *the quantified self* and *lifelogging*, as more people record large portions of their lives through wearable tech and an increasing array of apps.† Yes, lifelogging is still in its infancy but, as Martin Kallstrom, CEO of the Swedish start-up Memoto, writes in *Wired*, it "has the potential to transform the way we remember and track our lives."[2]

Machine Learning and the Internet of Things

Management at data-driven companies like Amazon, Apple, Facebook, General Electric, Google, and eBay realize that Big Data has arrived—and isn't going anywhere. The current opportunity is massive, only to be surpassed by what's coming. For instance, GE is betting heavily on the Internet of Things, aka the *Industrial Internet*. The company is "merging big iron with Big Data to create brilliant machines." In so doing, GE believes that it can eliminate a whopping $150 billion in waste.§

The Internet of Things changes nothing and everything at the same time. Yes, we'll still upload billions of videos and photos, blog, tweet, like, +1, and poke. We'll keep watching billions of hours of videos on YouTube, Netflix, and Hulu. But we humans will have plenty of company in generating ungodly amounts of data. As more and more devices connect to the Internet, the amount of data generated and consumed will keep exploding and force us to keep inventing new terms like *brontobyte* (a 1 followed by 27 digits). Machine-to-machine

---

* I gave Glass a whirl in Las Vegas in July 2013. For my humorous take on the experience, see http://tinyurl.com/phil-google-glass.

† For instance, the new iPad app mem:o transforms data into striking images rooted in Dutch graphic design.

§ For more on this, see http://tinyurl.com/ge-waste.

learning will continue to advance. Web-enabled devices will keep proliferating and getting smarter. Making sense of an exponentially growing amount of data will require even more powerful data-visualization tools.

With the arrival of smart grids, we will be able to look at detailed data around our peak electricity and water-usage times. In other words, we won't just be looking at data as employees, but increasingly as consumers and citizens. And we will take action based upon that data. Many products today give us an exciting glimpse of the future. DropCam lets us monitor our homes and watch what's happening in real time from any device. The Nest Thermostat learns how warm or cold we like our homes. IntelliTouch systems with ScreenLogic let us control pools and spas from anywhere on earth. Products like these and others portend an exciting and data-rich future. More and more physical objects will be seamlessly integrated into information networks. We will increasingly interact with smart objects over the Internet. It will become second nature for us to look at the data generated by these objects and make desired changes.

Multidimensional Data

What's the *shape* of your data? Does it look like Figure C.1?

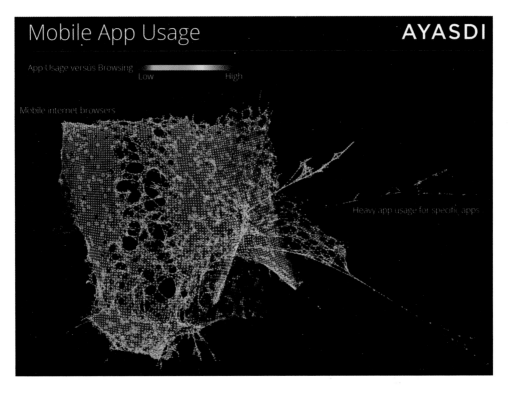

Figure C.1 Mobile App Usage
Source: Ayasdi

Today, that seems like a weird question to ask. Go ahead and say those words to someone at the office tomorrow. I'll bet that the response will be either "Pardon?" or "What?"*

That query should become much more commonplace in five or ten years, courtesy of the dataviz tools and emerging data sources discussed in this book. Dataviz will continue to evolve. This is especially likely given the rise of smartphones, crowdsourced mapping applications like Waze, real-time geolocation data, open APIs, and the ability to fuse them together. And the evolution of data and dataviz won't stop there. Some very smart cookies believe that the field will become more *topological*.

By way of background, topology is the nearly 300-year-old, admittedly obscure subset of mathematics that focuses on the study of shapes. While the field isn't new, its application to data is. In the words of *New York Times* graphics editor and dataviz wiz Mike Bostock, "A topology improves shape simplification by avoiding artifacts that would be caused by simplifying shapes independently. It also enables applications like map coloring and selective meshing, and makes the format more compact by removing redundant coordinates."[3]

Technical specifications like these are important, but let's forget about them for a moment and focus on business need. Specifically, what's driving the increasing popularity of topology? In short, it's our need to discover. To do this, we need to understand, analyze, and visualize Big Data in new ways.

Topology—in particular, Topological Data Analysis (TDA)—may provide the potential to discover insights that current dataviz tools simply cannot. TDA represents a fundamental advance in machine learning. As Jeff Bertolucci writes in *InformationWeek,* TDA has the ability "to empower business users to find value in very large data sets without having to consult data scientists or write algorithms or models."[4] Without getting all Euclidian here, TDA lets laypersons make more sense of what's happening because they can see data represented in three-dimensional images. The *shape* of the data is helping both humans and machines comprehend different complex phenomena and the data behind them. (If you're having a hard time getting your arms around three-dimensional data, don't worry. In the coming years, we'll be spending more and more time on the z-axis, particularly as 3D printers become commonplace.)

Start-up Ayasdi is applying these shapely principles to Big Data. (Ayasdi is pronounced *ai-yaz-dee* and means "to seek" in Cherokee.) Founded at Stanford University in 2008, the company is bringing a groundbreaking approach to solving the world's most complex problems. It has already landed blue-chip clients GE and Citi, as well as five of world's top 20 global pharmaceutical companies. Ayasdi's core technology is based on the work of Stanford University

---

*I live in Vegas. We have to bet. It's in the state constitution or something.

mathematics professor and company cofounder Gunnar Carlsson.* In Carlsson's words:

> By applying TDA to datasets like next-generation sequencing, financial information, and sensor data, individuals can now discover the subtle nuances inherent in *complete* datasets. People are doing much more than answering single questions that they have formulated.

> Along with machine-learning algorithms, TDA automatically represents datasets as shapes in the form of a topological network that presents many of the features associated to shape. This permits the easy interrogation of the dataset, and suggests a collection of natural questions based on the shape's theoretical features. As a result, anyone can easily analyze the dataset and perform tasks such as data segmentation.

> This new method of analysis is transforming the way individuals look at, understand, and mine data. Domain experts and data scientists alike now have the ability to see complex data as connected systems. They are able to easily view and understand the relationships that even individual data points have with all other data points in complex datasets.[5]

Brass tacks: the shape of data is changing.

The Forthcoming Battle over Data Portability and Ownership

The technology landscape is littered with companies that have struggled to maintain their erstwhile positions of prominence. Compared to 15 years ago, AOL, MySpace, Microsoft, Yahoo, Dell, HP, and others have fallen from grace. In the case of Yahoo, the company's missteps have been well documented. From 2004 to 2012, its stock remained essentially stagnant, and no wonder. The once-mighty Internet heavyweight missed the boat in a number of key areas. Today, Yahoo lacks each the following:

- A mobile operating system like Android or iOS
- A true platform à la Amazon, Apple, Facebook, Google, and Twitter
- Hardware (tablets, smartphones, and so on)
- A viable social network

Yahoo still does search, but its market share continues to dwindle. This has forced the company to rely largely upon partnerships to fight irrelevance. Adding salt to the wound, few people think that banner ads are effective, and prices reflect that. And its senior leadership game of musical chairs has been

* See Carlsson's introductory talk on the topic at http://tinyurl.com/Gunnar-Carlsson.

nothing less than embarrassing. A multitude of CEOs has come and gone over the past decade. Carol Bartz, Terry Semel, Jerry Yang, Ross Levinsohn, Scott Thompson, and others have each had a distinct vision of what Yahoo is and where it should go.*

On July 16, 2012, Yahoo's board of directors tried to stop the bleeding once and for all by hiring former Google rock star Marissa Mayer as its CEO. Mayer was not even 40 years old, but Yahoo believes that it is finally bringing long-term stability to the C-suite. Yahoo sees Mayer as someone with a real vision and plan to transform the company.

Say what you will about Mayer, but her time at Yahoo has been anything but boring. Almost from day one, she began shaking things up. She has made at least 20 major acquisitions as of this writing, most notably blogging platform Tumblr for nearly $1 billion. She effected policy changes, most notably banning remote work. In so doing, she inadvertently ignited a national debate on the subject. Mayer gave birth to her first child—and then went back to work three weeks later. She bought every employee a new Apple, Samsung, Nokia, or HTC smartphone—no BlackBerrys. Collectively, Mayer's moves are designed to change the company's culture and infuse excitement into its moribund brand. She launched a new corporate logo and redesigned its home page. Today, much of the old-guard senior leadership is gone, either by their choice or Mayer's.

By at least one critical measure, the changes are working. The stock has soared a "whopping 73 percent since Mayer become CEO, [although] that gain is almost entirely attributable to investments the company has in two Asian companies: the Chinese e-commerce giant Alibaba and Yahoo Japan."[6]

In late January 2013, Mayer gave an extended interview at the World Economic Forum in Davos, Switzerland. She talked about many things, including the benefits of—and need for—data portability.† Mayer was unyielding in her belief that users should "own" the data they generate on search engines, mobile devices, apps, social networks, and the like. What's more, since it's *their* data, users should be able to easily take it with them wherever and whenever they want.

In Mayer's ideal world, data portability would be as simple as snapping one's fingers. Users would be able to click a mouse a few times and *voila*! All of the data from, say, Facebook, automatically would port into some type of Yahoo service or application. Users would not need to manually repost pictures or reupload videos upon joining a new social network. All comments from friends instantly would appear with relevant metadata (time, date, location, and so on) User relationships, social networks, events, and entire

---

* To see the company's CEO timeline, go to http://tinyurl.com/yahoo-ceos.

† Watch the entire 30-minute video at http://tinyurl.com/davos-mm.

Web-browsing history would just magically show up in the new service, app, device, or network. Users would not have to key in this information, reestablish existing relationships, or write a bunch of code. Nothing would get lost in translation.

Mayer proselytized the benefits of data portability and, for all I know, those words represent her honest beliefs. Let's not make her out to be a martyr, though. She's not waving the flag for the data-deprived or -enslaved masses. Data-heavy companies Amazon, Apple, Facebook, Google, and Twitter have amassed untold petabytes of extremely valuable user and customer data. Data may or may not be the new oil, but few intelligent folks question its potential value.

And Yahoo would benefit tremendously by accessing that trove of data. True data liberation and portability would allow Mayer to effectively piggyback off the work of Yahoo's competitors, not to mention their data. Yahoo might even be able to build a better mousetrap in the process. If Mayer were running Facebook, she would be singing a very different tune.

Is Mayer right? Who owns this data anyway? If you take a photo and post it on Facebook or Twitter, does it still belong to you? If you create a presentation with Google Docs, does Google now legally own the content in those slides? Generally speaking, do you have the right to take your data with you when you stop using a social network or a cloud-based service? Should companies that provide free services have the right to monetize user data however they want in perpetuity?

Mayer is hardly the only one asking these fundamental questions, and I don't know the right answers to them. I am reminded here of the late Nelson Mandela's quote: "Where you stand depends on where you sit."

One thing is for certain: The issue of data ownership is becoming increasingly thorny. This battle is just getting started.

FINAL THOUGHTS: NOTHING STOPS THIS TRAIN

Like the arms race around Big Data, the dataviz train shows no signs of stopping. Expect innovation from most of the usual suspects, plus ones currently not on anyone's radar. The trends mentioned throughout this book will only intensify. Big Data and dataviz will only become more important not only in the workplace, but in more facets of our personal lives.

Collectively, Big Data and dataviz will allow Visual Organizations to do many currently unimaginable things, and even a few scary ones. At a minimum, Visual Organizations will be able to model complex systems better. They will be able to see how systems *really* interact with one another and discover things their competition cannot. They will make better predictions. Through Big Data and dataviz, Visual Organizations will continue to distance themselves from the pack. They will ask better questions and find better answers than their visually challenged counterparts. They will understand their businesses, customers, employees, and the world at large more holistically.

NOTES

1. Tubbs, Waynette, "Data Visualization: A Wise Investment," All Analytics, August 7, 2013, http://www.allanalytics.com/author.asp?section_id=2210 &doc_id=266454&f_src=allanalytics_sitedefault, Retrieved August 7, 2013.
2. Kallstrom, Martin, "How Lifelogging Is Transforming the Way We Remember, Track Our Lives," *Wired*, June 10, 2013, http://www.wired.com/insights/2013/06/how-lifelogging-is-transforming-the-way-we-remember-track-our-lives, Retrieved June 18, 2013.
3. Bostock, Mike, "How to Infer Topology," September 2, 2013, http://bost.ocks.org/mike/topology, Retrieved September 2, 2013.
4. Bertolucci, Jeff, "Ayasdi Analyzes Shape of Big Data," InformationWeek, July 29, 2013, http://www.informationweek.com/big-data/news/big-data-analytics/ayasdi-analyzes-shape-of-big-data/240159072, Retrieved August 14, 2013.
5. Personal conversation with Carlsson, September 11, 2013.
6. Gustin, Sam, "Yahoo CEO Marissa Mayer's One-Year Report Card: The Clock Is Ticking," *Time* magazine, July 16, 2013, http://business.time.com/2013/07/16/yahoo-ceo-marissa-mayers-one-year-report-card-the-clock-is-ticking/#ixzz2eb7wQMoE, Retrieved September 11, 2013.

My Life in Data

We can't run from who we are. Our destiny
chooses us.

—Martin Landau, *Rounders*

I
n a way, this book represents the sum total of many of my life's experiences.
Let me explain.

I began building my data chops early, long before I ever heard or used the
term *data*. As a kid, I enjoyed sports and looking at stats, especially on the back
of baseball and football cards. I played poker on a regular basis, and I loved cal-
culating odds on the fly. My dad has always been great with numbers, and the
apple didn't fall far from the tree. Math just made sense to me, as did gadgets.
I first started using a computer at the ripe old age of 11. (Yes, I was the very
definition of an early adopter.) My parents bought my sister and me a then-
amazing Commodore 64 in 1986. In high school, I did very well in accounting,
typing (yes, they taught that back then), algebra, and pre-calculus.

At age 18, I attended Carnegie Mellon University, a school known for its
strengths in computer programming, technology, engineering, and robotics.
Even the poets there knew how to code. I enrolled in CMU's College of Social
and Decision Sciences. In my sophomore year, I took a class called Empirical
Research Methods. Among the books assigned by pony-tailed Professor Miller
was *The Visual Display of Quantitative Information*, the classic by Edward Tufte.
The book really opened my eyes. I remember being amazed at the power of
scale—that is, how relatively small changes in the x- and y-axes could alter
the story told by the data. For instance, let's say that a company's stock price
appeared relatively stable over the long term. With some manipulation of each
axis, it wasn't terribly difficult to make the same stock appear much more vola-
tile. As the late economist Ronald Coase famously once said, "If you torture the
data long enough, it will confess."

My journey with data would continue after graduating from CMU. During the summer of 1996, I took a summer internship in the human resources department at Data General, a now-defunct tech company headquartered outside of Boston, Massachusetts. I worked with enterprise systems and different reporting tools, and I played with data for a good part of the day. Occasionally, I would sneak in looks at these cool new things called *websites*. Rather than presenting employee compensation and recruiting data to my manager in basic spreadsheets, I would throw it into a graph or chart for her. In Microsoft Excel, that was easy enough to do.

Back then, enterprise technology wasn't terribly sophisticated or democratic compared to today. Excel allowed tech-savvy employees like me to play with relatively small amounts of data. It didn't take a rocket scientist to create simple graphs, bar charts, and histograms. However, to do anything that would qualify as cool, employees usually needed to call the IT department. Invariably, the process took far too much time. A great deal of back and forth often took place between functional business users and IT. Being able to speak each user's language was then—and still is—extremely valuable. Some things never change.

In 1997, I graduated from Cornell University with my master's in industrial and labor relations. I took a full-time job in corporate HR. I was eager to apply the numbers-oriented approach to the field that I learned at Cornell. I considered myself part of the "new breed" of HR professionals. I quickly realized, however, that theory and practice diverged. Forget sophisticated statistical analyses on what motivated employees and why they left companies. I found that most HR departments were stuck in the *personnel* age. In hindsight, it was like watching an episode of *Mad Men*. Many of my like-minded friends agreed with me. Generally speaking, back then most HR departments and professionals lacked several essential elements, which prohibited them from being taken seriously in other pockets of the organization:

- Comprehensive and accurate employee data

- Contemporary systems that would store this information

- Reporting tools that would let employees access, interpret, and act upon it

- Worst of all, the realization that any of the above actually mattered

In my last proper HR role, my repeated requests for basic data irritated many of my colleagues and the IT department. *Why do you want to know how many people work here?* I must have been sick the day we covered the "science" of headcount at Cornell. It didn't take me too long to realize that I needed to change careers—and fast. I couldn't keep switching jobs in search of an enlightened HR department. I wasn't even sure that one existed. I was raised on data, technology, numbers, and analytics. It's hard to turn those facets of your personality off. I needed to find a line of work that reflected my interests, strengths, and personality.

In 2000, I started consulting for Lawson Software, an enterprise software vendor. I helped organizations implement HR and payroll systems. For several reasons, this type of work was a much better fit for me. First and most important, my interests in data technology were no longer liabilities; they were assets. My clients actually *needed* the skills that I brought to the table. Before long, some more senior Lawson colleagues were coming to me with questions. I had a knack for learning new applications and systems, as well as explaining them to others. (While not consulting, I taught classes to clients and newly hired consultants.) My analytical mind could easily get to the root of most issues, and I rapidly became skilled at data conversions. On a totally different level, if one client's culture was particularly dysfunctional or toxic, I knew that it was only a matter of time before I was on the road again.

I left Lawson to hang my own shingle in 2002. As I moved from client to client, the configurations, systems, application versions, databases, politics, and players invariably changed. If there was one constant, it was the primacy of enterprise data. Before I started any new engagement, I would always request direct access to my clients' databases. I knew that that essential bridge would soon help me be productive and solve key problems. No, it wasn't an elixir, but access to real-time enterprise data would always prove invaluable. Without it, I knew that I wouldn't be able to do my job. In the immortal words of W. Edwards Deming, "In God we trust, all others must bring data."

By 2003, a very skilled systems integrator. Over my consulting career, some pretty prominent companies brought me to perform magic with ones and zeros, and most appreciated my straightforward, no-nonsense approach to solving problems. In a few cases, I resolved incredibly thorny data issues that had confounded much pricier consultants from prestigious firms. In some cases, these issues nearly made my brain explode. I couldn't help but smile when a few of my tech-challenged clients quasi-seriously asked me if I had invented the computer. As my confidence grew, I was able to raise my rates. What's more, I was able to more than hold my own with pure techies. Not bad for a guy who used to work in corporate HR.

Of course, being a road warrior gets old. The appeal of travel wanes over time. A decade of integrating systems started to wear on me. Since 2010, I have not done very much enterprise system consulting. I have moved on to writing, public speaking, thought leadership, and more strategic advising. But just because I haven't built an Access database, written a Crystal Report, or run an SQL statement in the past three years doesn't mean that I ignore the world of data. Far from it. I recognize that data is more important than ever. Some have even said that "data is the new oil."

You'll get no argument from me. To varying extents, I've emphasized the significance of data in my first four books, and my fifth explored the nascent trend of Big Data. Beyond my books, I have written nearly 1,000 blog posts and articles on data-related issues. When I speak to audiences, the subject of data is never far from my mind.

Business is changing faster than ever, and none of us can accurately and reliably predict the future. I can say for certain, though, that the Visual Organization has arrived.

Now, what are you going to do?

Supplemental Dataviz Resources

The following table provides a slew of useful dataviz resources. The tools, forums, blogs, and other sites listed here do *not* represent a comprehensive directory of all dataviz resources. Such a list would be impossible to compile—and would change tomorrow. (It's no substitute for Google.) Rather, it should serve as a starting point for further exploration.

Tool	Description
BigSheets	IBM's tool integrates gigabytes, terabytes, or petabytes of unstructured data from Web-based repositories. It works in conjunction with Many Eyes (see below).
Chart.js	An easy way to include animated graphs on websites. Its open-source HTML5 charts use the <canvas> tag.
Chartio	A BI tool that bills itself as extremely simple to set up and easy to use. It claims to provide easy access to the world's most popular data sources.
Create.ly	Allows users to easily create flowcharts, mind maps, Unified Modeling Language (UML) diagrams, org charts, database models, and mockups.
DataHero	Start-up that allows users to connect to a wide array of datasets and sources. Its Data Decoder analyzes patterns in data and automatically generates relevant visualizations that help users unmask the answers within.
DataMarket	Helps professionals find and understand data. It brings together complex and diverse data in one place and one format so it can be searched, compared, visualized, and shared across teams, organizations, and the world.
Daytum	Conceived by data heavyweights Ryan Case and Nicholas Felton (see Feltron Report, below) as an elegant and intuitive tool for counting and communicating personal statistics.
DbVisualizer	A database management and analysis tool for all major databases (for example, Oracle, SQL Server, DB2, Sybase, MySQL, SQLite) on Windows, Mac OS, and Linux.
Easel.ly	Allows users to create and share visual ideas online. Its visual themes or "vhemes" allow users to easily create and share visual ideas. Just drag and drop a vheme onto an existing canvas or create your own.

(continued)

Tool	Description
Feltron Report	An annual glowing example of how seemingly mundane information can tell a beautiful story with just a little artistic treatment. Felton's work on Facebook's Timeline has helped the rest of us visualize (as much as we might like to forget it) the minutiae of our past.
FlowingData	Site that explores how designers, statisticians, and computer scientists are using data to understand one another better—mainly through dataviz.
Gapminder	Presents important global data in dynamically and clear graphs. Users can watch the history of the world unfold through the magic of statistics. Gapminder uses a platform called Trendalyzer that Google bought in 2007. It uses data from global institutions like the OECD, the World Bank, and the International Labor Organization.
Google Public Data Explorer	Search through databases from around the world, including the World Bank, OECD, Eurostat, and the U.S. Census Bureau. After you find what you want, filter through categories to make graphs with the axes you want. Google's Public Data Explorer then displays the data in a line graph, bar graph, scatterplot, or on a map.
Google Maps	Offers a wide array of APIs that let users embed robust maps, images, and even Street View into webpages without requiring JavaScript.
Hohli Charts	Based on the Google Chart API, this tool allows users to create a variety of great charts including lines, bar and pie charts, Venn diagrams, radar charts, and scatterplots.
Infogr.am	An online tool that allows you to easily create your own infographics.
Many Eyes	IBM's online data visualizer and chart-making tool.
Mapfluence	Lets users render transit lines, stations, and detailed attributes on a map of the Washington, DC, area. To ensure contextual relevance, rail layers reflect local transit naming conventions and designations.
MATLAB	A high-level language and interactive environment for numerical computation, visualization, and programming. Using MATLAB, you can analyze data, develop algorithms, and create models and applications. The language, tools, and built-in math functions enable you to explore multiple approaches and reach a solution faster than with spreadsheets or traditional programming languages, such as C/C++ or Java.
Pixlr	A free online photo editor that allows you to create your own charts, infographics, and images.
Polymaps	A free JavaScript library for making dynamic, interactive maps in modern Web browsers.
Processing	A programming language, development environment, and online community. Since 2001, Processing has promoted software literacy within the visual arts and visual literacy within technology. Initially created to serve as a software sketchbook and to teach computer programming fundamentals within a visual context, Processing evolved into a development tool for professionals. Today, there are tens of thousands of students, artists, designers, researchers, and hobbyists who use Processing for learning, prototyping, and production.*

---

* For more on this, see http://www.processing.org.

Tool	Description
Visier	Specializes in Big Data and dataviz for HR.
Visualizing.org	A community of creative people making sense of complex issues through data and design.
Weave	A platform that visualizes trend and geographical data. Developed at the University of Massachusetts Lowell with support from IBM, Weave supports a wide range of uses. It is intended for both novice and advanced users.
Wordle	One of the many word cloud tools that marketing folks seem to love. It contains a surprising number of customizable options for a free tool.
Zoho Creator	Online database creation tool.
Zoomdata	Allows users to connect to internal and external data sources; combine, merge, and crunch data streams; visualize the results in real time; and provide instant access to colleagues.

Selected Bibliography

Cairo, Alberto. *The Functional Art: An Introduction to Information Graphics and Visualization*. Berkeley: New Riders, 2013.

Carr, Nicholas. *The Big Switch: Rewiring the World, from Edison to Google*. New York: W. W. Norton & Company, 2008.

Christensen, Clayton M. *The Innovator's Dilemma: The Revolutionary Book That Will Change the Way You Do Business*. New York: HarperCollins, 2003.

Cleveland, William S., and McGill, Robert. "Graphical Perception: Theory, Experimentation, and Application to the Development of Graphical Methods", *The Journal of the American Statistical Association*. September 1984.

Few, Stephen (2013): Data Visualization for Human Perception. In: Soegaard, Mads and Dam, Rikke Friis (eds.). *"The Encyclopedia of Human-Computer Interaction*, 2nd Ed.*"* Aarhus, Denmark: The Interaction Design Foundation. Available online at http://www.interaction-design.org/encyclopedia/data_visualization_for_human_perception.html.

Few, Stephen. *Information Dashboard Design: The Effective Visual Communication of Data*. Sebastopol, CA: O'Reilly Media, 2006.

Few, Stephen. *Show Me the Numbers: Designing Tables and Graphs to Enlighten*, Second Edition. Burlingame, CA: Analytics Press, 2012.

Fisher, Tony. *The Data Asset: How Smart Companies Govern Their Data for Business Success*. Hoboken, New Jersey: John Wiley & Sons, 2009.

Franks, Bill. *Taming the Big Data Tidal Wave: Finding Opportunities in Huge Data Streams with Advanced Analytics*. Hoboken, NJ: John Wiley & Sons, 2012.

Johansson, Frans. *The Click Moment: Seizing Opportunity in an Unpredictable World*. New York: Portfolio/Penguin, 2012.

Lankow, Jason; Ritchie, Josh; Crooks, Ross, *Infographics: The Power of Visual Storytelling*. Hoboken, NJ: John Wiley & Sons, 2012.

May, Matthew. *The Laws of Subtraction: 6 Simple Rules for Winning in the Age of Excess Everything*. New York: McGraw-Hill, 2013.

McCandless, David. *The Visual Miscellaneum: A Colorful Guide to the World's Most Consequential Trivia*. New York: HarperCollins, 2009.

Moore, David S. and McCabe, George P., *Introduction to the Practice of Statistics*, Seventh Edition. New York: W. H. Freeman, 2010.

PricewaterhouseCoopers. "PwC's 5th Annual Digital IQ Survey: Digital Conversations and the C-suite," 2013, http://www.pwc.com/us/en/advisory/2013-digital-iq-survey/download-the-report.jhtml.

Raymond, Eric S., *The Cathedral & the Bazaar, Sebastopol,* CA: O'Reilly Media, 2001.

Siegel, David. *Pull: The Power of the Semantic Web to Transform Your Business.* New York: Penguin Group, 2009.

Silver, Nate. *The Signal and the Noise: Why So Many Predictions Fail—but Some Don't.* New York: Penguin Press, 2012.

Simon, Phil. *The Age of the Platform: How Amazon, Apple, Facebook, and Google Have Redefined Business.* Henderson, NV: Motion Publishing, 2011.

Simon, Phil. *Too Big to Ignore: The Business Case for Big Data.* Hoboken, New Jersey: John Wiley & Sons, 2013.

Smolan, Rick; Erwitt, Jennifer. *The Human Face of Big Data.* Sausalito, CA: Against All Odds Productions, 2012.

Steiner, Christopher. *Automate This: How Algorithms Came to Rule Our World.* New York: Portfolio/Penguin, 2012.

Stone, Brad. *The Everything Store: Jeff Bezos and the Age of Amazon,* New York: Little, Brown and Company, 2013.

Tapscott, Don. *Grown Up Digital: How the Net Generation Is Changing Your World.* New York: McGraw-Hill, 2009.

Tufte, Edward. *The Visual Display of Quantitative Information,* 2nd Edition. Cheshire, CT: Graphics Press, 2001.

Ware, Colin. *Information Visualization, Third Edition: Perception for Design.* Waltham, MA: Morgan Kaufmann, 2012.

Yau, Nathan. *Data Points: Visualization That Means Something.* Indianapolis: John Wiley & Sons, 2013.

About the Author

Phil Simon is a recognized management and technology expert, a sought-after keynote speaker, and the author of six books, including the award-winning *The Age of the Platform*. While not writing and speaking, he advises organizations on strategy, technology, and data management. His contributions have been featured in the *Harvard Business Review*, CNN, *Wall Street Journal*, NBC, CNBC, the *New York Times*, *InformationWeek*, *Inc. Magazine*, *Bloomberg Businessweek*, The *Huffington Post*, *Forbes*, *Fast Company*, and many other mainstream media outlets. He holds degrees from Carnegie Mellon and Cornell University. His home page is www.philsimon.com. Needle him on Twitter at @philsimon.

Index